◆ Sarah Bell ◆

The British Columbia & Alberta
Bed & Breakfast
Guide

A guide to over 400 B&Bs in Western Canada

Also by Sarah Bell

The British Columbia Lodge & Resort Guide
Also includes the Banff/Jasper area and the Yukon

The British Columbia & Alberta Adventure Travel Guide
Guided outdoor trips and more

Gordon Soules Book Publishers Ltd.
West Vancouver, Canada
Seattle, U.S.

Canadian Cataloguing in Publication Data

Bell, Sarah.
The British Columbia and Alberta Bed & Breakfast Guide

Includes index.
ISBN 0-919574-91-2

1. Bed and breakfast accommodations—British Columbia—
Guidebooks. 2. Bed and breakfast accommodations—Alberta—
Guidebooks. 3. British Columbia—Guidebooks 4. Alberta—
Guidebooks. I. Title. II. Title: British Columbia and Alberta
bed and breakfast guide.
TX907.5.C22B735 1996   647.94711'03   C96-910447-2

Published in Canada by
Gordon Soules Book Publishers Ltd.
1354-B Marine Drive
West Vancouver, BC V7T 1B5
(604) 922-6588 or (604) 688-5466
Fax: (604) 688-5442
E-mail: books@gordon.soules.com

Published in the United States by
Gordon Soules Book Publishers Ltd.
620—1916 Pike Place
Seattle, WA 98101
(604) 922-6588 or (604) 688-5466
Fax: (604) 688-5442
E-mail: books@gordon.soules.com

Cover designned by Harry Bardal
Printed and bound in Canada by Printcrafters Inc.

Contents at a Glance
(for full contents, see pages 4 to 9)

4

Contents

Information for Users of This Book

1. Information in any guidebook is subject to change and error. It is advisable to confirm important information when making reservations.

2. While great care has been taken to ensure the accuracy of the information in this book, neither the author nor the publisher can accept responsibility for any outdated information, omissions, or errors.

3. Rates are in Canadian currency.

4. All distances are approximate.

5. B&Bs are open year round unless otherwise indicated.

6. Ensuite bathroom describes a bathroom accessible directly from a guest room or suite, for the exclusive use of the guests in that room or suite.

7. Private bathroom describes a bathroom for the exclusive use of the guests of one room or suite; the guests must exit their room or suite to get to it.

8. Shared guest bathroom describes a bathroom shared by some or all guests; the hosts do not use this bathroom.

9. Shared bathroom describes a bathroom shared by guests and hosts.

10. Kitchen describes, at minimum, a sink, a stove, and a fridge.

11. Self-contained describes a room, suite, or cottage that has its own cooking facilities and bathroom.

12. Maps of British Columbia and Alberta are available from many sources, including bookstores, gas stations, automobile associations, and tourist information offices. (Retailers, automobile associations, and tourist information offices can order maps of British Columbia and Alberta from Gordon Soules Book Publishers Ltd. at wholesale prices. Addresses are given on the copyright page of this book.)

A B & C B&B Agency

Norma McCurrach
4390 Frances Street
Burnaby, BC V5C 2R3
(604) 298-8815 Fax: (604) 298-5917
Toll-free: 1-800-488-1941

• One person $45–85; two people $65–135.
King-sized beds, queen-sized beds, double beds,
and twin beds. Private and shared guest bathrooms. Additional person $15. Off-season rates.
• A B&B reservation service covering British
Columbia, including Vancouver and Victoria. Modest to luxurious accommodation. Close to
major tourist attractions. Honeymoon accommodation is the agency's specialty. Some B&Bs
with Jacuzzis and swimming pools. Full breakfasts. Cancellation notice seven days. Com-
missionable. Credit cards. No pets. **In the agents' own words:** "We have been in the tourist
business for twenty years, and our aim has always been customer satisfaction."

AA-Accommodations West

Doreen Wensley
660 Jones Terrace
Victoria, BC V8Z 2L7
(250) 479-1986 Fax: (250) 479-9999
(Area code 604 before October 1996.)

• One person $45–75; two people $55–125.
King-sized beds, queen-sized beds, and double
beds. Additional person from $15. Child from $5.
• A B&B reservation service covering Victoria,
Vancouver Island, and some of the nearby islands.
Cottages and houses with sea views, antiques, hot tubs, and swimming pools. Accommodation for one or more nights. All B&Bs are inspected and are selected with attention to cleanliness, hospitality, and breakfasts. Descriptions given over the phone. Detailed brochure
available. Office is open Monday to Saturday from 7:00 a.m. to 10:00 p.m. and Sunday from
2:00 to 8:00 p.m. No booking fees. **In the agents' own words:** "Country comfort, magnificent sea views, cottages, and regal heritage houses. Our reservation service has been family
owned since 1985. Your requirements are given caring, careful attention to ensure your satisfaction."

Abbotsford/Fraser Valley B&B Reservation Service

34745 Arden Drive
Abbotsford, BC V2S 2X9
(604) 853-5398 Fax: (604) 850-5069

• One person $45–90; two people $60–100.
King-sized beds, queen-sized beds, double beds,
and twin beds. Shared guest, private, and ensuite
bathrooms. Additional person $15. Child $10.
Off-season and extended stay rates.

• A B&B reservation service covering Abbotsford, Mission, Aldergrove, Langley, Surrey, and
Vancouver. Simple to honeymoon-style accommodation. Some B&Bs welcome children,
pets, and/or smoking. Some B&Bs are wheelchair accessible. All B&Bs are inspected and
are selected with attention to cleanliness and friendliness. Detailed brochure available. Full
breakfasts. Visa, MasterCard. **In the agents' own words:** "We are right in the heart of the
Fraser Valley. One call does it all."

Alberta and Pacific B&B Reservation Service

June M. Brown
Mail: Box 15477, M.P.O.
Vancouver, BC V6B 5B2
(604) 944-1793 Fax: (604) 552-1659

• A B&B reservation service covering Alberta and
British Columbia. In Alberta, Circle Tour
information and bookings are available in Calgary, Banff, Lake Louise, the Columbia Icefields,
Jasper, and Edmonton. In British Columbia,
bookings are available for Vancouver Island, the
coast from Victoria to Prince Rupert, Vancouver, the Okanagan, and Kamloops. **In the
agents' own words:** "We offer comfort and hospitality in personally inspected houses—the
personal approach to travel since 1981."

Alberta's Gem B&B and Reservation Agency

Gordon and Betty Mitchell
11216 Forty-eighth Avenue
Edmonton, AB T6H 0C7
(403) 434-6098 Fax: (403) 434-6098

• One person from $45; two people from $60.
• A B&B reservation service covering Alberta and
British Columbia, including Calgary, Canmore,
Banff, Lake Louise, the Columbia Icefields,
Jasper, Hinton, Evansburg, Edmonton, Red Deer,
Didsbury, Drumheller, Rosebud, the Peace River,
Grande Prairie, and many points in B.C. Tourist information available. Reservations for
B&Bs in Canada and the U.S. Reservations made for hotels and motels in areas without
B&B accommodations. Deposit required. Visa, MasterCard. **In the agents' own words:**
"Your one-stop reservation service for bed and breakfast accommodation in Canada."

All Seasons B&B Agency Inc.

Kate Catterill
Mail: Box 5511 Station B
Victoria, BC V8R 6S4
(250) 655-7173 Fax: (250) 655-7193
(Area code 604 before October 1996.)

• $65–190.
• A B&B reservation service covering Victoria,
the Saanich Peninsula close to Sidney and the
Butchart Gardens, Vancouver Island, and the Gulf
Islands. An accommodation style for everyone,
including heritage houses of architectural interest, houses with gardens, and waterfront prop-
erties. Brochure and tourist information available. Visa, MasterCard. **In the agents' own
words:** "We are a personalized service geared to the needs of the discriminating traveller. It
is important to us that you enjoy yourself."

Canada-West Accommodations B&B Registry

Ellison Massey
Mail: Box 86607
North Vancouver, BC V7L 4L2
(604) 929-1424 Fax: (604) 929-6692
Toll-free from within the U.S.:
   1-800-561-3223
Victoria office: (250) 652-8685
Kelowna office: (250) 763-2797
(Area code 604 before October 1996.)
Whistler office: (604) 932-2755
E-mail: canwest@netnation.com

• One person $50–65; two people $65–125.
• A B&B reservation service covering British Columbia and parts of Alberta, the Yukon, and Alaska, including Greater Vancouver, Victoria, Vancouver Island, the Okanagan, Whistler, Jasper, Banff, Calgary, Prince George, Prince Rupert, Dawson Creek, Fort St. John, White-horse, and Dawson City. Offices in Vancouver, Victoria, Kelowna, and Whistler. Each office arranges bookings in all of the areas covered. The B&Bs have one to three rooms. Accommodation for skiers at Whistler; at Sun Peaks near Kamloops; and at Big White, Silver Star, and Apex in the Okanagan. Deposit by credit card required to hold reservation. Cancellation notice seven days or, during the ski season at Whistler, thirty days. **In the agents' own words:** "We extend an invitation to call on us when planning to visit any location in B.C., Jasper, Banff, or Calgary."

Old English B&B Registry

Vicki Tyndall
1226 Silverwood Crescent
North Vancouver, BC V7P 1J3
(604) 986-5069 Fax: (604) 986-8810

• Rooms. Two people $75–175, private and en-suite bathrooms; two people $75–125, shared guest bathrooms.
Self-contained suites. Two people $75–120.
Rate for one person is usually $10 less. Additional person $20.
Minimum stay two nights on holiday weekends.

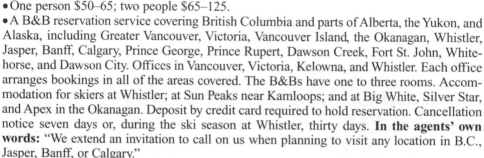

• A B&B reservation service covering Vancouver, North Vancouver, and West Vancouver. Most B&Bs are within twenty minutes of the city centre. Deposit required to hold reservation. Deposit less $20 administration fee is refunded if reservation is cancelled fourteen days before arrival. Cash, traveller's cheques, credit cards. **In the agents' own words:** "All our B&Bs have been personally inspected with attention given to cleanliness, hospitality, and breakfasts. Our free professional reservation service offers European-style B&Bs with warm, friendly West Coast ambience and with lots of breakfast table conversation about places to explore and things to do. What is offered is definitely more than just a place to stay."

Reservations Jasper Ltd.

Karen Kovich and Debi Derksen
Mail: Box 1840
Jasper, Alberta T0E 1E0
(403) 852-5488 Fax: (403) 852-5489
E-mail: resjas@ycs.ab.ca
Web site: http://www.ycs.ab.ca/market/
resjas/index.htm

• A reservation service covering in-house accommodation without breakfast, B&Bs, hotels, motels, cabins, and bungalows in the Jasper area;
B&Bs, hotels, motels, cabins, and bungalows in Banff; and hotels, motels, cabins, and bungalows in the Lake Louise area. $15 booking fee for one reservation in one place. $20 booking fee for multiple reservations. Additional $5 booking fee for overseas clients. Visa. Noncommissionable. **In the agents' own words:** "We offer a fast, reliable, and informative service for our clients. You need only make one call for your Canadian Rockies vacation accommodations."

Town and Country B&B Reservation Service

Helen Burich
Mail: Box 74542
2803 West Fourth Avenue
Vancouver, BC V6K 1K2
(604) 731-5942 Fax: (604) 731-5942

• One person $55–85; two people $75–190.
Queen-sized beds, double beds, and twin beds.
Private and shared bathrooms.
• A B&B reservation service covering Vancouver,
Victoria, and Vancouver Island. B&Bs range
from modest to luxurious. Character houses to contemporary. B&Bs in residential areas are usually within fifteen to twenty minutes of city centres. Most are within walking distance of neighbourhood shops, restaurants, and parks. Some self-contained units and cottages. Personally selected and inspected. Deposit required. Cancellation notice seven days. **In the agents' own words:** "Our service has been established since 1980. We know our hosts and houses personally and do our best to meet your requirements according to facilities and availability."

WestWay Accommodation Registry

Zarina Jadavji
Mail: Box 48950 Bentall Centre 3
Vancouver, BC V7X 1A8
(604) 273-8293 Fax: (604) 278-6745

• One person $35–110; two people $50–225. Additional person $10–25.

• A B&B reservation service covering British Columbia (including Greater Vancouver, Greater Victoria, the Sunshine Coast, the Gulf Islands, Whistler, the Rockies, the Kootenays, and the Okanagan Valley) and Alberta (including Edmonton, Calgary, Jasper, Banff, and Canmore). One hundred and fifty-seven B&Bs, from modest to luxurious and from Victorian to modern. Self-contained suites and cottages. Some have swimming pools, Jacuzzis, fireplaces, saunas, views, and waterfront locations. Close to airports, ferries, ski hills, beaches, recreational facilities, sightseeing, and bus routes. Available daily, weekly, and monthly. Accommodations are checked for comfort, cleanliness, and courtesy. B&Bs in Greater Vancouver are from five minutes' to an hour's drive from downtown Vancouver, Stanley Park, the Vancouver Aquarium, theatres, shopping malls, restaurants, the Vancouver Art Gallery, English Bay, Kitsilano, Fantasy Garden World, Grouse Mountain, beaches, skiing, golfing, and fishing. In Greater Vancouver and Greater Victoria, car rentals and sightseeing tours are arranged. **In the agents' own words:** "We look forward to serving you and welcoming you to beautiful houses. Our congenial hosts from different backgrounds and countries speak French, German, Spanish, Italian, and other languages."

West Bay B&B

Ralf and Yvette Craig
715 Suffolk Street
Victoria, BC V9A 3J5
(250) 386-7330 Fax: (250) 389-0280
(area code 604 before October 1996)

• From downtown Victoria, follow Pandora Street southwest over the blue Johnson Street bridge and onto Esquimalt Road. Go 1 kilometre, turn right onto Dalton, and turn left onto Suffolk Street.

• One or two people $85–125. Queen-sized bed; twin beds (or a king-sized bed). Ensuite bathrooms. Additional person $25.

• A house on a ridge, with a view of Victoria, the ocean, and the Olympic Mountains. Within walking distance of restaurants, pubs, entertainment, tennis courts, and jogging trails. Two kilometres from the Empress Hotel. Downtown Victoria and the Empress Hotel can be reached by harbour water taxi or a twenty-minute walk along an ocean boardwalk. Guest rooms have microwaves and small fridges. Breakfast, including a main course and homemade breads or other baked goods, is served between 8:00 and 9:30 a.m. in the dining room, which has a view of the ocean. Check-in between 4:00 and 6:00 p.m. MasterCard, American Express. French, German, and some Spanish spoken. Not suitable for children under six or for pets. No smoking. **In the hosts' own words:** "We welcome you to our large, modern house perched high on a ridge—your holiday home."

Agra House B&B

Gulshan and Abdul Adatia
679 Herald Street
Victoria, BC V8W 1S8
(250) 380-1099 Fax: (250) 380-1099
(area code 604 before October 1996)

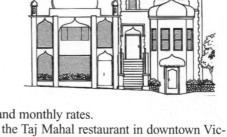

• In downtown Victoria, a few steps from Douglas Street, two blocks from city hall.

• Ten rooms. One person $50–70; two people $60–80. Queen-sized bed. Ensuite bathrooms. Breakfast ingredients supplied. Additional person $5–15. Off-season rates. In winter, weekly and monthly rates.

• A B&B with domes and minarets, attached to the Taj Mahal restaurant in downtown Victoria. Two blocks from city hall, Wharf Street, and the waterfront; three blocks from a public swimming pool; five blocks from the Inner Harbour and the Parliament Buildings; and a few minutes' walk from shopping. Near public transportation. Each guest room has a small stove, a coffeemaker, a kettle, a teapot, a fridge, and a TV. Some of the guest rooms are ornately decorated. Coin laundry. Ingredients for Continental breakfast are supplied in the guest rooms. Reservations recommended. Deposit of one night's rate required to hold reservation. Cancellation notice forty-eight hours. Check-out time 11:00 a.m. Visa, MasterCard. No pets. No smoking. **In the hosts' own words:** "Friendly and clean, our B&B is ideally located on a quiet street right in the centre of Victoria."

Andersen House B&B

Janet and Max Andersen
301 Kingston Street
Victoria, BC V8V 1V5
(250) 388-4565 Fax: (250) 388-4563
(area code 604 before October 1996)

• At Kingston and Pendray streets, one and a half blocks west of the Parliament Buildings.
• Four suites. Two people $75–175. Queen-sized bed; king-sized bed. Ensuite bathrooms and ensuite bathrooms with showers. Additional person $35.
• A Victorian house built for a sea captain in 1891, with ornately plastered high ceilings, stained glass windows, and a garden with ninety-year-old pear, apple, and willow trees. Within walking distance of Victoria's attractions. Suites have original paintings, Peruvian rugs, and home-fired Raku pottery. Each suite has a view of mountains, gardens, or the downtown skyline. One of the ensuite bathrooms has a Jacuzzi; another has an extra-long claw-foot tub. Full breakfast, with homemade jams, fruit, and herbs from the garden, is served by the fireplace in an oak-furnished dining room. Cancellation notice seven days. Visa, MasterCard. No pets; cat in residence. Smoking on decks and patio. **In the hosts' own words:** "We are ideally located a short walk from Victoria's best-known attractions, and we can ensure that you also enjoy the secret Victoria so many visitors miss."

Heathergate House B&B and Cottage

Ann Easton
122 Simcoe Street
Victoria, BC V8V 1K4
(250) 383-0068 Fax: (250) 383-4320
(area code 604 before October 1996)

• Ten minutes' walk from the Seattle and Port Angeles ferries.

• Three rooms. In summer (May 15 to September 30) one person or two people $95–115. In winter, one person or two people $65–90. Queen-sized bed; twin beds. Ensuite and private bathrooms.

Two-bedroom cottage (accommodates six people). Two people $125. Queen-sized bed and twin beds. Hide-a-bed. Private bathroom. Additional person $20. Winter monthly rates, October 1 to April 30.

• A B&B in the James Bay area of Victoria. Within fifteen minutes' walk of the Inner Harbour, the Parliament Buildings, a conference centre, the Royal British Columbia Museum, Fisherman's Wharf, shops, and restaurants. Guest rooms have down comforters, bathrobes, hair dryers, ceiling fans, and telephones for local calls. Silver tray service for coffee or tea before breakfast in the guest rooms. Guest lounge with fireplace, books, and TV. Cottage has a kitchen with washer and dryer, a dining room, a living room with TV, a private patio, down comforters, and bedroom ceiling fans. Full breakfast is served in the dining room, with different entrées each day. Continental breakfast is delivered to the cottage. Visa, MasterCard. Adult oriented. Children over nine welcome in the cottage. No pets. No smoking. **In the hosts' own words:** "A city retreat for honeymoons and those special holidays. Enjoy casual luxury in the heart of Victoria—a combination of old world antiques and traditions and warm West Coast hospitality."

At Craig House B&B

Jim Hill
52 San Jose Avenue
Victoria, BC V8V 2C2
(250) 383-0339
(area code 604 before October 1996)

• Go south on Douglas Street to the end. Turn right onto Dallas Road and continue for eight blocks. Turn right onto San Jose Avenue.

• One person $50–70; two people $55–75. Queen-sized bed; double bed. Additional person $15.

• A B&B in the James Bay area of Victoria, within fifteen minutes' walk of Beacon Hill Park, the Empress Hotel, the Parliament Buildings, and the Inner Harbour. Guest rooms have TVs and are on a floor exclusively for guests' use. One of the guest rooms accommodates up to four people and has a fireplace. Full breakfast of juice, a fresh fruit cup, a hot entrée, tea, and coffee is served. Cancellation notice seven days. Traveller's cheques, Visa, Master-Card. Children over seven welcome. No pets. Smoking on the sun deck. **In the hosts' own words:** "Comfort, relaxation, and hospitality await you. Our newly decorated guest rooms are spacious and traditionally furnished for the comfort of our guests. Awake refreshed."

Fran's B&B

Fran Thoburn
20 San Jose Avenue
Victoria, BC V8V 2C2
(250) 380-7145
(area code 604 before October 1996)

• From downtown Victoria, follow Menzies Street or Government Street to Dallas Road and turn right. San Jose is two blocks from Menzies and Dallas and five blocks from Government and Dallas.

• Two rooms. One person $55–65; two people $65–75. Twin beds (or king-sized bed); queen-sized bed. Shared guest bathroom.

• A small, 1930s renovated house close to downtown Victoria, on a quiet, family-oriented street in the James Bay area. Ten minutes' walk from the Parliament Buildings and from ferries to Port Angeles. A few steps from the ocean, parks, and beaches. Close to bus service. Living/dining room with wood stove. Breakfast usually consists of fresh fruit, nuts, jams, and daily homemade muffins. Other items available on request. Children welcome, although guest rooms are too small to accommodate a cot. Pets welcome. No smoking. **In the hosts' own words:** "Two things make this B&B special: the location—close to the ocean, parks, and downtown—and the warm, friendly, and relaxed atmosphere."

B&M/Breland B&B

Anita Breland
544 Toronto Street
Victoria, BC V8V 1P2
(250) 383-0927
(area code 604 before October 1996)

• Two blocks south of the Parliament Buildings. Five blocks from Beacon Hill Park.
• Two rooms. One person $39–49; two people $49–59. Queen-sized bed; double bed and one twin bed. Shared guest bathroom. Child 7 to 12 $10. Seasonal rates. Open May to November.
• An older, colonial-style house in the James Bay area of Victoria, five minutes' walk from the Parliament Buildings and ten minutes' walk from the Royal British Columbia Museum, the Inner Harbour, and Beacon Hill Park. Guest rooms have TVs. A guest bathroom on the main floor has a claw-foot tub. Pickup can be arranged from the bus terminal, the Airporter bus stop at the Empress Hotel, and the ferry from Port Angeles, Washington. Light breakfast is served in the dining room. Diets are accommodated. German and Dutch understood. No pets; the host has allergies.

Lily House B&B

Lily, Greg, and Lynn
143 Government Street
Victoria, BC V8V 2K6
(250) 920-0891 Fax: (250) 920-0891
(area code 604 before October 1996)

• Suites. Two people $65–140. Ensuite bathrooms. Additional person $15.
• A 1911 house on one of the oldest streets in the city centre. Two blocks from the ocean, Beacon Hill Park, the downtown Inner Harbour, and the Empress Hotel. Within walking distance of tourist attractions. Each suite has a kitchen and a TV. Cancellation notice five days. Children welcome.

Battery Street Guest House

Pamela Verduyn
670 Battery Street
Victoria, BC   V8V 1E5
(250) 385-4632
(area code 604 before October 1996)

• Near Battery and Douglas streets.

• Six rooms. One person $45–65; two people $65–85. Queen-sized bed; two double beds; queen-sized bed and one twin bed. Two ensuite half bathrooms and two shared guest bathrooms. Additional person $20. Child $15.

• A 1898 house on a quiet street, within walking distance of downtown Victoria, the Inner Harbour, the Royal British Columbia Museum, and the Empress Hotel. One block from Beacon Hill Park and the ocean. Guest living room on the ground floor. Full breakfast is served between 7:00 and 9:00 a.m. Traveller's cheques, personal cheques. Dutch spoken. Non-smokers. **In the hosts' own words:** "Our comfortable, established heritage guest house is centrally located in a quiet, peaceful area."

Dashwood Seaside Manor

Derek Dashwood
1 Cook Street
Victoria, BC V8V 3W6
(250) 385-5517 Fax: (250) 383-1760
(area code 604 before October 1996)
Toll-free, for reservations: 1-800-667-5517

● From downtown Victoria, follow Douglas Street south and turn left onto Dallas Road. Continue through Beacon Hill Park. The B&B is at the corner of Dallas Road and Cook Street.

● Fourteen suites. Two people $65–285. Queen-sized bed; queen-sized bed and sofa bed. Ensuite bathrooms. Breakfast ingredients supplied. Off-season and extended stay rates.

● A B&B in a Tudor-style mansion. Suites have views of the ocean and the Olympic Mountains. In the mornings, seals, killer whales, eagles, and sea otters can be seen from the suites. Songbirds can be heard. The suites have TVs and kitchens stocked with breakfast ingredients. Some suites have sofa beds. Most suites have a fireplace, a Jacuzzi, a balcony, a beamed ceiling, leaded glass, or a chandelier. The house was built in 1912 on property once owned by Governor Sir James Douglas, bought from the Hudson's Bay Company. On Victoria's marine drive (Dallas Road), five minutes' drive from downtown or twenty minutes' walk through Beacon Hill Park. Within walking distance of restaurants and stores in Cook Street Village. Breakfast ingredients supplied. Deposit of one night's rate required to hold reservation. Cancellation notice one week. Check-in by 2:00 p.m., or 10:00 p.m. at the latest; check-out 11:00 a.m. Visa, MasterCard, American Express, personal cheques. **In the hosts' own words:** "We—myself, my family, and staff—will delight in guiding you to Victoria's many secret places and help you to create your own special experience here. Or you may simply want to relax in the privacy of your own suite. Whatever your vacation intentions, let our manor be a part of your special memories."

The Vacationer B&B

Anne and Henry DeVries
1143 Leonard Street
Victoria, BC V8V 2S3
(250) 382-9469 and (250) 384-6553
(area code 604 before October 1996)

• End of Cook Street, across from Beacon Hill Park.
• Rooms. One person $50; two people $65. Queen-sized bed; twin beds.
Shared guest bathrooms.
• A Victorian-style house across the street from Beacon Hill Park's gardens, tennis courts, and walking paths. Two blocks from a beach; around the corner from a bus stop; five minutes' walk from shopping and restaurants; and fifteen minutes' walk from the Inner Harbour, the city centre, and the Royal British Columbia Museum. Guest rooms have TVs. The living room has a stone fireplace. Guests use the backyard and bicycles. Pickup from downtown, ferry, and bus. Off-street parking. The hosts operate a B&B service offering a variety of other accommodations. Four-course breakfast includes homemade croissants, muffins, and jams. Visa, MasterCard. Dutch and German spoken. Not suitable for children. No pets. No smoking. **In the hosts' own words:** "We welcome travellers with a choice of tastefully decorated bedrooms. Our four-course breakfast is sumptuous."

The Beaconsfield Inn

Con and Judi Sollid
998 Humboldt Street
Victoria, BC V8V 2Z8
(250) 384-4044 Fax: (250) 384-4052
(area code 604 before October 1996)

- At the corner of Vancouver and Humboldt streets.
- Six rooms and three suites. One person or two people $175–325. Additional person $65. Ensuite bathrooms.
- A 1905 English-style manor in a residential area, one block from Beacon Hill Park's 120 acres and four blocks from the ocean, the Inner Harbour, downtown shops, galleries, and restaurants. The house has fourteen-foot-high beamed ceilings, mahogany wainscoting, and hardwood floors. Guest rooms and suites have down comforters, antiques, and fresh flowers. Some of the guest rooms and suites have fireplaces, Jacuzzi tubs, and stained glass windows. A sunroom overlooks the front garden. Full breakfast is served in the dining room. Tea and homemade cookies are served in the afternoon. Later, sherry is served by a fireplace in a library. No children. No pets. No smoking. **In the hosts' own words:** "Our heritage-designated house lives up to its reputation as one of Victoria's most beautiful turn-of-the-century restorations. Once the private house of a prominent family, it now offers guests the chance to go back in time to a more gentle era."

Abigail's Hotel

Frauke and Daniel Behune
906 McClure Street
Victoria, BC V8V 3E7
(250) 388-5363 Fax: (250) 388-7787
(area code 604 before October 1996)
Toll-free from within North America: 1-800-561-6565

• At the corner of Quadra and McClure streets. Turn onto McClure Street from Vancouver Street.

• Sixteen rooms. One person or two people $127–249. Ensuite bathrooms. Additional person $30.

Celebration and honeymoon packages.

• A European-style country inn surrounded by gardens, in a residential area three blocks from downtown and the Inner Harbour. Guest rooms have antique furniture, down comforters, and flowers. Some have fireplaces, sitting areas, and canopied beds. Some have Jacuzzis or soaker tubs. Snacks are available in the library, which has a stone fireplace. At six p.m., sherry and hors d'oeuvres are served by the fire. Full breakfast is served in the dining room. Cash, Visa, MasterCard, American Express. German spoken. No children under ten. No pets. No smoking. **In the hosts' own words:** "Smiling faces greet you in this Tudor-style mansion, which has been lovingly restored. Charm, comfort, and sophistication are what make staying here a quality experience."

The Postern Gate Inn

Hazel Lara Prior
1145 Meares Street
Victoria, BC V8V 3J9
(250) 744-8787 Fax: (250) 383-0462
(area code 604 before October 1996)

• From Fort Street, turn right onto Cook and left onto Meares.
• Suites. One person or two people $98–140. Ensuite bathrooms. Additional person $25. Children under 10 free.
Daily, weekly, and monthly rates and packages.
• A B&B that was once the groom's cottage of Craigdarroch Castle, ten minutes' walk from downtown Victoria. Around the corner from Craigdarroch Castle, antique row, and Government House. The host advises guests about dining, shopping, and exploring on the island. Suites have fireplaces, TVs, telephones, and kitchens; some suites have Jacuzzis. Guest entrance. Parking in a courtyard. Full breakfast is delivered to the suites. **In the hosts' own words:** "Romantic ambience combined with all the conveniences of a small European inn."

Pitcairn House B&B

Paul and Diana McCarthy
1119 Ormond Street
Victoria, BC V8V 4J9
(250) 744-8078
(area code 604 before October 1996)
Toll-free from within Canada and the U.S.:
1-800-789-5566

• In central Victoria, one block from downtown.
• Three rooms. One person $60–75; two people $80–95. Queen-sized bed or twin beds, shared guest bathroom; queen-sized bed, ensuite bathroom.
• A 1901 Victorian house with lace curtains, period wallpaper, and original stained glass windows. Guest rooms are decorated with antiques from the early nineteenth century. Guest sitting room has TV and books. Patio and English garden. Full breakfast. Visa, MasterCard. Accessible to the physically challenged, though not wheelchair accessible—three stairs inside. Children over ten welcome. No pets. No smoking. **In the hosts' own words:** "Our heritage house offers a quiet, relaxing environment minutes from downtown."

Friends B&B

Jie and George Morrow
651 Trutch Street
Victoria, BC V8V 4C3
(250) 480-5504 Fax: (250) 480-5288
(area code 604 before October 1996)

• Five blocks from the harbour, at the corner of Richardson and Trutch.
• Rooms. One person $65; two people $75–105. Queen-sized bed. Ensuite
bathrooms. Additional person $15. Child $10.
• A 1912 house on a quiet tree-lined street, ten minutes' walk from the Empress Hotel, Beacon Hill Park, Dallas Road waterfront, Craigdarroch Castle, shopping, and antique row. The house has a panelled hallway, hardwood floors, leaded stained glass windows, and original fireplaces and light fittings. Each guest room has an ensuite bathroom, a TV, a fridge, and a down duvet. Full English breakfast with fresh-squeezed orange juice, fresh fruit salad, and cereal is served in the east-facing dining room, which overlooks the garden. Cancellation notice three days. Visa. Children welcome. A non-smoking house. **In the hosts' own words:** "We enjoy meeting old friends and look forward to making new friends. Our aim is to make our guests feel at home."

Wellington B&B

Inge Ranzinger
66 Wellington Avenue
Victoria, BC V8V 4H5
(250) 383-5976 Fax: (250) 383-5976
(area code 604 before October 1996)

• Four blocks east of Beacon Hill Park, off Dallas Road between Linden and Howe streets. Take the Number 5 bus from downtown Victoria to Dallas Road and Wellington or walk from downtown, twenty minutes through the park.
• Four rooms. One person $45–75; two people $65–100. Queen-sized bed; king-sized bed. Ensuite and private bathrooms. Additional person $20. Child over 12 $20.
• A 1912 Edwardian house in Fairfield, half a block from a bus stop, ocean beaches, and a walking and jogging trail. Four blocks from Beacon Hill Park and tennis courts. Twenty minutes' walk from downtown Victoria through the park. Near shops and restaurants. Guest rooms have down quilts, lace, and walk-in closets. Some of the guest rooms have fireplaces. The host is an interior designer. Breakfast, including fresh fruit, muffins, waffles, and home-made preserves, is served in the dining room. The best time to reach the host is between 8:00 and 10:30 a.m. No pets. No smoking. **In the hosts' own words:** "Our 1912 Fairfield character house has been designed for your comfort and enjoyment. Guests may read or relax in the living room, on a sun porch, or on a sun deck. You'll be delighted to stay here."

The Sea Rose B&B

Joanne and Arnie Davis
1250 Dallas Road
Victoria, BC V8V 1C4
(250) 381-7932 Fax: (250) 480-1298
(area code 604 before October 1996)
Toll-free: 1-800-307-7561

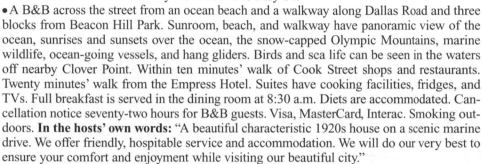

• From downtown Victoria, follow Douglas
Street to Mile 0 of Highway 1. Turn left onto
Dallas Road and continue to Howe.
• Four suites. Two people $95–155. Ensuite bath-
rooms.
Off-season and extended stay rates.
Furnished suites rented monthly November 1 to May 14.
• A B&B across the street from an ocean beach and a walkway along Dallas Road and three
blocks from Beacon Hill Park. Sunroom, beach, and walkway have panoramic view of the
ocean, sunrises and sunsets over the ocean, the snow-capped Olympic Mountains, marine
wildlife, ocean-going vessels, and hang gliders. Birds and sea life can be seen in the waters
off nearby Clover Point. Within ten minutes' walk of Cook Street shops and restaurants.
Twenty minutes' walk from the Empress Hotel. Suites have cooking facilities, fridges, and
TVs. Full breakfast is served in the dining room at 8:30 a.m. Diets are accommodated. Cancellation notice seventy-two hours for B&B guests. Visa, MasterCard, Interac. Smoking outdoors. **In the hosts' own words:** "A beautiful characteristic 1920s house on a scenic marine
drive. We offer friendly, hospitable service and accommodation. We will do our very best to
ensure your comfort and enjoyment while visiting our beautiful city."

The Weekender B&B

Michael Maglio
10 Eberts Street
Victoria, BC V8S 5L6
(250) 389-1688
(area code 604 before October 1996)

• Three rooms. In summer (May to October),
one person $80–95, two people $85–99. In winter (November to April), one person $65–79, two
people, $72–82. Queen-sized bed. Ensuite bath-
rooms. November to April, open weekends only.
• A seaside B&B a few steps from the ocean along Victoria's beachside drive. Near Beacon
Hill Park, shopping, restaurants, Victoria's night life, and tourist attractions. One of the guest
rooms has ocean views and a private sun deck. Guest living room and sun deck. Continental breakfast is served in the dining room. Cancellation notice seven days. Check-in 4:30 to
6:00 p.m. or by arrangement; check-out by 11:00 a.m. Visa, MasterCard. Adult oriented. No
pets. No smoking. **In the hosts' own words:** "We offer warm hospitality at this quality bed
and breakfast by the sea."

Dogwood Manor

Anne-Marie and Haji Dawood
1124 Fairfield Road
Victoria, BC V8V 3A7
(250) 361-4441 Fax: (250) 382-1618
(area code 604 before October 1996)

• Between Cook and Trutch streets.
• Eight suites. One person $75–95; two people
$90–135. Queen-sized bed and sofa bed. Ensuite
bathrooms. Breakfast ingredients supplied. Additional person $15–25. Child under 13 $15.
Off-season rates October to May. Extended stay rates in winter.
• A 1910 house in a garden setting, six blocks from the Empress Hotel and the Inner Harbour and two blocks from Beacon Hill Park. Each suite has a private entrance, a kitchen, a
TV, and a telephone. Some of the suites have fireplaces. Coin laundry. Suites are supplied
with ingredients for Continental breakfast. Reservations recommended. Deposit of one
night's rate required to hold reservation. Cancellation notice three days. Check-in between
1:00 and 6:00 p.m. or by arrangement; check-out by 11:00 a.m. Visa, MasterCard. French,
German, and Spanish spoken. No pets. No smoking. **In the hosts' own words:** "Your home
away from home."

Lilac House Victorian B&B

Gail Harris
252 Memorial Crescent
Victoria, BC V8S 3J2
(250) 389-0252
(area code 604 before October 1996)

• From Blanshard Street, follow Fairfield Road
east for 3 kilometres. Turn right onto Memorial
Crescent. The B&B is the fourth house.
• Two to three rooms. One person $40–60; two
people $60–85. Shared guest bathroom and
shared bathroom. Additional person $20.
• A restored Victorian (1892) house near the sea, in the turn-of-the-century neighbourhood
of Fairfield. Guest rooms have antiques and original watercolour paintings and overlook
Moss Rocks Park and the historical Ross Bay Cemetery. Breakfast includes homemade
baked goods and is served in a Pre-Raphaelite–style dining room. Deposit of one night's rate
required to hold reservation. Cancellation notice seven days. Check-in 5:30 to 6:30 p.m. or
by arrangement. Visa, MasterCard, traveller's cheques. Children over twelve welcome. No
smoking. **In the hosts' own words:** "We offer warm hospitality to the discriminating traveller."

The Shire

Kenn Hollingsworth and Martha Page
464 Stannard Avenue
Victoria, BC V8S 3M5
(250) 598-0406
(area code 604 before October 1996)

• From downtown Victoria, go east on Fort
Street, turn right onto Cook Street, and turn left
onto Richardson. The B&B is on the corner of
Richardson and Stannard avenues.

• Rooms. One or two people $55–95. Queen-
sized bed. Ensuite bathrooms. Additional person $15.

• A turn-of-the-century house surrounded by a garden, below the grounds of the Lieutenant
Governor's official residence, in the quiet, historical Ross Bay/Fairfield/Rockland area. Five
minutes' drive from downtown Victoria and the ocean. Guest rooms have TVs and down
comforters. Cancellation notice three days. Check-in 4:00 to 6:00 p.m. or by arrangement;
check-out by 11:00 a.m. **In the hosts' own words:** "Delicious, wholesome breakfasts and
at-home comfort in a warm, relaxed setting."

Marion's B&B

Thomas and Marion Simms
1730 Taylor Street
Victoria, BC V8R 3E9
(250) 592-3070
(area code 604 before October 1996)

• Five minutes from downtown Victoria. From
Victoria International Airport or the Swartz Bay
ferry terminal, follow the Patricia Bay Highway
(which becomes Blanshard Street) to Hillside
Avenue and turn left. Turn right onto Shelbourne
Street and then take the first left onto Myrtle, which becomes Taylor. The B&B is the fifth
house on the left.

• Three rooms. One person $35–40; two people $50–55, double bed; two people $55–60,
queen-sized bed. Shared guest bathroom and shared bathroom. Additional person $20.
Child $10.

• A B&B on a quiet street, five minutes from downtown Victoria. Guests have breakfast in
a dining room that overlooks an open field, originally part of Victoria's first airport, with
Mount Tolmie in the distance. Living room with view of the Olympic Mountains. Beds with
comforters, percale sheets, and homemade quilts. Jacuzzi. Full breakfast is served on bone
china with silver cutlery. Reservations recommended. Cancellation notice two days. Cash,
traveller's cheques. Small dog in residence. Smoking outdoors. **In the hosts' own words:**
"Home accommodation with a friendly atmosphere."

Chez Raymonde

Raymonde Lortie
1762 Midgard Avenue
Victoria, BC V8P 2Y7
(250) 472-1768
(area code 604 before October 1996)

• Two rooms. One person $45; two people $75. Double bed; twin beds. Shared bathrooms. Additional person $20. Child 7 to 12 $10. Roll-away beds and playpen available.
• A quiet split-level house with large trees in the university district of Victoria, half a block from the University of Victoria. Close to shopping centres, bus route, and beach. Fifteen minutes from downtown Victoria. Guest lounge with TV. Sun deck and large backyard. Parking. French cuisine is served on silver tableware. Visa, MasterCard. French spoken. Children welcome. A non-smoking house. **In the hosts' own words:** "We are renowned for the quality of our food; many guests book for one night and stay for more. Come see us soon. You will not be disappointed."

Country Heritage B&B

Ruth and Allan Holmes
4366 Blenkinsop Road
Victoria, BC V8X 2C4
(250) 477-0011
(area code 604 before October 1996)

• From the Swartz Bay ferry terminal, take the Patricia Bay Highway (17) to the McKenzie Avenue overpass. Turn left onto McKenzie and continue for 3 kilometres. Turn left onto Blenkinsop Road and continue for 1.5 kilometres. The B&B is on the left.
• Two rooms. $75–85, queen-sized bed, shared guest bathroom. $85–95, extra-long twin beds, ensuite bathroom. Child over 12 $15.
• A restored 1916 farmhouse on acreage with mountain and valley views and horses and cattle in the fields. Ten minutes from downtown Victoria. Five minutes from Cordova Bay Beach. Close to eight hundred acres of hiking and nature trails in Mount Douglas Park. A few minutes' walk from a par three golf course, miniature golf, and a driving range. Antiques, handcrafted furniture, and stencilled walls. Guest living room on the main floor with window seats and a granite fireplace. Guest room with queen-sized bed has a sink. Shared guest bathroom has a shower and a claw-foot bathtub. Flowers from the garden are delivered to guest rooms every day. Full breakfast, including home-grown organic fresh fruit and preserves, is served in the kitchen. Low-fat breakfast foods available. Deposit of one night's rate required to hold reservation. Cancellation notice seven days. Cash, traveller's cheques. No pets; black lab in hosts' quarters. Smoke-free environment. **In the hosts' own words:** "A friendly welcome awaits you; afternoon tea is served in our English country garden, where fragrant old roses and sweet peas bloom."

Swan Lake Chalet

Captain Alan and Linda Donohue
948 McKenzie Avenue
Victoria, BC V8X 3G5
(250) 744-1233 Fax: (250) 744-2510
(area code 604 before October 1996)

• Five kilometres from downtown Victoria, near Saanich Road, between Highway 17 and Quadra Street.

• Three rooms. Two people $65–110. Two double beds, ensuite bath; queen-sized bed, ensuite bath; double bed, private bath. Additional person $20.

• A modern chalet-style house across from Swan Lake nature sanctuary. Guests walk around the lake in the nature sanctuary and see panoramic views from the top of Christmas Hill. Within walking distance of a neighbourhood pub, restaurants, and shops. One of the guest rooms has two double beds and a sitting area with TV and opens onto a deck. A second guest room has a queen-sized bed and has access to the deck through a gallery. A third guest room has a double bed and a private bathroom with Jacuzzi. Full breakfast, including homemade muffins and homemade preserves, is served in the dining room, which has antique furnishings, or on the deck. Children over ten welcome. No pets. No smoking.

Bender's B&B

Glenda Bender
4254 Thornhill Crescent
Victoria, BC V8N 3G7
(250) 472-8993 Fax: (250) 472-8995
(area code 604 before October 1996)

• Eight kilometres from city centre. From downtown Victoria, take Johnson Street east. As Johnson curves north, its name changes to Begbie and then to Shelbourne. Turn east onto Kenmore. The first right off Kenmore is Thornhill Crescent.

• Six rooms. Two people $40–45, two double beds, shared guest bathroom; two people $45–50, queen-sized bed, shared guest bathroom; two people $50–55, double bed, ensuite bathroom; two people $55–60, double bed and one twin bed, shared guest bathroom; two people $60–65, double bed and one twin bed, ensuite bathroom. Additional person $20.

• A B&B with six guest rooms, eight kilometres from Victoria's city centre and close to tourist attractions. Two minutes' walk from bus stop. Two of the guest rooms have TVs and ensuite bathrooms. Living room, sun deck, and guest family room. Full breakfast is served in a solarium before 10:00 a.m. Check-in by 10:00 p.m.; check-out by 10:00 a.m. Children welcome. No smoking. **In the hosts' own words:** "Our attractive house has a choice of pretty bedrooms."

Eagle's Nest B&B

Pat and Kathy McGuire
4769 Cordova Bay Road
Victoria, BC V8Y 2J7
(250) 658-2002 Fax: (250) 658-0135
(area code 604 before October 1996)

• Fifteen minutes' drive from downtown Victoria. From Victoria International Airport or the Swartz Bay ferry terminal, follow the Patricia Bay Highway (17). Take the exit for Royal Oak Drive and then turn left at the stop sign and cross over an overpass. Continue on Royal Oak Drive until the intersection of Blenkinsop Road and Cordova Bay Road. Turn left onto Cordova Bay Road, continue for half a kilometre, and turn right into the B&B's driveway.

• Two rooms and one self-contained suite. Two people $70–95. King-sized bed, ensuite bathroom; queen-sized bed, shared guest bathroom; queen-sized bed, bathroom in suite. Additional person $15. Use of kitchen facilities in suite $15. Weekly and seasonal rates.
Honeymoon packages.

• A new house with a sun deck and ocean views, five minutes' walk from beachcombing by the ocean. Five minutes' drive from three golf courses, the Commonwealth Games pool, and a shopping centre. Near Mount Douglas Park and other walking and hiking trails. Deer, raccoons, squirrels, eagles, and other wildlife can be seen. On bus route. Most beds have duvets. One of the guest rooms has a king-sized bed and an ensuite bathroom with Jacuzzi. Suite has kitchen facilities, a TV, a private deck, and a private entrance. Coffee available in the sunroom. Varied, full breakfast. Most diets accommodated. Cancellation notice forty-eight hours. Visa, Mastercard, American Express. Children welcome. No pets. Smoking on sun deck. **In the hosts' own words:** "We are well travelled and offer advice on sightseeing and restaurants. Our home is truly your home away from home."

Cedar Shade B&B

Olga and Ken Richardson
6411 Anndon Place
Victoria, BC V8Z 5R9
(250) 652-2994 Fax: (250) 652-2994
(area code 604 before October 1996)

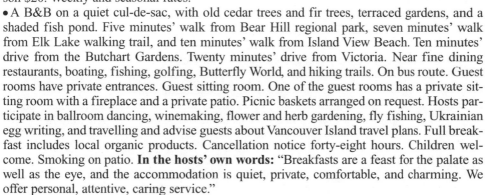

• From the Swartz Bay ferry terminal or the Sidney ferry terminal, take Highway 17. Turn right onto Tanner Road, turn right onto Rodolph Road, and turn onto Anndon Place.

• Three rooms. One person $50; two people $70–80. Queen-sized bed; twin beds. Private and shared guest bathrooms. Additional person $20. Weekly and seasonal rates.

• A B&B on a quiet cul-de-sac, with old cedar trees and fir trees, terraced gardens, and a shaded fish pond. Five minutes' walk from Bear Hill regional park, seven minutes' walk from Elk Lake walking trail, and ten minutes' walk from Island View Beach. Ten minutes' drive from the Butchart Gardens. Twenty minutes' drive from Victoria. Near fine dining restaurants, boating, fishing, golfing, Butterfly World, and hiking trails. On bus route. Guest rooms have private entrances. Guest sitting room. One of the guest rooms has a private sitting room with a fireplace and a private patio. Picnic baskets arranged on request. Hosts participate in ballroom dancing, winemaking, flower and herb gardening, fly fishing, Ukrainian egg writing, and travelling and advise guests about Vancouver Island travel plans. Full breakfast includes local organic products. Cancellation notice forty-eight hours. Children welcome. Smoking on patio. **In the hosts' own words:** "Breakfasts are a feast for the palate as well as the eye, and the accommodation is quiet, private, comfortable, and charming. We offer personal, attentive, caring service."

Benvenuto B&B

Pat and Cathie Monahan
1024 Benvenuto Avenue
Brentwood Bay, BC V8M 1A1
(250) 652-9254 Fax: (250) 652-4003
(area code 604 before October 1996)

• Twenty minutes' drive from Victoria.

• Two rooms. One person $65; two people $75. Ensuite bathrooms. Additional person $15. Cots available.

• A B&B in a rural setting on the Saanich Peninsula, at the entrance to the Butchart Gardens. Beside Todd Inlet Provincial Park, where there are walking trails. In the area are restaurants, kayaking, canoeing, and golfing. Fifteen minutes from shopping and restaurants in Sidney. Twenty minutes from Victoria. Pickup from ferry. The guest area is separate from the hosts' living area. Guest sitting room with fireplace, books, TV, VCR, movies, and games. Full, varied breakfast. Dinner available by arrangement. Check-in by arrangement; check-out by 11:00 a.m. Visa, MasterCard. Children welcome. No pets. Outside smoking area. **In the hosts' own words:** "We have created a feeling of country charm and look forward to catering to your comfort."

Brambley Hedge B&B

David and Jane Boal and Family
7152 Maber Road
Saanichton, BC V8M 1S9
(250) 652-3211 Fax: (250) 652-0322
(area code 604 before October 1996)
E-mail: hedge@octonet.com

• Ten minutes from the Swartz Bay ferry terminal. Twenty minutes from downtown Victoria.
• Three rooms. One person $40–85; two people $65–85. Queen-sized bed; twin beds. Ensuite
and shared guest bathrooms. Additional person $20. Cots and crib available.
Off-season rates.
• A country house surrounded by small farms, five minutes' drive from the Butchart Gardens and Butterfly World. Five minutes' walk from bus stop. Guests walk in the garden, sit on the patio, and watch the G-scale garden railway train running through rhododendrons and annuals. Fireplace. Full breakfast includes homemade muffins, homemade jam, fresh fruit, and breads. Cancellation notice seven days. Deposit of one night's rate required to hold reservation. Visa. Children welcome. No pets; dog and cat in residence. A non-smoking establishment. **In the hosts' own words:** "Please come and visit so that we can share our island with you. Relax in front of a fire with your tea and gingersnaps and we will tell you about all of the places you can discover on Vancouver Island."

The Shires

Gwen and Tom Cooper
6924 Wallace Drive
Brentwood Bay, BC V8M 1G3
(250) 652-1421
(area code 604 before October 1996)

• Twenty minutes' drive from either downtown Victoria or the Swartz Bay ferry terminal. Fifteen minutes from Victoria International Airport.
Follow the signs for the Butchart Gardens onto Wallace Drive.
Buses for Brentwood Bay via Sidney leave from the parking lot of the Swartz Bay ferry terminal.
• Two rooms. One person $50; two people $55–60. Queen-sized bed; double bed. Shared guest bathroom.
• A B&B with a sunroom and deck overlooking a garden with roses, lavender, daffodils, tulips, impatiens, hyacinths, and flowering fruit trees. Four minutes' drive from the Butchart Gardens and Butterfly World. Within walking distance of restaurants and marina facilities. Sitting room with TV. Cookies and drinks provided before bed. Full or Continental breakfast includes homemade baked goods and preserves. Reservations recommended. Cash, traveller's cheques. No pets. No smoking in the guest rooms; smoking in a separate area. **In the hosts' own words:** "We extend to all our guests the finest English hospitality."

Island View Beach

Sylvia Nicholson
7242 Highcrest Terrace
Saanichton, BC V8M 1W5
(250) 652-6842
Cellular: (250) 744-7413
(area code 604 before October 1996)

• Fifteen minutes from the Swartz Bay ferry terminal. From the ferry terminal, take the Patricia Bay Highway (17). Turn left onto Island View Road and continue for one block. Turn left onto Puckle. Turn right onto Lamont Road, which becomes Highcrest Terrace.
• Self-contained suite. Two people $69.
• A B&B with a self-contained suite overlooking Haro Strait and Mount Baker. The suite has a private entrance, a kitchen, a bathroom, a sunroom, laundry facilities, and a living room with TV and VCR. Fifteen minutes' drive from ferries, the Butchart Gardens, and Victoria. Coffee and tea supplies and homemade cookies and squares are provided in the suite. Breakfast, served in the suite's sunroom, often includes blackberry cake, muffins, and fresh fruit with yogurt and cream. Children welcome. Smoking outside. **In the hosts' own words:** "An ideal location for a second honeymoon or for families to have a quiet holiday, birdwatching or just walking on our beach."

Venross B&B

Inez and Don Louden
1905 Venross Place
Saanichton, BC V8M 1K4
(250) 652-2348 Fax: (250) 652-2349
(area code 604 before October 1996)

• From the Swartz Bay ferry terminal, go south on the Patricia Bay Highway, west on Mount Newton X Road, north on Simpson Road, and east on Venross Place.
• Self-contained one-bedroom suite. Two people $49. Twin beds. Bathroom with shower in suite. Additional person $20. Roll-away cots available. Off-season and extended stay rates.
• A ground-level self-contained suite with a private entrance. Suite has a bedroom with twin beds, a kitchen, a laundry room, and a living room with gas fireplace, TV, and telephone. Fifteen minutes from Victoria, ferry terminal, and golf course. Ten minutes from Victoria International Airport and Sidney. Five minutes from restaurants, pubs, and grocery store. Coffee and tea supplies provided in the suite. Continental breakfast is served in the suite at guests' convenience. Children welcome. No pets. No smoking. **In the hosts' own words:** "Make our B&B your home away from home."

Honoured Guest B&B

Donna and David Petroski
8155 Lochside Drive
Saanichton, BC V8M 1V1
(250) 544-1333 Fax: (250) 544-1333
(area code 604 before October 1996)

• Eighteen kilometres north of Victoria off Highway 17.
• Two-bedroom suite. In summer, two people $150, four people $225. In winter, two people $90, four people $140. Double bed and twin beds (or a king-sized bed).
• A B&B on one acre on the Saanich Peninsula, with a private sandy beach and Oriental gardens, on the shores of the Cordova Channel. Panoramic view of the ocean, islands, and mountains. Near the Butchart Gardens, Sidney, Victoria, Victoria International Airport, the Swartz Bay ferry terminal, and the Sidney ferry terminal. On bus route. A five-hundred-square-foot suite has a private entrance, a patio, an outdoor hot tub, a Jacuzzi, and a lounge with TV, VCR, and books. Guest fridge has water, soda, and juices. Tea, coffee, and hot chocolate available in the suite. Chocolates and lemon iced water served when guests arrive. Honeymoon, anniversary, and birthday guests receive a chilled bottle of champagne with silver goblets. Cotton bathrobes, extra towels, toiletries, and a pant press. Pickup from ferry and plane. Full buffet breakfast. Cash, cheques. Adult oriented. **In the host's own words:** "Our house, built in 1994, offers quiet and privacy and was designed to take advantage of its dramatic views and setting. The suite is a sophisticated blend of elegant architecture and contemporary décor. Enjoy our large picture windows that take in a sweep of views, from the moon rise over Mount Baker to the sunrise over the ocean. Honoured guest, we welcome you through winding Oriental gardens to your suite overlooking the ocean."

Silver Sea Waterfront B&B

Sylvia and Peter Gamble
8271 Lochside Drive
Saanichton, BC V8M 1T9
(250) 652-8169
(area code 604 before October 1996)

• Three rooms. From $85. King-sized bed, ensuite bathroom; queen-sized bed, shared guest bathroom; twin beds, shared guest bathroom.
• A quiet waterfront B&B with views of the Gulf of Georgia and the San Juan Islands, a few minutes from B.C. and Washington ferries, Victoria International Airport, fine dining restaurants, and the Butchart Gardens. Patio and garden. Shore walks and birdwatching. Guest rooms have antiques, collectibles, and views of the ocean. One of the guest rooms has an ensuite bathroom with Jacuzzi. Living room with fireplace and a view of the garden and the ocean. Eastern exposure provides views of moon and sunrises. On bus route. Boat anchorage. Adult oriented. **In the hosts' own words:** "Enjoy a restful night, a bountiful breakfast, and West Coast hospitality at its best."

Pineneedle Place B&B

Joan Buchanan
9314 Lochside Drive
Sidney, BC V8L 1N6
(250) 656-2095
(area code 604 before October 1996)

• Twenty-five minutes from Victoria. From the Swartz Bay ferry terminal, go 3 kilometres south on Highway 17. Turn left onto Beacon Avenue. Turn right onto Fifth Street and continue south for 1.6 kilometres. Fifth becomes Lochside Drive.

• Suite. Two people $79. Queen-sized bed. Private bathroom. Additional person $20. Double bed and single bed available. Weekly and off-season rates.

• A house on half an acre of beachfront, with a garden. Ground-floor suite has a private entrance and a lounge with fireplace and TV. Covered outdoor room with barbecue. Tea and coffee provided at any time. Full breakfast is served at a time that suits guests. Wheelchair accessible. Children welcome. No smoking indoors. **In the hosts' own words:** "A peaceful place. Come stroll my garden paths and beachcomb on the beach."

Orchard House

Gerry Martin
9646 Sixth Street
Sidney, BC V8L 2W2
(250) 656-9194
(area code 604 before October 1996)

• From Highway 17, turn east onto Beacon Avenue. Turn south onto Fifth Street and continue for three blocks. Turn west onto Orchard Avenue and continue for one block to Sixth Street.

• Four rooms. One person $49–59; two people $59, double bed; two people $69, queen-sized bed. Additional person $15.

• A house built in 1914 by the founding family of Sidney, with beamed ceilings, built-in cabinets, and flower gardens. Ten minutes' drive from the Butchart Gardens. Five minutes' walk from beaches and parks and from Sidney's shops and restaurants. Two blocks from ferries to Anacortes, Washington. Twenty minutes' drive from downtown Victoria. Full breakfast is served in a formal dining room. Children over twelve welcome. No pets. Smoking outdoors. **In the hosts' own words:** "Come stay with us in our beautiful heritage house and enjoy the small-town character of Sidney by the Sea."

Seventh Haven B&B

Valerie Freeman
9617 Seventh Street
Sidney, BC V8L 2V4
(250) 655-4197
(area code 604 before October 1996)

• Between Orchard and Ocean avenues, south of
Beacon Street and west of Fifth Street. The B&B
has a white picket fence.

• Two rooms. One person $45–50; two people
$55–60. Queen-sized bed, ensuite bathroom;
twin beds, shared bathroom. Additional person $10.

• A 1950-built, recently updated cottage with hardwood floors, coved ceilings, and antique
furniture, within walking distance of shops, dining, the Anacortes ferry, and the seashore.
Ten minutes' drive from the Swartz Bay ferry terminal and Victoria International Airport.
Twenty minutes from the Butchart Gardens. Thirty minutes from Victoria. Living room with
TV. Varied, hot breakfast includes fruit. Reservations recommended. Cash, traveller's
cheques. No pets. Smoking on the patio. **In the hosts' own words:** "Val's Villa of Vancouver has become Seventh Haven of Sidney. You will enjoy this seaside mecca and my cheerful home."

Saanich Inlet B&B

Marjorie A. Copeland
610 Seacliffe Road
Sidney, BC V8L 5W1
(250) 652-3016
(area code 604 before October 1996)

• From the ferry terminal at Swartz Bay, go
south on Patricia Bay Highway (17) to the fourth
traffic light. Turn right onto Mount Newton X
Road and continue past a hospital, a neighbourhood pub, and Saanichton Elementary School to
West Saanich Road. Turn right and continue for 1.8 kilometres to Seacliffe Road.

• Two rooms. Two people $100. Double bed; twin beds. Ensuite bathrooms.

• A cedar house in a rural setting among firs and rhododendrons, on the slopes of Mount
Newton, with a view of Saanich Inlet. Five minutes from Victoria International Airport; ten
minutes from Sidney and the Butchart Gardens; thirty minutes from downtown Victoria; two
minutes from Admore Golf Course and Glen Meadows Golf and Country Club; and within
ten minutes of beaches, marinas, and fine dining restaurants. Guest rooms, a deck, and a
patio overlook Saanich Inlet. Sauna, guest lounge, off-street parking. Full breakfast includes
corn fritters, Quebec maple syrup, and Scandinavian rosettes. Deposit of one night's rate required to hold reservation. Cancellation notice seven days. Check-in by 6:00 p.m. or by
arrangement; check-out by 11:00 a.m. Payment on arrival. Adults only. No pets. Smoke-free
residence. **In the hosts' own words:** "The views of Saanich Inlet are simply wonderful and
the sunsets are absolutely fabulous. A wonderful home with quality furnishings and first-
class hospitality."

Lovat House Seaside B&B

Fran and Chris Atkinson
9625 Second Street
Sidney, BC V8L 3C3
(250) 656-3188
(area code 604 before October 1996)

• Three rooms. One person $45; two people $50–70. Double bed and single bed; queen-sized bed. Ensuite and private bathrooms. Additional person $20.

• A B&B in a quiet area of Sidney, within walking distance of shopping, restaurants, and marinas and with panoramic views of the ocean, islands, and mountains. Within a few minutes of B.C. and U.S. ferries, Victoria International Airport, and the Butchart Gardens. Near beach access. Boat charters, lessons, and whale watching can be arranged. Guest rooms have TVs. Two of the guest rooms have sea views. Sitting area and patio. Full breakfast. Children over eleven welcome. No pets. No smoking.

The Latch Country Inn

Bernd and Heidi Rust
2328 Harbour Road
Sidney, BC V8L 2P8
(250) 656-6622 Fax: (250) 656-6212
(area code 604 before October 1996)

• Twenty minutes from Victoria. Five minutes from the Swartz Bay ferry terminal and the Anacortes ferry.

• Five suites. One person or two people $125–280. King-sized bed; queen-sized bed. Ensuite bathrooms.

Dinner packages. Sailing and fishing cruises.

• A newly restored timber lodge that was built by Samuel Maclure in the 1920s as a summer residence for the lieutenant governor of British Columbia, who once hosted visiting royalty there. Guest suites have antiques, original art, duvets, TVs, and telephones. Some suites have fireplaces. Bark-paneled guest sitting room with a fireplace and a view of the ocean. Near Tsehum Harbour, golf courses, and sailing and fishing cruises. Continental breakfast. Credit cards. German and French spoken. Adult oriented. No pets. Smoking outside. **In the hosts' own words:** "We provide privacy in a country setting, with in-house cuisine featuring a Euro-Pacific menu. Our chef uses locally harvested products and emphasizes Pacific flavours with European-style preparation."

Top o' Triangle Mountain

Henry and Pat Hansen
3442 Karger Terrace
Victoria, BC V9C 3K5
(250) 478-7853 Fax: (250) 478-2245
(area code 604 before October 1996)

• From Highway 1, take Highway 14 west for 5.5 kilometres. Turn left onto
Fulton Road. At the top of the hill, keep left on Fulton. Turn left onto Karger
and continue to cul-de-sac.

• Two rooms and a two-room suite. One person $45; two people $65–85.
Queen-sized bed; queen-sized bed and double hide-a-bed. Ensuite bathroom
and ensuite bathrooms with showers. Additional person $20. Child under 12 $5.
Rollaway and crib available. Off-season rates.

• A cedar house on a small mountain with a view of Victoria, the Strait of Juan de Fuca,
Mount Baker, and the Olympic Mountains. Twenty minutes' drive from downtown Victoria.
Within fifteen minutes' drive of golfing, fishing, swimming, hiking trails, and provincial and
regional parks. Garden and wrap-around sun deck. Open-plan living area. Guest rooms and
suite have TVs. One of the guest rooms and the suite face a back garden with trees. The suite
has a sitting room with double hide-a-bed. Another guest room has a view of the ocean and
mountains and has a sliding glass door to the sun deck. Full hot breakfast is served in a solarium or in the dining room, which has a view of the ocean and mountains. Visa, Master-
Card. No pets. Smoking in designated areas. **In the hosts' own words:** "Our solid cedar
house's natural warmth and charm quickly make our guests feel at home. We offer sincere
hospitality, comfortable beds, and great food."

Our Home on the Hill B&B

Grace and Arnie Holman
546 Delora Drive
Victoria, BC V9C 3R8
(250) 474-4507 Fax: (250) 474-4507
(area code 604 before October 1996)

• From Highway 1 north, take Highway 14 exit
to Colwood. Continue for 5 kilometres to
Metchosin Road and turn left. Turn right onto
Wishart Road, right onto Cairndale, left onto
Mary Anne Crescent, and left onto Delora Drive.
• Three rooms. One person $50; two people $60, double bed, shared guest bathroom; two
people $65, twin beds (or a king-sized bed), private bathroom.
Family rates. Seventh night free.
• A house with a treed yard and sheltered guest hot tub, close to local beaches, parks, trails,
and golf. Twenty minutes' drive from downtown Victoria. Guest sitting room with a TV and
a glass-fronted wood stove overlooks the back garden. Parking. Breakfast includes homemade jam, muffins, and a hot entrée. Diets are accommodated. Children welcome. No pets.
No smoking. **In the hosts' own words:** "Enjoy treed seclusion, bedrooms with antiques, and
a delicious, hearty breakfast. It's worth the short drive from downtown to stay with us."

Pacific Sunrise B&B

Peter and Chris Adamek
3631 Upper Park Drive
Mail: Park Drive RR 4
Victoria, BC V9C 3W3
(250) 474-0158 Fax: (250) 474-3373
(area code 604 before October 1996)

• From Victoria, take Highway 1 to the
Colwood/Sooke exit, turn onto Highway 14, and
continue for 4.5 kilometres. Turn left onto
Metchosin Road and continue for 3.5 kilometres.
Turn left onto the Farhill Road connector, turn left again, and immediately turn right onto
Upper Park Drive.
• Two rooms. One person $65–70; two people $70–75. Queen-sized bed; double bed.
Ensuite bathrooms. Additional person $15. Children under 6 free. Crib $10.
• A new West Coast–style house with an ocean view, in a mature Douglas fir forest. Guest
rooms have ocean views and private decks. One of the guest rooms has a six-foot Jacuzzi.
Guest entrance. Guest telephone, fridge, and microwave. Five minutes' walk from a beach.
A few minutes' drive from golf clubs, beaches, parks, walking and bicycle trails, and salmon
fishing. Fishing charters can be arranged. Five minutes' drive from the Juan de Fuca
Recreation Centre, lawn bowling, and the velodrome venue for the Commonwealth Games.
Twenty minutes' drive from the Butchart Gardens and downtown. Breakfast, including
homemade muffins, fresh fruit plate, and a choice of made-to-order main courses, is served
in the guest rooms at guests' convenience. Traveller's cheques, Visa, MasterCard. No pets.
No smoking. **In the hosts' own words:** "Our guest rooms are bright, clean, and comfortable. After a busy day of sightseeing, hiking, fishing, or maybe golf, you'll want to relax at
our B&B. Enjoy a beautiful ocean view in a classic West Coast setting."

Gracefield Manor

Shirley Wilde
3816 Duke Road RR 4
Victoria, BC V9B 5T8
(250) 478-2459 Fax: (250) 478-2447
(area code 604 before October 1996)

• From Victoria, take Highway 1 west to the Colwood/Sooke exit (to Highway 14). Turn left onto Metchosin Road, go 7 kilometres, and turn left onto Duke Road. The B&B's address number is on an old tree at the end of a long driveway.

• Three rooms. One person or two people $85–100. Double bed; twin beds. Ensuite bathrooms.

• A colonial plantation–style manor with antique furnishings, restored in 1991, on eleven acres of pasture with apple trees, sheep in the fields, and views of the Olympic Mountains and Juan de Fuca Strait. Ten minutes' walk from a park, hiking trails, and a beach. Ten minutes' drive from golf courses and fishing. Twenty minutes' drive from downtown Victoria. Living room and front terrace. One of the guest rooms has a fireplace. Breakfast is served on fine china in a formal dining room. Reservations required. Cancellation notice seven days. Check-in 3:00 to 5:00 p.m. or by arrangement; check-out by 11:30 am. Cash, Visa. Adult oriented. No pets; dog in residence. Smoking outdoors. **In the hosts' own words:** "If you like the quiet country, fabulous ocean and mountain views, fresh sea air, and clean beaches, then come to our manor."

M'Chosin Haven B&B

Sandra and Tony French
3922 Gilbert Drive RR 4
Victoria, BC V9B 5T8
(250) 478-0558 Fax: (250) 478-1814
(area code 604 before October 1996)

• From Victoria, take Highway 1 west to the Colwood/Sooke exit onto Highway 14. Turn left onto Metchosin Road and continue for 4 kilometres. Turn left onto Duke Road, continue for 2 kilometres to Gilbert Drive, and turn right.
• Three rooms. One person $55–75; two people $75–85. Queen-sized bed, ensuite bathroom; twin beds (or a king-sized bed), private bathroom; one twin bed, private bathroom.
Extended stay rates in winter.
• A country house surrounded by arbutus and oak trees in rural Metchosin, five minutes' walk from beaches and trails for walking, jogging, and bicycling. A few minutes' drive from golf and fishing; fishing charters available. Guest rooms are on the ground floor. One of the guest rooms has a queen-sized bed, an ensuite bathroom, and a sitting area. Another guest room has twin beds or a king-sized bed, a private bathroom, and a sitting area. Living room, sun deck, and garden. Full or light breakfast is served at guests' convenience. Deposit required to hold reservation. Cash, traveller's cheques, Visa. Pets outdoors. Smoking outdoors. **In the hosts' own words:** "Our guarantee is gracious hospitality, scrumptious breakfasts, relaxation, privacy, and beautiful surroundings."

Wooded Acres B&B

Elva and Skip Kennedy
4907 Rocky Point Road RR 2
Victoria, BC V9B 5B4
(250) 474-8959 or 478-8172
(area code 604 before October 1996)

• In Metchosin, between Victoria and Sooke. From Highway 14, turn onto
Metchosin Road, right onto Happy Valley, and left onto Rocky Point.
• Two suites. Two people $110. Queen-sized bed. Bathrooms in suites.
• A log house in a country setting, thirty minutes' drive from downtown Victoria, surrounded
by three acres of forest and close to beaches, wilderness parks, golf courses, fishing, birdwatching, and trails for walking, hiking, and mountain bike riding. Twenty minutes' drive
from Sooke. Suites have antiques, down duvets, and hot tubs with views of the wilderness;
robes provided. Full breakfast, with homemade baked goods, scones, biscuits, and fresh eggs
from the hosts' chickens, is served at guests' convenience. Diets are accommodated. Cash,
cheques. Adult oriented. No pets. Smoking restricted. **In the hosts' own words:** "A honey-
mooner's delight, with friendly hospitality, home-like relaxing atmosphere, privacy, and
good food."

Blue Castle B&B

Valerie and Gerry Walther
1009 Glen Forest Way
Mail: RR 1 Box 54
Victoria, BC V9B 5T7
(250) 478-2800
(area code 604 before October 1996)

• From Highway 14, take Metchosin Road. Turn right onto Happy Valley
Road and right onto Glen Forest Way. Continue for 1 kilometre. Keep right at
checkerboard.

• One suite. Two people $130. King-sized bed. Ensuite bathroom.
Two rooms. One person $60–65; two people $70. Queen-sized bed; twin beds.
Shared guest bathroom.
Additional person $25. Winter and weekly rates.

• A Victorian house on Mount Metchosin, with views of mountains and the ocean. Deer visit
the property regularly. Veranda with wicker furniture. Sitting room. Suite has a seven-foot
claw-foot bathtub, a solarium, and a balcony with a panoramic view. Two guest rooms have
mountain views. One of the guest rooms is decorated with white wicker and has a queen-
sized bed and a sitting area. Ten minutes from beach and parks. A few minutes from golf
courses, riding stables, hiking and biking trails, fishing, and whale watching. Twenty minutes' drive from Victoria and Sooke. Afternoon coffee or tea is served. Full breakfast is
served in the dining room. German spoken. Children over eleven welcome. No pets; cat in
residence. Smoking on the lower veranda. **In the hosts' own words:** "Come, relax, enjoy our
home—stay a while."

Swallow Hill Farm B&B

Gini and Peter Walsh
4910 William Head Road
Mail: RR 1
Victoria, BC V9B 5T7
(250) 474-4042 Fax: (250) 474-4042
(area code 604 before October 1996)
E-mail: gwalsh@intertrek.com

• From Victoria, take Highway 1 north to Highway 1A. Take Highway 1A west to Highway 14. Follow Highway 14 towards Sooke. Turn south onto Metchosin Road, which becomes William Head Road. The B&B's sign is 2 kilometres past Metchosin country store.

• Two suites. In summer (May to October), one person $65–75, two people $75–95. In winter, one person $55, two people $65–70. Queen-sized bed, en-suite bathroom; queen-sized bed and twin beds, private bathroom. Additional person $20. Extended stay rates.

• A small working farm with chickens, geese, ducks, sheep, a vegetable garden, a duck pond, and orchards with fourteen varieties of apples from around the world. Views of the ocean and the Olympic Mountains. Surrounded by open fields and meadows. Near trails, beaches, parks, and wildlife. Decorated with handcrafted furniture and antique Canadiana. One of the suites, separate from the house, has a private entrance, a deck, a microwave, and a wet bar. The other suite has two rooms upstairs and a private balcony with view. Sauna. Tea and coffee supplies and homemade cookies are provided. Breakfast includes farm-fresh eggs and juice from home-grown apples. Cancellation notice five days. Check-in 4:00 to 6:00 p.m. or by arrangement. Cash, credit cards. No pets; dog in residence. Non-smokers.

Skookum B&B

Robert and Kathleen Watkins
2085 Harbour View Road
Mail: Box 16
Sooke, BC V0S 1N0
(250) 642-4825 Fax: (250) 642-4264
(area code 604 before October 1996)

- Thirty-five minutes from Victoria. From Highway 14, turn right onto Harbour View Road.
- Three rooms. One person $50, double bed; two people $60, double bed; two people $70, twin beds (or a king-sized bed). Shared guest bathrooms.
- A Cape Cod–style house with wrap-around porch, on three wooded and landscaped acres. Resident deer visit daily. Next to the Galloping Goose Regional Park hiking and mountain bike trail. The hosts arrange bike rentals and fishing charters. The house has a vaulted cedar ceiling, cedar-framed windows, a fireplace, and a formal dining room with hardwood floor. On the upper level are the guest rooms and a guest sitting room with books on the area, a TV, and a VCR. Beverages and homemade cookies. Full breakfast, including fresh fruit in season, homemade baked goods, homemade preserves, and a hot entrée, is served in the dining room. Deposit of one night's rate required to hold reservation. Cash, traveller's cheques, Visa. Cancellation notice seven days. No pets. Smoking on the porch. **In the hosts' own words:** "Our home provides you with the quiet of a country setting and yet is just a short drive from the attractions of Lower Vancouver Island. Let our home be your home away from home."

Hartmann House B&B

Ray and Ann Hartmann
5262 Sooke Road
Sooke, BC V0S 1N0
(250) 642-3761 Fax: (250) 642-7561
(area code 604 before October 1996)

• Thirty minutes' drive from Victoria, on the west coast of Vancouver Island, in the village of Sooke.

• Two rooms. $100, double bed, private bathroom; $120, king-sized bed, ensuite bathroom. Twin beds available.

• Honeymoon suite. Two people, $180. King-sized bed. Ensuite bathroom.

A handcrafted English cottage with ocean and sunset views, surrounded by gardens and lily ponds. Across the road from beaches and trails for hiking and walking. Five minutes' drive from restaurants, tearooms, craft shops, and a golf course. Twenty minutes' drive from windsurfing. Fishing charters can be arranged by the hosts. A guest living area has books and a Count Rumford fireplace. Guest veranda with white wicker chairs. Guest rooms have canopied beds and eiderdown quilts. One of the guest rooms has a four-post double bed. A new seven-hundred-square-foot honeymoon suite has a fireplace, a private courtyard, and a whirlpool bath for two. Bathrooms have robes, shampoo, lotions, and hair dryers. Champagne and fruit plate served when guests arrive. Breakfast includes strawberry waffles, homemade muffins, and omelettes. Entrées change daily. Off-street parking. Cancellation notice three days. Cash, traveller's cheques, Visa. German spoken. Adult oriented. No pets. Smoking on the veranda. **In the hosts' own words:** "Treat yourself to the charm of a country B&B. A unique romantic getaway."

Cooper's Cove Guesthouse B&B

Angelo Prosperi-Porta and Ina Haegemann
5301 Sooke Road
Sooke, BC V0S 1N0
(250) 642-5727 Fax: (250) 642-5749
(area code 604 before October 1996)

• Thirty minutes west of Victoria, via Highway 14.
• Three rooms. One person $75–100; two people $95–125. King-sized bed; queen-sized bed; twin beds. Ensuite bathrooms. Additional person $20. Weekly rates.
Special occasion packages.
• A waterfront house with guest rooms with ocean views. A footpath leads to the water's edge. Two of the guest rooms have private decks. One of the guest rooms has a private entrance, and one has a fireplace. Guest outdoor hot tub in a garden deck is surrounded by flowers and overlooks the water. Guest lounge with fireplace, stereo, telescope, and fridge. Full breakfast includes entrée, homemade baked goods, fresh fruit, cereals, preserves, tea, and coffee. Check-in 4:00 p.m. or by arrangement; check-out 10:00 a.m. Traveller's cheques, Visa, MasterCard. German spoken. No pets. No smoking. **In the hosts' own words:** "Enjoy our European hospitality, world-class food (prepared by Culinary Team Canada chef Angelo Prosperi-Porta), and panoramic view of the Sooke Basin and surrounding hills, on the edge of the famous Galloping Goose Trail. Wir sprechen deutsch."

Belvista B&B

Joe and Pauline Cziraky
6397 Belvista Place
Mail: RR 3
Sooke, BC V0S 1N0
(250) 642-5005 Fax: (250) 642-4599
(area code 604 before October 1996)

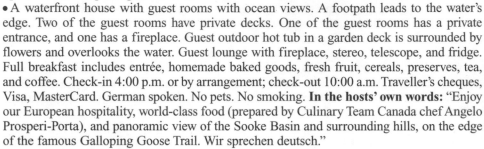

• Thirty-two kilometres west of Victoria on Highway 14. Cross Sooke River Bridge and turn left onto Belvista Place.
• Room, two-bedroom suite, and self-contained one-bedroom cottage. Two people $95–130. Breakfast not included in cottage.
• A waterfront B&B with a walk-on beach, in the coastal village of Sooke, with a view of the sea and the snow-capped Olympic Mountains. Bald eagles, seals, and otters can be seen. The B&B has a guest room, a suite, and a cottage, each with a view of the ocean, a private entrance, a bathroom, a beachside patio, a TV, a VCR, a stereo, and a barbecue. The guest room has an adjoining glass- and cedar-enclosed Jacuzzi. The suite has two bedrooms, a living room, and a fireplace. The one-bedroom beachfront cottage has supplies for coffee and tea; other breakfast ingredients are not supplied. For guests staying in the guest room and the suite, breakfast is served on the guests' private patios or in the dining room. Deposit of one night's rate required to hold reservation. Cancellation notice three days. Guest room and cottage are wheelchair accessible. Children welcome. **In the hosts' own words:** "The West Coast of your dreams. Let our peaceful and natural location be yours to enjoy."

Sooke River Estuary B&B

Linda and Hugh Audet
2056 Glenidle Road RR 1
Sooke, BC V0S 1N0
(250) 642-4655 Fax: (250) 642-4621
(area code 604 before October 1996)

• From Victoria, go 32 kilometres west on Highway 14. Turn left onto Kaltasin Road at Saseenos Elementary School. Turn right onto Glenidle Road. Follow the B&B's long driveway to the house.

• Room. Two people $140. Queen-sized bed. Ensuite bathroom. Two-bedroom suite. Two people $125. Queen-sized bed, double bed and/or twin beds, and queen-sized sofa bed. Breakfast ingredients supplied. Additional person $25. Child $10. Rollaway cot available.

• A B&B on two acres of waterfront overlooking Sooke Harbour, with views of the Olympic Mountains. Landscaped gardens and forest. Eagles, herons, swans, geese, ducks, and otters can be seen. Waterfront patio with lawn furniture, a cooler, and a barbecue. Forty minutes from downtown Victoria. Five minutes from Sooke. Whale watching and salmon charters can be arranged. Ten minutes from golf, hiking trails, beachcombing, and fine dining restaurants. Guest room has a view of sunsets over Sooke Harbour, a queen-sized four-post bed, a small fridge, swivel chairs, a private entrance, a patio, and an ensuite bathroom with sauna, Jacuzzi, and separate marble shower. Wine, flowers, and a basket of fruit are provided. Fourteen-hundred-square-foot two-bedroom suite overlooks gardens and forest and has a bedroom with a queen-sized bed, a bedroom with a double bed and/or twin beds, and a living room with a queen-sized sofa bed. The suite has a washer, a dryer, a freezer, a wood stove, a TV, and kitchen facilities including fridge, stove, microwave, dishwasher, ironing board, iron, and coffeemaker. Children are welcome in the suite; crib, highchair, and wading pool are available. For guests staying in the guest room, breakfast is served in the guest room or in the dining room. For guests staying in the suite, breakfast ingredients for the first morning are provided, including farm-fresh eggs, bacon, sausages, pancake mix, bread, milk, cereal, syrup, juice, fresh fruit, tea, and coffee. One night's rate required to hold reservation. Cancellation notice seven days. Check-in 4:00 p.m.; check-out 11:00 a.m. Cash, traveller's cheques. Children welcome in the suite. No smoking near the house. **In the hosts' own words:** "Treat yourself to the West Coast experience—abundant wildlife, gorgeous sunsets, and warm hospitality."

Lakeside Hideaway B&B Waterfront Cabins

Don and Diana Hunt
Poirier Lake, Otter Point Road
Mail: Box 76
Sooke, BC V0S 1N0
(250) 642-2527 Fax: (250) 642-2527
(area code 604 before October 1996)

• Fifty minutes from Victoria. Take Highway 14
to Sooke. At the only traffic light, turn right onto
Otter Point Road and continue for 6 kilometres.
The B&B's sign is on the left.

• Three cabins. Two people $129–149. Queen-sized bed. Additional person $15.

• A B&B five minutes from Sooke, with three self-contained cedar cabins on four acres by
a private lake. Each cabin has a queen-sized brass bed, a fireplace, and a hot tub. Hiking,
canoeing, and swimming from the B&B. Breakfast is served in the cabins. **In the hosts' own
words:** "Designed for those who enjoy privacy and relaxation or a romantic getaway."

Burnside House B&B

Renate and Heinz Tilly
1890 Maple Avenue
Sooke, BC V0S 1N0
(250) 642-4403 Fax: (250) 642-4403
(area code 604 before October 1996)

• Less than 1 kilometre past Sooke; 37 kilometres west of Victoria.

• Four rooms. One person $65–85; two people
$75–95. Queen-sized bed; double bed. Private
bathroom. Additional person $20.

Off-season rates October 1 to May 1, excluding weekends and holidays.

• A restored Georgian-style country house on two acres of lawn and gardens. Built by John
Muir in 1870, the B&B is the oldest inhabited house in Sooke. Two of the guest rooms have
couches to accommodate an additional person. Some guest rooms have ocean and mountain
views. Jacuzzi in a gazebo. Near golfing, swimming, hiking, and trout and salmon fishing.
Picnic lunches and bicycles available. Whales and seals can sometimes be seen from the
beaches. Accessible by public transit. Full breakfast is served in the guest living room, which
has a fireplace, a TV, and games. Vegetarian breakfast available. Deposit of one night's rate
required to hold reservation. Cancellation notice three days. Visa, MasterCard. German spoken. Children over eleven. Pets welcome. Non-smokers preferred. **In the hosts' own words:**
"An ideal base for exploring the Sooke area. We'd love to spoil you."

Whiffin Spit Lodge B&B

Al and Sheila Carter
7031 West Coast Road
Sooke, BC V0S 1N0
(250) 642-3041 Fax: (250) 642-4181
(area code 604 before October 1996)

• Thirty-seven kilometres west of Victoria. From Victoria, take Highway 1A and watch for the Sooke-Colwood turnoff to the right. Follow Highway 14 to Sooke. Continue past traffic light for 1.5 kilometres to the corner of West Coast Road and Whiffin Spit Road. On bus route No. 61 Sooke.

• One suite and two rooms. One person $75–115; two people $85–125. Queen-sized bed; queen-sized bed and double sofa bed. Ensuite bathrooms. Additional person $20. Child $10. Rollaway bed available.

Self-contained cottage. Two people $110. Breakfast ingredients supplied. Minimum stay two nights. Weekly rates.

• A country-style house built in 1918 and recently renovated, on three-quarters of an acre of gardens. Two guest rooms are on the main floor. Attic suite has a sunken bedroom with skylights, a sitting room with TV and double sofa bed, and an ensuite bathroom with skylights and a marble Jacuzzi. Guest lounge has beamed ceiling, fireplace, TV, and VCR. Breakfast room has beamed ceiling and fireplace. Within two kilometres of Sooke Harbour House Restaurant and Whiffin Spit Beach. Five minutes' walk from Sooke Harbour Marina; salmon fishing and whale-watching charters can be arranged. Close to natural beaches, mountain biking, and hiking trails including the West Coast Trail, the Juan de Fuca Marine Trail, and Galloping Goose Trail. Guests take day trips from the B&B. Off-street parking. Full breakfast and afternoon tea. For guests staying in the cottage, breakfast ingredients are provided in the cottage's kitchen. Deposit of one night's rate required to hold reservation. Cancellation notice three days. Check-in 6:00 p.m. or by arrangement; check-out 11:00 a.m. Visa, MasterCard. No pets. Smoking on the front porch and in the garden. **In the hosts' own words:** "Enjoy a warm British welcome—always."

Sooke Harbour House

Frederique and Sinclair Philip
1528 Whiffen Spit Road
Sooke, BC V0S 1N0
(250) 642-3421 Fax: (250) 642-6988
(area code 604 before October 1996)
Toll-free: 1-800-889-9688
E-mail: shh@islandnet.com
Web site: http://www.sooknet.com/sooke/shh

• Thirty-two kilometres west of Victoria.

• Thirteen rooms. Two people $225–295. King-sized bed; queen-sized bed. Private bathrooms. Lunch included. Children under 12 free. Hideaway beds. Off-season and mid-week rates.

Self-contained three-bedroom cottage. Two people $275. One and a half bathrooms in cottage. Breakfast ingredients supplied in cottage; lunch at main B&B inn. Additional person $25. Children under 12 free. Off-season, mid-week, and weekly rates. Minimum stay two nights; three nights on long weekends.

Conference, dinner, wedding, and romance packages.

• A clapboard inn with a fine dining restaurant on a bluff overlooking the ocean and a self-contained B&B cottage on a nineteenth-century farm, fifteen kilometres from the inn. The inn is surrounded by a kitchen garden with over four hundred varieties of herbs, greens, edible flowers, and trees. Near salmon fishing charters, golf courses, hiking, whale watching, beaches, and cross-country skiing. Each guest room in the inn has an ocean view, a fireplace, a balcony or terrace, a wet bar, a radio, and a telephone. Some of the guest rooms have skylights, an outdoor hot tub, a double Jacuzzi, a double bathtub, or a claw-foot bathtub. TV and VCR on request. Full breakfast including a hot entrée and baked goods is served in the guests' rooms. A set menu lunch for guests of the B&B inn and the cottage is served in the restaurant. The cottage has three bedrooms, a claw-foot tub and separate shower, a fireplace, a six-person outdoor gazebo hot tub, a kitchen, a stocked pantry, a radio, and a telephone. Breakfast ingredients supplied in the cottage. Newspaper, iron, robes, hair dryer, toiletries, baked goods, fruit, and port provided for guests of the B&B inn and the cottage. Reflexology, massage therapy, baby-sitting, and beauty consulting available. Room service. Facilities for conferences, weddings, receptions, and private parties. One night's deposit required. Cancellation notice fourteen days. Service in French and German with advance notice. The restaurant and one of the guest rooms are wheelchair accessible. Children welcome. Pets welcome; $20 per pet per day. No smoking indoors.

Eagle Cove B&B

David Williamson
8061 West Coast Road
Sooke, BC V0S 1N0
(250) 642-7433
(area code 604 before October 1996)

• Seven minutes west of Sooke's only traffic light, on Highway 14 (West Coast Road). The B&B's eagle sign is on the left.
• Self-contained two-room suite. One person or two people $100. Queen-sized bed. Bathroom in suite. Seventh night free.
• A self-contained two-room suite on the shore of the Strait of Juan de Fuca with views of the ocean and the Olympic Mountains. The suite is on the lower floor of the house and has a private deck overlooking the ocean and access to the host's private beach. Sitting room with fridge, bar sink, and coffeemaker. Bedroom with TV, phone, and sliding glass door that opens onto the deck. Breakfast includes coffee or tea, juice, dry cereal, and milk, already in the fridge, and a choice of hot entrée served in the suite at guests' convenience. Visa. Adults only. No pets. No smoking. **In the hosts' own words:** "A honeymoon haven."

Ocean Wilderness

Marion Rolston
109 West Coast Road
Sooke, BC V0S 1N0
(250) 646-2116 Fax: (250) 646-2116
(area code 604 before October 1996)
Toll-free from within Canada and the U.S.: 1-800-323-2116

• Forty-five kilometres west of Victoria. From Highway 1, turn onto Highway 14. Go through Sooke and continue for 14 kilometres.

• Nine rooms. Two people $115–175. Ensuite bathrooms. Additional person $15 (cot) or $25 (hide-a-bed). Off-season rates.

Fishing and tour charters.

Seafood buffet package.

• An oceanfront house on five acres of old-growth forest, with views of the forest, the Strait of Juan de Fuca, and the Olympic Mountains. Orca whales, grey whales, seals, bald eagles, and deer grazing under cedars can be seen. Guest rooms have sitting areas, antiques, and canopied beds. Some of the guest rooms have soaker tubs for two overlooking the ocean. Fishing charters, whale tours, trail hiking, beachcombing, scuba diving, snorkelling, golfing, and dining. The hosts help with arrangements for weddings at the B&B. Coffee or tea on a silver service with fresh flowers is delivered to guests' rooms before breakfast. Full breakfast with cinnamon rolls, biscuits, farm-fresh eggs, and homemade jams and jellies is served in the log dining room or, if guests prefer, in their rooms. Reservations recommended. Cancellation notice seven days. Credit cards. No smoking indoors. **In the hosts' own words:** "Wander the gardens or have a luxurious soak in a hot tub in a Japanese gazebo overlooking the ocean and mountains."

The Beach House

Ellie Thorburn
369 Isabella Point Road
Salt Spring Island, BC V8K 1V4
(250) 653-2040 Fax: (250) 653-9711
(area code 604 before October 1996)

• Fifteen kilometres from Ganges. Two kilometres from the Fulford Harbour ferry terminal and village. Follow the road around the top of the harbour and go straight along the water's edge, past the Fulford Inn (on the right), for 1.3 kilometres. The B&B is on the left.

• Rooms. $115–130. Queen-sized bed; king-sized bed. Ensuite bathrooms. Self-contained one-bedroom suite. Two people $110–$130. Queen-sized bed, twin beds, and queen-sized sofa bed. Breakfast service optional. Additional person $10–20. Weekly and off-season rates.

• A B&B with beach access, on the shore of Fulford Harbour, in a rural setting. Country décor and local artwork. Eleven steps lead down to a shell beach for beachcombing, crabbing, kayaking, and swimming. Each guest room has a private entrance, a patio, a sitting area with a fireplace, and a view of the shoreline. One of the guest rooms has a Jacuzzi tub and a king-sized bed. A room with a double bed is available for a third person accompanying the guests staying in either of the guest rooms. One-bedroom suite has an oceanside deck, a kitchen, and a living room with a queen-sized sofa bed. Gas barbecue, outdoor fire pit, guest laundry facilities, and beach gear including gumboots, pails, and shovels. Hot beverages. Reservations recommended. Credit cards. Rooms are adult oriented and are not suitable for pets. The suite is suitable for families. Pets in the suite by arrangement. Smoking outside. **In the hosts' own words:** "Tasty, creative breakfasts served oceanside provide memorable moments. Our location offers seclusion, tranquillity, and excellent seascape views. At low tide our beach invites hours of beachcombing, with numerous treaures to collect. A front-row seat to magnificent sunrises and glistening reflections of moonlight. A taste of paradise that is yours to enjoy."

Ocean Spray B&B by the Sea

Ilse and Harry Leader
1241 Isabella Point Road
Salt Spring Island, BC V8K 1T5
(250) 653-4273
(area code 604 before October 1996)

• Located 5.5 kilometres south of the Fulford Inn.

• Self-contained suite. Two people $75. Twin beds and double sofa bed. Bathroom in suite. Breakfast ingredients supplied. Additional person $20.

• A cedar house on Satellite Channel, with five acres of forested waterfront and a panoramic view of the Gulf Islands and Mount Baker. Self-contained suite has a bedroom with twin beds, a sitting room with double sofa bed, a kitchen, a dining area, and a private entrance. A deck off the bedroom has a view of Satellite Channel; marine wildlife can be seen. Ingredients are supplied for guests to have breakfast in the suite. Visa, MasterCard. **In the hosts' own words:** "We supply ample and wholesome food for your breakfast."

Weston Lake Inn B&B

Susan Evans and Ted Harrison
813 Beaver Point Road
Salt Spring Island, BC V8K 1X9
(250) 653-4311
(area code 604 before October 1996)

• Located 3.6 kilometres from Fulford Harbour, on the road to Ruckle Park.
Eleven kilometres from Ganges.

• Three rooms. One person $80–100; two people $95–115. Queen-sized bed;
queen-sized bed and one twin bed. Ensuite bathrooms. Additional person $25.
Charters on the hosts' 36-foot sailboat.

• A country house on a knoll with flowering trees and shrubs, on a ten-acre hobby farm with gardens, woodlands, and pastures, overlooking Weston Lake. A long driveway beside a split-rail fence winds past cows grazing in pasture. Guest rooms have flowers and down duvets. Guest lounge has a fireplace, books, TV, VCR, and movies. Guest hot tub on a deck faces the lake. Full breakfast, including home-grown organic produce and farm-fresh eggs, is served in an antique-furnished dining room, with classical music in the background. Cancellation notice seven days. Check-out 11:00 a.m. Visa, MasterCard. Adult oriented. No pets; sheep dog in residence. No smoking indoors.

Daffodil Cove Cottage

John Gilman
146 Meyer Road
Salt Spring Island, BC V8K 1X4
(250) 653-4950
(area code 604 before October 1996)

• On Satellite Channel, adjacent to the ecological reserve on the south end of Salt Spring Island. Seven kilometres from the Fulford Harbour ferry terminal.

• Self-contained cottage (sleeps four). Two people $95. Queen-sized bed and twin beds. Private bathroom. Additional person $20. Cereals, tea, and coffee supplied; perishables not supplied. Minimum stay two nights. Weekly and off-season rates.

• A self-contained cedar and glass cottage on the ocean, adjacent to a nature reserve. A kitchen and a sunroom dining area lead off a living room that has a glass-front wood stove, a wrap-around deck, and a panoramic view of the ocean and forest. Guest rooms have electric heat. Cedar, ceramic tile, and other natural materials. The cottage accommodates up to four people and has a bedroom with a queen-sized bed, a loft with twin beds, and a bathroom. Food staples, including tea, coffee, cereals, sugar, flour, and oil, are provided for guests to prepare meals. Children welcome. No pets. A non-smoking establishment. **In the hosts' own words:** "The cottage is nestled amongst fir, arbutus, garry oak, and wildflowers typical of this very special mediterranean ecological niche, on seven sunny, parklike acres. The adjacent unmarked nature and marine reserves provide an array of wildlife at the door. Come and enjoy the beauty and seclusion of this region from the comfort of our very private cottage."

Beddis House B&B

Terry and Bev Bolton
131 Miles Avenue
Salt Spring Island, BC V8K 2E1
(250) 537-1028 Fax: (250) 537-9888
(area code 604 before October 1996)

• Eight kilometres south of Ganges. Call for directions.

• Three rooms in a coach house separate from the hosts' house. Two people
$140–170. King-sized bed; queen-sized bed; twin beds. Ensuite bathrooms.
One-person, weekly, and winter rates.

• A restored turn-of-the-century oceanfront farmhouse with a walk-on beach. The house is
between the sea and an apple orchard and is surrounded by one and a quarter acres of flower
gardens, lawns, and fruit trees. Deer, otters, seals, and eagles and other seabirds can be seen.
Guest rooms are in a coach house separate from the hosts' house. Each guest room has a private oceanfront deck, a wood stove, a sitting area, and a Victorian-style ensuite bathroom
with claw-foot tub and pedestal sink. Guest sitting room in the main house has a wood stove,
a games table, and books. Afternoon tea is served in the sitting room or on the decks.
Breakfast, including foods in season and homemade baked goods, is served in the seaside
dining room in the main house. Cancellation notice ten days. Visa, MasterCard. Adult
oriented. No pets. Non-smoking. **In the hosts' own words:** "Whether you choose rest,
romance, or revitalization, you'll escape to quieter times in a spot that is truly magical all
year round."

The Armand Way B&B

Odette and Michael Indridson
221 Armand Way
Ganges, Salt Spring Island, BC V8K 2B6
(250) 653-9650 Fax: (250) 653-9650
(area code 604 before October 1996)

• Eight kilometres south of Ganges, off Fulford-Ganges Road. Turn onto Dukes Road, and then left onto Seymour Heights, which leads onto Armand Way.

• Three rooms. In winter, two people $75. In summer, two people $95–115. Ensuite bathrooms.

• A B&B surrounded by arbutus, pine, and fir trees, on a mountainside, with views of the Gulf Islands and the mainland mountains from each room. Close to ferries, marinas, lakes, beaches, and a golf course. Ten minutes' drive from shopping and restaurants. Guest living room and den with TV and VCR. Guests watch sunrises and sit under the stars on upper and lower decks. Full breakfast includes cappuccino and homemade baked goods. Adult oriented. No pets. Smoking outdoors. **In the hosts' own words:** "Pamper your body and soul with a relaxing stay at our B&B. Breathtaking views, comfortable rooms, and scrumptious breakfasts will make your getaway memorable."

Pauper's Perch B&B

Libby and Michel Jutras
225 Armand Way
Salt Spring Island, BC V8K 2B6
(250) 653-2030 Fax: (250) 653-2045
(area code 604 before October 1996)
E-mail: libby@saltspring.com

• Six kilometres south of Ganges. Three kilometres from the highway.

• Three rooms. $125–165. Queen-sized bed. Ensuite bathrooms.

• A new, architect-designed West Coast contemporary house, with private entrances and decks, one thousand feet above sea level. Sunrises and view extend from the Sunshine Coast to the San Juan Islands. At night, the lights of Vancouver, White Rock, and Bellingham can be seen across the Strait of Georgia, fifty-five kilometres away. Each guest room has an ensuite bathroom with a double Jacuzzi, twin shower heads, or a double soaker tub. Beds have duvets and feather pillows. One host is a watercolour artist and instructor. The hosts arrange bookings and rentals for sailing, scuba diving, boating, fishing, horseback riding, kayaking, tennis, golf, mopeds, theatre, and artists' studio tours. Five-course breakfast includes farm-fresh eggs, homemade jams, and seafoods or vegetarian alternatives. Check-in 4:00 to 6:00 p.m. Visa, MasterCard. Adult oriented. No pets. Smoke-free environment.

Mallard's Mill B&B

Jack Vandort and Jan Macpherson
521 Beddis Road
Mail: Box 383
Ganges, Salt Spring Island, BC V8K 2W1
(250) 537-1011 Fax: (250) 537-1030
(area code 604 before October 1996)

- Six minutes south of Ganges.
- Three rooms and a cottage. Two people from $98–155. King-sized bed; queen-sized bed. Ensuite bathrooms. Additional person $30.
- A quiet country inn with a seventeen-foot spring-fed waterwheel on the side of the inn. Guest rooms have fireplaces and hand-made quilts. Guest lounge has a fireplace, games, and books. Outdoor hot tub; bathrobes provided. Cottage with king-sized bed, fireplace, separate tub room for two, living/dining area, books, and a dock on a pond. Hot beverages and cookies. Island maps, local restaurant menus, and travel information material. In the area are kayaking, golfing, horseback riding, boating, hiking, a farmers' market, galleries, studios, and fine dining restaurants. After breakfast, guests have a ride on a miniature train that circles the property. Three-course breakfast includes fresh bread, fruit, and an entrée such as French toast. Visa, MasterCard. Adult oriented. **In the hosts' own words:** "Let us take you on a magical first-class excursion and pamper you. All aboard."

Alice's Outlook

Alice and Eric Bundock
142 Mount Baker Crescent
Salt Spring Island, BC V8K 2J7
(250) 537-4684
(area code 604 before October 1996)

- Five minutes' drive from Ganges. From Fulford-Ganges Road, turn west onto Charlesworth Road and take the second right.
- Self-contained one-bedroom suite. Two people $85–100. Queen-sized bed and double sofa bed. Ensuite bathroom with shower. Breakfast ingredients supplied. Additional person $15. Infants free. Weekly rates; stay seven nights, pay for six.
- A B&B overlooking Ganges Harbour, with a view of Mount Baker and the Gulf Islands, a few minutes' walk from the town of Ganges. Self-contained one-bedroom suite with private deck, private entrance, kitchen facilities, dining area, and living room with TV and VCR. Breakfast ingredients, including homemade bread, prepared fresh-fruit plate, fresh-squeezed juice, milk, cream, eggs, bacon, waffles, cereals, coffee, and tea, are supplied in the suite. MasterCard. Children and pets welcome. Border collie in residence. Smoking outside. **In the hosts' own words:** "We invite you to enjoy our extensive views of Ganges Harbour, Mount Baker, the Gulf Islands, and more."

Water's Edge B&B

Helen Tara
327 Price Road
Salt Spring Island, BC V8K 2E9
(250) 537-5807 Fax: (250) 537-2862
(area code 604 before October 1996)

• Four kilometres south of Ganges. Take Fulford-Ganges Road to Beddis Road. Turn southeast onto Beddis Road and continue for 2 kilometres to Price Road. Turn left onto Price and continue for 1 kilometre to the waterfront.

• One room and one two-bedroom suite. One person $95–105; two people $110–125. Queen-sized bed and one twin day bed; two queen-sized beds. Ensuite and private bathrooms. Additional person $35.

• A house with country gardens on Ganges Harbour, a few steps from a beach. Guest room and two-bedroom suite have views of the ocean. Guest sitting room with books, paintings, and a fireplace has a fridge, a toaster oven, a microwave, kettles, and dishes for preparing light meals. Guest entrance. Rowboat. While eating breakfast, guests watch birds, sea life, boats, and other marine traffic. Breakfast, including fresh fruit, homemade cereals, yogurt, muffins, and scones, is served on a covered brick patio or in the guest sitting room overlooking the water. MasterCard. Children and pets welcome by arrangement. Smoking outdoors. **In the hosts' own words:** "Watch the sun rise over the water, stroll the beach, or row the boat along the shore."

The Partridge House

Lynne Partridge
131 Salt Spring Way
Salt Spring Island, BC V8K 2G3
(250) 537-2822 Fax: (250) 537-1443
(area code 604 before October 1996)

• Three kilometres south of Ganges, off Fulford-Ganges Road.
• Room. One person $55, two people $65. Twin beds. Shared guest bathroom.
Studio suite. Two people $85. Queen-sized bed and queen-sized hide-a-bed.
Shared guest bathroom. Additional person $15.
Room, suite, and bathroom (entire floor; sleeps six people). $120–165.
Weekly rates.
• A B&B with a view of Active Pass, islands, Mount Baker, and Vancouver's North Shore mountains. Guest entrances. Guest porch and covered outdoor hot tub. Studio suite has kitchen, fireplace, and sitting area with TV. The entire floor (room, suite, and bathroom) accommodates up to six people and is separate from the rest of the house. Full breakfast includes juice, fruit, yogurt, cereals, and a hot entrée, different each day, such as pancakes or soufflés. Cash, traveller's cheques, Visa, MasterCard. Children welcome. No pets; Japanese spaniel in residence. Smoking on the deck. **In the hosts' own words:** "Comfortable beds, fabulous sunrises, and attention to the smallest details have our guests returning again and again."

Sand Dollar B&B

Yvette and Jack Clements
102 Goodrich Road
Salt Spring Island, BC V8K 1L2
(250) 537-9752
(area code 604 before October 1996)

• Half a kilometre from the Vesuvius Bay ferry terminal. Eight kilometres from the Long Harbour ferry terminal. Six kilometres from Ganges.
• Self-contained studio suite separate from the hosts' house. One person or two people $70. Queen-sized bed, chesterfield bed, and fold-out futon. Ensuite bathroom. Additional person $25.
Child 3 to 12 $10.
• A B&B with a studio suite separate from the hosts' house, with a sun deck overlooking Vesuvius Bay Beach. Another sun deck overhangs the beach, is glassed in on one side, is surrounded by trees, and has a barbecue and picnic tables. Near golf, tennis, kayaking, and fine dining restaurants. Within walking distance of a restaurant that specializes in seafood, a neighbourhood pub that serves meals, and a convenience store. Artisans' studios and shops on the island. Guests come by bike or bring bikes on their vehicles. The suite has a bedroom with a brass queen-sized bed; a sitting room with a chesterfield bed, a fold-out futon, a TV, and a wood heater; and a kitchen with a sink, a microwave, a fridge, and an electric frying pan. Pickup from ferry terminal can be arranged. Full breakfast is served in the hosts' dining room. Smoking on the deck. **In the hosts' own words:** "Relax on our sun deck overhanging the beach and let your cares vanish."

White Fig Orchard B&B and Cottage

John and Carol Langston
135 Goodrich Road
Salt Spring Island, BC V8K 1L2
(250) 537-5791
(area code 604 before October 1996)

• From the Vesuvius Bay ferry terminal, take Vesuvius Bay Road for two blocks.
Turn right onto Bay View and continue for one block. Turn left onto Goodrich.
From Fulford Harbour and Long Harbour ferry terminals, take Vesuvius Bay
Road. Turn left onto Bay View and then left onto Goodrich.

• Rooms. One person $70; two people $80. Queen-sized bed; twin beds.
Private and shared guest bathrooms.
Cottage (sleeps four). Two people $95. Private bathroom. Breakfast not included.

• A B&B with a view of the ocean, on two acres of landscaped grounds with an orchard. Two
to five minutes' walk from a public beach, a pub, a restaurant, and a store. The main house
is furnished with antiques. Guest lounge has a TV, a VCR, and a stone fireplace. A cottage
has a bedroom, a living room, kitchen facilities, and a sun deck. Cancellation notice fourteen days. Visa, MasterCard. Smoking restricted. **In the hosts' own words:** "The best eggs
Florentine this side of Florence and the best Belgian waffles this side of Brussels."

Red Tin Roof Cottage

Joan and Dan Clements
140 Goodrich Road
Salt Spring Island, BC V8K 1L2
(250) 537-9864
(area code 604 before October 1996)

• Six kilometres from Ganges. Ten kilometres
from Long Harbour. Near the Vesuvius Bay
ferry terminal. Turn onto Bayview Road and
then left onto Goodrich Road.
• Self-contained cottage. Two people $75.
Queen-sized bed. Private bathroom. Breakfast ingredients supplied.
• A self-contained cottage on a hilltop overlooking Stuart Channel, at the edge of the village
of Vesuvius Bay, surrounded by farmland and meadows. Two hundred metres from a sheltered beach. Within walking distance of a public wharf, a grocery, a family restaurant, and a
pub. The cottage has stained glass windows, a handmade door, a bathroom with claw-foot
bathtub, and a bed-sitting room with brass queen-sized bed, down duvet, fridge, microwave,
sink, frying pan, electric kettle, and toaster. Breakfast ingredients are provided in the fridge.
No pets. No smoking. **In the hosts' own words:** "A romantic oasis for two."

Blencathra House

Margaret and Alan Wooldridge
125 Mountain View Drive
Salt Spring Island, BC V8K 1G1
(250) 537-1606 Fax: (250) 537-1606
(area code 604 before October 1996)

• Two kilometres from Vesuvius Bay. Fourteen
kilometres from Ganges. Off Sunset Drive.
• Two rooms. Two people $115–125, queen-sized
bed; two people $95–105, twin beds (or a king-
sized bed). Ensuite bathrooms.
• A post-and-beam cedar house in a grove of fir and arbutus, with a view of Sansum
Narrows, Duck Bay, and Vancouver Island. Guest entrance. Private balconies. Guest sitting
room has TV, books, magazines, fruit in season, and homemade cookies. Fridge, microwave,
toaster, and coffeemaker. Laundry facilities. Full breakfast. Visa, MasterCard. Children welcome by arrangement. No pets. No smoking. **In the hosts' own words:** "Wonderful views
down Sansum Narrows, into Duck Bay, and across to Vancouver Island—one can guess the
time by the ferry going back and forth all day. Very private and very peaceful."

Anne's Oceanfront Hideaway B&B

Rick and Ruth-Anne Broad
168 Simson Road
Salt Spring Island, BC V8K 1E7
(250) 537-0851 Fax: (250) 537-0861
(area code 604 before October 1996)

• Eight kilometres north of Vesuvius, off Sunset Drive; beside Stone Cutter's Bay on the northwest shore of Salt Spring Island.
• Four rooms. In winter, $125–165. In summer, $165–200. Queen-sized bed; twin beds. Ensuite bathrooms.
Sailing packages.
• A new seven-thousand-square-foot house with an elevator, a guest library with a fireplace, and a guest living room with a TV and a VCR. Covered veranda, exercise room, and outdoor hot tub are for guest use only. Guest entrance and east-facing deck. Each guest room has an ocean view, an individual thermostat, recliners, down duvets, percale sheets, a fruit tray, and terry robes. Each ensuite bathroom has a hydromassage tub. One of the guest rooms has a balcony overlooking the ocean, a fireplace, a queen-sized canopied bed, a hydromassage tub for two, and a separate shower for two. Guest canoes and bicycles. Refreshments on arrival. Coffee is served in guests' rooms or on sun deck before breakfast. Full breakfast. Allergy aware; diets are accommodated with advance notice. Reservations recommended. Cancellation notice seven days. Visa, MasterCard. Wheelchair accessible. Adult oriented. No pets. Smoke-free establishment. **In the hosts' own words:** "Words are inadequate to describe the ever-changing ocean views, the sunsets, and our home. Come, share the experience."

J. CURRAN

The Bellhouse Inn

Andrea Porter and David Birchall
29 Farmhouse Road
Mail: Box 16, Site 4
Galiano Island, BC V0N 1P0
(250) 539-5667 Fax: (250) 539-5316
(area code 604 before October 1996)
1-800-970-RING (7464)

• On Galiano Island, 1 kilometre from the ferry dock. Follow the signs to Bellhouse Provincial Park.

• Three rooms. In winter, two people $89–140. In summer, two people $110–150. Queen-sized bed; double bed. Ensuite bathrooms.

Self-contained two-bedroom cottage $125. Two double beds and a hide-a-bed. Private bathroom. Minimum stay three nights. Extended stay rates.

• A B&B on six grassy acres on Bellhouse Bay, with a sandy beach facing south to Active Pass. The property has been a farm since about 1870, when the land was cleared, and has been an inn, originally known as the Farmhouse Inn, since about 1920. The house was built at the turn of the century and was rebuilt in 1928. It has recently been renovated and is furnished with antiques. Guest rooms have private balconies with ocean views. One of the guest rooms has a Jacuzzi. Two of the guest rooms have soaker tubs. The cottage has a kitchen, a woodstove, and an ocean view. Guests watch eagles, killer whales, otters, and seals from the grass and private balconies. Golfing, fishing, kayaking, hiking, cycling, and diving. One host used to be a professional dancer, the other a race car driver. Suitable for weddings, retreats, and board meetings. Full breakfast with homemade bread, muffins, and jams and entrées such as eggs Benedict. Visa, MasterCard. Adults only. Children welcome in cottage. No pets; dog and cat in residence. No smoking. **In the hosts' own words:** "An idyllic waterfront romantic retreat."

Moonshadows Guest House

Pat Goodwin and Dave Muir
771 Georgeson Bay Road
Mail: RR 1 Site 16 C–16
Galiano Island, BC V0N 1P0
(250) 539-5544 Fax: (250) 539-5544
(area code 604 before October 1996)

• Three kilometres from Sturdies Bay. On Sturdies Bay Road, after 2 kilometres, follow the curve to the left to Georgeson Bay Road.

• Two rooms. One person $90; two people $100. Queen-sized bed; double sofa bed. Ensuite bathrooms. Additional person $20. Off-season rates mid-October to mid-May.

Suite. Two people $125. Queen-sized bed. Ensuite bathroom. Minimum stay two nights.

• A B&B on two acres overlooking a hundred-acre horse farm. Two upstairs guest rooms have high ceilings and down duvets. Three-hundred-square-foot suite on the main floor has French doors that open to a private gardenside covered patio overlooking a pond and pasture. The suite has a TV, a VCR, a stereo, a walk-in shower, a Jacuzzi, and an exercise bike. Guest lounge with books and games. Living room with TV, VCR, and videos. Fireplaces in the living room and dining room and a wood stove in the entry hall. The hosts make arrangements for biking, walking, kayaking, golfing, fishing, picnics, and dinners. Pickup from ferry. Full breakfast, including fruit, baking, a hot dish, coffee, tea, and juice, is served at a time that suits guests. Cancellation notice seven days. Check-in times are flexible. Visa, MasterCard. Adult oriented. No pets. Smoking outdoors. **In the hosts' own words:** "We encourage our guests to be themselves, feel at home, and enjoy our outstanding hospitality."

Dragonfly B&B

Catherine and Ken Maneker
RR 2
Galiano Island, BC V0N 1P0
(250) 539-2084
(area code 604 before October 1996)

• From the Sturdies Bay ferry terminal, take Sturdies Bay Road for 3 kilometres to Porlier Pass Road. Turn right onto Porlier Pass Road and continue for 8 kilometres. Turn right onto McClure Road and take next right up hill. At top of hill, turn left.

• Three rooms. One person $55–65; two people $65–75. Queen-sized bed. Shared guest bathroom. Child over 6 $15. Weekly, extended stay, and retreat rates.

Sailing and kayaking packages.

• A quiet hilltop B&B with views of the ocean, islands, and mountains, on twenty acres of forest. Flower gardens, lawns, fruit trees, grape arbour, and tea house. Close to hiking, swimming, and the pebble beaches of Galiano's east coast. Two-floor guest wing of house has private entrances, a guest dining room, and a guest sitting room. Guest rooms have ocean views. Meditation room available. Japanese art, wood floors, and windows with south facing views. Tea and coffee available all day. Vegetarian menu; breakfast includes homemade breads and muffins, garden vegetables, farm eggs, organic coffee, homemade granola, and jams. Children welcome. Friendly pets welcome; dog and cats on the premises. No smoking. **In the hosts' own words:** "A relaxing, private retreat on a high ridge running through the centre of Galiano Island. Ideal for meditation, spiritual, creative, and stress-reducing retreats."

Orca View

Brian and Trish Cowperthwaite
20675 Porlier Pass Road RR 2
Galiano Island, BC V0N 1P0
(250) 539-3051
(area code 604 before October 1996)

• On the north end of Galiano Island, 20 kilometres from the ferry terminal.
• Suite. One person $85; two people $95. Queen-sized bed, ensuite two-piece bathroom. Private bathroom. One twin bed in second bedroom for additional person $40. Crib and highchair available. Open May to October.
• A B&B on the waterfront with a third-floor suite overlooking Trincomali Channel, with a southwest view of Vancouver Island and sunsets. Hot tub on ground-floor deck. Barbecue and picnic table overlooking the ocean. Pool table and dartboard. Five kilometres from Dionisio Point Provincial Park, where there are sandy beaches, hiking, and trail riding. Near kayak and bicycle rentals and golf. Diving can be arranged. Packed lunches available. Suite has two balconies that overhang the water; seals, otters, and sometimes orcas can be seen. Fridge, microwave, coffee pot, kettle, and toaster. Coffee and tea supplies provided. Breakfast, including fresh fruit, homemade jams and breads, and (when available) smoked salmon, is served in the suite or on a balcony. Check-in after 2:00 p.m.; check-out 11:00 a.m. Personal cheques; no credit cards. Because it is on the third floor, the suite is suitable for school-aged children and pre-walking babies only. No pets; dog and cats in residence. Smoking outdoors. **In the hosts' own words:** "Go to sleep to the sound of the waves and enjoy the spectacular ocean view on awakening. Peace, privacy, and comfort make this an ideal honeymoon haven."

Fernhill Lodge

Brian and Mary Crumblehulme
610 Fernhill Road
Mail: RR 1 C–4 Fernhill Road
Mayne Island, BC V0N 2J0
(250) 539-2544
(area code 604 before October 1996)

• From the ferry terminal, turn left onto the main road. At the Trading Post grocery store, turn right onto Fernhill Road. Continue past a school, Fernhill Centre, and the Horton Bay Road intersection. At the top of a steep, short hill, turn right onto the B&B's driveway.

• Seven rooms. One person $75–124; two people $90–139. Ensuite bathrooms. Additional person $20. Child under 8 $10. Child 8 to 12 $15.

• A lodge with a herb garden on five acres on a hilltop in the country. Within walking distance of beaches, tennis courts, and restaurants. Half an hour's walk or three minutes' drive from the village of Miners' Bay. On the island are fishing charters, art galleries, hiking, cycling, and swimming. Some guest rooms have private decks with outdoor hot tubs. Library and piano. Sauna. Full breakfast with a choice of entrée. Dinner available most nights by reservation. Licensed dining room. Children welcome by arrangement. Smoking outdoors. **In the hosts' own words:** "What really makes our B&B memorable is old-fashioned, attentive, personal service."

Breezy Bay B&B

Irene Muir
131 Payne Road
Mail: Box 40
Saturna Island, BC V0N 2Y0
(250) 539-5957 and (250) 539-3339
Fax: (250) 539-5957
(area code 604 before October 1996)

• Two kilometres from the ferry terminal. Take East Point Road to Payne Road. Turn right onto Payne Road and continue on winding Payne Road to Mill Road. Turn left. The B&B's sign is on the gate.

• Four rooms. One person $55; two people $65–75. Shared guest bathroom. Additional person $15. Children under 7 free.

• An 1890s house surrounded by orchards, flower gardens, and scented lindens, on a fifty-acre farm. Victorian wainscoting, period wood panelling, and stone fireplace. Guest library on the second floor and guest lounge on the first floor. A veranda for reading and bird-watching runs the length of the house and overlooks an orchard and a pond used by tame geese and wild waterfowl. Private beach for kayak launching and sunbathing. Facilities are suitable for groups. Full breakfast. Diets are accommodated. Children welcome. **In the hosts' own words:** "Our majestic Lombardy poplars welcome guests at the gate, which opens up onto beautiful sheep pastures and the original homestead barn."

Poppy Hill Farm B&B

Janet Comstock
104 Payne Road
Mail: Box 44
Saturna Island, BC V0N 2Y0
(250) 539-5002 Fax: (250) 539-5002
(area code 604 before October 1996)

• One kilometre from the ferry terminal. Take East Point Road to Payne Road. Turn right onto Payne Road. The B&B's driveway is the first on the right.

• Three rooms. One person $55–75; two people $65–80. Double bed; double bed and double hide-a-bed. Ensuite, private, and shared guest bathrooms. Additional person $10.

• An eighty-year-old farmhouse on two and a half acres overlooking Boot Cove. Guest rooms are furnished with antiques and have ocean or garden views; some have separate entrances. A wrap-around veranda has a view of Boot Cove and an apple orchard. Full breakfast includes local produce in season. Visa, MasterCard. Children welcome. No pets; cat and dog in residence and wildlife, birds, chickens, and sometimes cows and sheep on the property. Smoking on the veranda. **In the hosts' own words:** "Relax over a gourmet breakfast in our restored farmhouse."

Maple Tree Lane B&B

Dot and Jim Garbet
440 Goulet Road RR 2
Mill Bay, BC V0R 2P0
(250) 743-3940 Fax: (250) 743-3959
(area code 604 before October 1996)

• From the Island Highway, turn east onto Hutchinson Road, towards Arbutus Ridge. Turn right onto Telegraph, left onto La Fortune Road, right onto Kilipi Road, and left onto Goulet Road. Watch for signs on all corners.

• Two rooms. One person $45–55; two people $55–70. Twin beds; queen-sized bed. Private bathrooms. Additional person $20. Child 6 to 14 $10. Double hide-a-bed. Crib and cot. Family and weekly rates.

• An oceanfront house thirty-five minutes' drive from Victoria, with ocean views, a swimming pool in summer, and a beach. Guests walk on the beach, collect shells and driftwood, and go canoeing and kayaking from the front door. Five to ten minutes' drive from golfing, fishing charters, hiking trails, Brentwood and Shawnigan College schools, shopping, and restaurants. Twenty minutes from Duncan; thirty minutes from Chemainus; fifty-five minutes from Nanaimo. Garden-level guest room has a queen-sized bed and a private entrance. Adjoining family room has a double hide-a-bed and TV. Main-floor guest room has twin beds and is wheelchair accessible. Full breakfast. Diets are accommodated. Children welcome. Pets by arrangement; two cats in residence. Smoking outdoors. **In the hosts' own words:** "Enjoy our country hospitality and scrumptuous breakfasts, in a beautiful setting on Vancouver Island."

Norton's Green B&B

Clifford and Mary Norton
663 Frayne Road RR 1
Mill Bay, BC V0R 2P0
(250) 743-8006
(area code 604 before October 1996)

• Half an hour from Victoria. Forty-five minutes from Nanaimo.

• Two rooms. One person $50; two people $55. Queen-sized bed; double bed. Shared guest bathroom.

• A green-coloured house with a white balcony and flowers, close to the ocean. Guests sightsee and shop in Victoria and go to see the Chemainus murals. Parking. TV. Four o'clock tea is served. Full breakfast with fruit is served by the fireplace in the dining room. No pets. No smoking. **In the hosts' own words:** "We were formerly the hosts of Norton's Green B&B of Gibsons, B.C. We give you a warm welcome. Experience comfort in a relaxed atmosphere. Stay with us—we love to spoil you."

Arbutus Cove B&B

Carole and Bob Beevor-Potts
2812 Wiltshire Road
Mail: RR 2
Mill Bay, BC V0R 2P0
(250) 743-1435
(area code 604 before October 1996)

• From the Island Highway (1), two traffic lights north of Mill Bay, turn east onto Kilmalu Road. Continue 1.5 kilometres, following the yellow line, to Whiskey Point Road. Turn left onto Wiltshire Road.

• Two rooms. One person $55; two people $75. Queen-sized bed. Ensuite bathrooms. Extended stay rates.

• A modern, oceanfront house on two wooded acres, with a natural beach. Within walking distance of a nature park. Five minutes' drive from shopping centre and Arbutus Ridge golf course. Fifteen minutes' drive from Duncan's totems, Native heritage centre, and a forest museum. Forty minutes' drive from Victoria. Canoe and bikes. Guest rooms have views of the ocean. Guest entrance. Guest lounge with TV, books, and fireplace. Billiard room. Tea and coffee provided in the guest lounge. Full breakfast is served in a modern kitchen that overlooks the bay; guests' preferences are accommodated. Visa, MasterCard. Adult oriented. No pets. No smoking. **In the hosts' own words:** "Come and enjoy our quiet country atmosphere and yet be so close to the attractions of the South Cowichan region and the charms of nearby Victoria."

Quail's Nest B&B

Vivian and Herb Cline
3160 Mutter Road RR 2
Mill Bay, BC V0R 2P0
(250) 743-2618
(area code 604 before October 1996)

• Forty-five kilometres north of Victoria. Turn right from the Island Highway onto Kilmalu Road, left onto Telegraph Road, right onto Meredith Road, and left onto Mutter Road.

• Three rooms. One person $50–60; two people $60–70. Queen-sized bed; twin beds, shared guest bathroom; twin beds and double hide-a-bed, private bathroom. Additional person $15–20.

Off-season and weekly rates.

Open March 1 to November 30.

• A new house, a few minutes from the highway, on acreage shared by a barn owl family and other birds. Deer can often be seen in the garden. Within one hour's drive of the Butchart Gardens, a Native heritage centre, the Chemainus murals, and two golf courses. Near Brentwood College, Shawnigan Lake school, and Maxwell International Baha'i School. A guest lounge and a ground-level guest room with a private bathroom are designed and equipped for wheelchairs. Full or Continental breakfast, including homemade muffins, jams, and jellies made from locally grown fruits and berries, is served, often in the solarium. Diets are accommodated. No pets; two old dogs in residence. No smoking. **In the hosts' own words:** "We look forward to meeting you and sharing with you our quiet, rural setting."

Whistlestop Shawnigan Lakeside B&B

Ken and Shirley Charters
1838 Baden Powell Road
Mail: Box 39
Shawnigan Lake, BC V0R 2W0
(250) 743-4896 Fax: (250) 743-3301
(area code 604 before October 1996)

• Forty minutes north of Victoria on the east shore of Shawnigan Lake.
• Four rooms. Two people $125; $225 for two nights. Ensuite bathrooms.
Three-room honeymoon suite. Two people $199; $375 for two nights. King-sized bed. Ensuite bathroom.
Off-season rates.
• A B&B on the east shore of Shawnigan Lake, accessible by float plane and car. Docks for boats and float planes are a 200-foot walk from the B&B. Close to E & N passenger train station. A few minutes' walk from the village of Shawnigan and a provincial park with walking/jogging trails and a beach. Guest rooms have down quilts, TVs, VCRs, and private decks with views of sunsets and the lake. Guest hot tub in a gazebo overlooks the lake and has privacy glass windows and a keyed entrance. Bathrobes provided. Croquet sets and rowboats. Living room with stone fireplace, sunroom, library, ice machine, and bar area. Suite has a private dining/bar area, a four-post king-sized bed, a two-person Jacuzzi, and a marble fireplace. Hosts help with arrangements for small weddings, honeymoons, anniversaries, birthdays, and conferences. A karafe of fresh-ground coffee and assorted baked goods are served on a tray left at guests' doors before breakfast. Guests choose from a full breakfast menu for either an 8:30 or a 10:00 a.m. seating. Diets are accommodated by arrangement. Deposit of fifty dollars required. Cancellation notice seven days. Check-in from 2:00 p.m. to midnight; check-out by noon. Visa, MasterCard, American Express. Smoking on decks and in courtyard. **In the hosts' own words:** "Rediscover the country spirit of days gone by on southern Vancouver Island. Nestled amongst magnificent ivy-covered maples on a secluded, sandy-beached acreage, our B&B offers luxuriously appointed character rooms, decorated in a railroad theme. Warm hospitality and privacy in a relaxing setting are the order of the day. Curl up by the fireplace or relax on the balcony and enjoy the beautiful grounds, courtyard, and lakeside views. Our full breakfasts will satisfy even the heartiest appetites. The perfect romantic getaway."

Hipwood House B&B

Sharon and Malcolm Spraggett
1763 Hipwood Road
Mail: Box 211
Shawnigan Lake, BC V0R 2W0
(250) 743-7855
(area code 604 before October 1996)

• Half a kilometre north of Shawnigan Lake Village. Forty-five minutes' drive from Victoria. One hour's drive from Nanaimo.
• Four rooms. One person $35–55; two people $55–65. Queen-sized bed, ensuite bathroom; double bed, shared guest bathroom; queen-sized bed and twin bed, shared guest bathroom. Additional person $15.
• A country house on two acres with walking paths, a 50-foot suspension bridge, a putting green, horseshoes, and badminton. Five minutes' walk from public beach and Shawnigan Lake Village. Five minutes' drive from two private schools—Shawnigan Lake School and Maxwell Baha'i School—and ten minutes from Brentwood College. Within walking distance of swimming, hiking trails, local artists' gallery, and museum. A few minutes' drive from sports equipment rentals, fishing, golfing, tennis, and restaurants. Living room with TV. Guest sun deck and outdoor garden seating. Full breakfast includes fruit, muffins or scones, waffles, and eggs strata. Entrées change daily. Adult oriented; children welcome by arrangement. No pets. Smoking outside. **In the hosts' own words:** "Relax and unwind in spacious rooms in a peaceful setting. Enjoy our friendly welcome and warm hospitality."

Marifield Manor, an Edwardian B&B

Cathy, Ian, and Kate Basskin
2039 Merrifield Lane RR 1
Shawnigan Lake, BC V0R 2W0
(250) 743-9930 Fax: (250) 743-9930
(area code 604 before October 1996)

• Fifty minutes north of Victoria. Fifty minutes south of Nanaimo, along Highway 1. Turn east onto Shawnigan-Mill Bay Road and continue to the four-way stop. Turn right onto Renfrew Road, continue past the store and past Shawnigan Lake School, take the next right onto Linden, and then immediately turn right onto Merrifield.
• From $65–135.
Two two-bedroom suites. Ensuite bathrooms.
Rooms. Queen-sized bed; double bed; twin beds. Private bathrooms.
Group rates for 10 or more guests. Off-season and extended stay rates.
• A restored Edwardian house with period furnishings and art. Close to Shawnigan Lake School, Brentwood School, Queen Margaret's School, and Cowichan Valley wineries and cidery. Sailing, rowing, swimming, cycling, running, hiking, tennis courts, and cricket. Guest entrances and guest lounge with fireplace. Verandas with lake view. Suites have sitting rooms and views over Shawnigan Lake to Mount Baldy. Some of the guest rooms have lake views. Accessible by car, train, float plane, or bus. High tea is served. Breakfast is served on the veranda, in the dining room, or in guests' rooms. Reservations recommended. Cash, traveller's cheques. No pets. No smoking indoors. **In the hosts' own words:** "Rediscover the pleasures of conversation and elegant hospitality in our wonderful manor as we strive to surprise and surpass your expectations."

Cobble House B&B

Ingrid and Simon Vermegen
3105 Cameron-Taggart Road RR 1
Cobble Hill, BC V0R 1L0
(250) 743-2672 Fax: (250) 743-2672
(area code 604 before October 1996)

• Forty-five minutes north of Victoria. One hour south of Nanaimo. Fifteen minutes south of Duncan.

• Three rooms. One person $50–60; two people $65–80. Queen-sized bed; queen-sized bed and double futon; twin beds. Ensuite bathrooms. Additional person $20. Child 6 to 12 $20.
Weekend package.

• A new house with a cedar deck and a separate wing for guests, on forty forested acres with a creek. One of the guest rooms has an ensuite bathroom with a Jacuzzi. In the area are wineries, private schools, golf, kayaking, swimming, hiking, mountain biking, fishing, and a Native heritage centre. One host is a former executive chef. Full breakfast includes fruit, baked goods, and homemade jams and bread. Deposit of 30 percent required to hold reservation. Cancellation notice four days. Dutch and some German spoken. Two dogs in residence. No smoking. **In the hosts' own words:** "Come, relax, and feel at home with us in peaceful, bright surroundings."

Rainbow's End B&B

Sheila and Gray Thomson
1745 Ordano Street
Mail: Box 111
Cowichan Bay, BC V0R 1N0
(250) 746-8320
(area code 604 before October 1996)

• Forty-five minutes north of Victoria. Forty-five minutes south of Nanaimo. From the Island Highway (19), turn onto Cowichan Bay Road and continue to Glen Road. Follow Glen Road to McGill Road. Turn left onto McGill Road, follow McGill to the end, and turn right onto Ordano Street.

• Three rooms. One person $45; two people $60, queen-sized bed or twin beds, shared guest bathroom; two people $70, queen-sized bed, ensuite bathroom. Weekly rates.

Fishing and sightseeing charters and evening cruises arranged.

• A country B&B with an outdoor pool and a barbecue, surrounded by tall trees. Wild birds in a nearby green belt are often seen and heard. Two minutes' drive from a maritime centre. Ten minutes' drive from a Native heritage centre, Duncan's totems, and a forest museum. Twenty minutes' drive from Chemainus's murals. Ten minutes' drive from downtown Duncan and shopping for art, crafts, and antiques. Five minutes' drive from boat rentals, a boat ramp, fine dining restaurants, two par three golf courses, and three other golf courses. The hosts arrange evening cruises and fishing and sightseeing charters. No pets; cat in residence. Smoking outside. **In the hosts' own words:** "In summer, bring your bathing suits and have your morning coffee by the outdoor pool."

Old Farm B&B

Barbara and George MacFarlane
2075 Cowichan Bay Road
Cowichan Bay, BC V0R 1N0
(250) 748-6410 Fax: (250) 748-6410
Cellular: (250) 416-9101
(area code 604 before October 1996)

• Forty-five minutes north of Victoria. Five minutes south of Duncan. From the Island Highway (1) turn onto Cowichan Bay Road, which is well marked from both directions. The B&B is 1 kilometre north of the village of Cowichan Bay, on the side of the road closer to the water.

• Three rooms. One person $65–110; two people $75–120. Queen-sized beds. Ensuite bathrooms. Additional person $20. Off-season rates.

• A restored century-old three-storey house, designed by architect Samuel Maclure for a retired English sea captain. Landscaped gardens, fruit trees, and a gazebo on two acres that slope down to tidal water. An estuary formed by the Cowichan and Koksilah rivers provides a sanctuary for resident and migrating birds. Guest lounge and reading room on the main floor, with fireplace, TV, VCR, and contemporary books. Guest rooms have high ceilings and are decorated in Laura Ashley style. One of the guest rooms has an ensuite bathroom with a Jacuzzi. Pre-breakfast coffee or tea is delivered to guest rooms. Breakfast, including farm-fresh and home-grown produce, is served, with silver and linen, at a time that suits guests. Diets are accommodated. Check-in and check-out times are flexible. Visa, MasterCard. Adult oriented. Dog and cat in residence. Smoking outdoors. **In the hosts' own words:** "We try to make sure that every guest will want to come back."

Fairburn Farm Country Manor

Anthea and Darrel Archer
3310 Jackson Road RR 7
Duncan, BC V9L 4W4
(250) 746-4637 Fax: (250) 746-4637
(area code 604 before October 1996)

• Eleven kilometres southwest of Duncan. Fifty kilometres north of Victoria and 50 kilometres south of Nanaimo.

• Six rooms. Two people $95–140. Queen-sized bed; twin beds; queen-sized bed and twin beds. Private and ensuite bathrooms. Additional person $15. Cots available.

Self-contained cottage. One person to four people $750 for six days. Breakfast not included. Additional person $10.

Single and family rates. Open April 1 to September 30.

• A nineteenth-century farmhouse and cottage surrounded by forested hills, on 130 acres of rolling countryside, with walking trails beside a mountain stream and through woodlands and meadows. Five thousand tree seedlings in a sustainable seventy-acre forest with birds, wildlife, and old-growth trees. An hour's drive north of Victoria. A base for touring the Cowichan region. Some guest rooms have fireplaces. Some bathrooms have whirlpool tubs and fireplaces. Robes provided. A room with a queen-sized bed and twin beds and two rooms beside each other at the end of a corridor are suitable for families. Guest veranda and two sitting rooms with fireplaces and books. The self-contained cottage, formerly the cottage of the farm manager, is available by the week and has a washing machine. The hosts answer questions about their country lifestyle, and guests may take part in farm chores. Breakfast includes homemade granola, muffins and bread made from the farm's wheat, butter and milk from the cows, preserves from the garden and orchard, bacon or sausage from the pigs, and fresh eggs from the hens. Reservations and deposit of one night's rate required. No pets; there are border collies for herding and livestock guardian dogs who live with the sheep. No smoking. **In the hosts' own words:** "We welcome you to step back in time, share our way of life, and experience the hospitality of a bygone era."

Grove Hall Estate B&B

Judy Oliver
6159 Lakes Road
Duncan, BC V9L 4J6
(250) 746-6152
(area code 604 before October 1996)

• From Victoria, go 58 kilometres north on Highway 1. In Duncan, turn right onto Trunk Road. Turn left onto Lakes Road and continue for 1.5 kilometres. The B&B is on the right. There is no B&B sign; look for the brass number 6159 on the entrance pillars to the driveway.

• Three rooms. One person from $90; two people from $120. Queen-sized bed; twin beds. Additional person $30.

One-bedroom cottage. $125. Minimum stay two nights. Weekly rate $750. Breakfast not included.

• A lakefront Tudor-style house, built in 1906, on seventeen acres. Guest rooms have fireplaces and are decorated with an Asian theme. One of the guest rooms has an ornate Chinese wedding bed; another has Balinese art and batiks. Antiques throughout, including an antique Brunswick billiard table. Guests play tennis, walk by the lake, and have tea or wine on a veranda that overlooks swans on the lake. Near several golf courses, sailing and fishing in Cowichan Bay and Maple Bay, murals and antiques in Chemainus, and the arts community of Salt Spring Island. Full breakfast is served in a wood-pannelled and wood-beamed dining room. Reservations required. Not suitable for children or for pets. No smoking indoors. **In the hosts' own words:** "Enjoy Edwardian elegance and the mysteries of the Orient in our historic mansion."

Bird Song Cottage B&B

Larry and Virginia Blatchford
9909 Maple Street
Mail: Box 1432
Chemainus, BC V0R 1K0
(250) 246-9910 Fax: (250 246-2909
(area code 604 before October 1996)

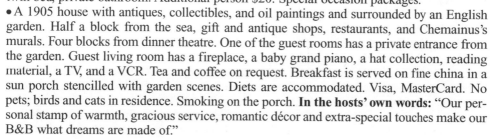

• Chemainus is one hour north of Victoria on the Island Highway (1).
• Three rooms. One person $65; two people $75–85. Queen-sized bed and single bed, ensuite bathroom; queen-sized bed and one twin day bed, private bathroom; double bed and one twin bed, private bathroom. Additional person $20. Special occasion packages.
• A 1905 house with antiques, collectibles, and oil paintings and surrounded by an English garden. Half a block from the sea, gift and antique shops, restaurants, and Chemainus's murals. Four blocks from dinner theatre. One of the guest rooms has a private entrance from the garden. Guest living room has a fireplace, a baby grand piano, a hat collection, reading material, a TV, and a VCR. Tea and coffee on request. Breakfast is served on fine china in a sun porch stencilled with garden scenes. Diets are accommodated. Visa, MasterCard. No pets; birds and cats in residence. Smoking on the porch. **In the hosts' own words:** "Our personal stamp of warmth, gracious service, romantic décor and extra-special touches make our B&B what dreams are made of."

Carleton House B&B

George and Sophie Carleton
10543 Chemainus Road
Mail: RR 1
Chemainus, BC V0R 1K0
(250) 246-2253
(area code 604 before October 1996)

• Sixty-five kilometres from Victoria. From Nanaimo, take Highway 1 south to Ladysmith. At the second traffic light, turn left onto Chemainus Road and continue for 6 kilometres. Watch for the B&B's sign.
• Three rooms. One person $35; two people $50–55. Queen-sized bed; double bed; twin beds. Shared guest bathroom. Additional person $15. Rollaway cot available.
• A B&B in a rural setting, four kilometres from shopping, theatre, and Chemainus's murals. Ground-level guest entrance. Guest sitting room with TV. Breakfast includes homemade baked goods, homemade preserves, fresh fruit, bacon and eggs, and waffles. German spoken. No pets. Smoke-free. **In the hosts' own words:** "Enjoy the peace and tranquillity of rural living. Come as a stranger—leave as a friend."

Once Upon a Time Inn

Kathy and Ward Yeager and Regina Ebert
9940 Cedar Street
Mail: Box 1505
Chemainus, BC V0R 1K0
(250) 246-1059 Fax: (250) 246-1059
(area code 604 before October 1996)

- One hour north of Victoria. Thirty minutes south of Nanaimo.
- Two rooms. One person $65; two people $75. Queen-sized bed. Private and
shared guest bathrooms. Additional person $20.
Suite. One person $95; two people $110. King-sized bed, one twin bed, and
one twin trundle bed. Ensuite bathroom. Additional person $20.
- A restored Victorian house built by a British sea captain in 1887, with views of the ocean
from wrap-around verandas. English flower gardens and putting greens. Antiques, a grand
piano, brass beds with down duvets, and original tubs and showers. Suite on the top floor has
a skylight, a king-sized bed, two sitting areas, a dining area with chandelier, and a separate
bedroom with twin beds. Two guest rooms on the main floor have queen-sized brass beds
and seventeenth- and eighteenth-century furniture. Guest entrance through guest kitchen.
Guest games room is separate from the main house and has a pool table, air hockey, darts, a
TV, a VCR, and movies. Two hundred steps from a beach. Three blocks from Chemainus's
murals, antique shops, gift shops, and galleries. Chemainus has a dinner theatre, an eighteen-
hole golf course, tennis, swimming, boating, and fishing. A base for exploring southern and
central Vancouver Island on day trips. Evening tea with homemade baked goods is served in
a guest kitchen on the second floor. Full breakfast, including fresh fruit, a hot entrée, homemade cinnamon buns, homemade preserves, cold and hot cereals, and juices, is served in a
formal dining room on the main floor. Visa. Children welcome. No smoking indoors.

The Treasure House by the Sea

Vic and Dorothy Forster
11203 Chemainus Road RR 4
Ladysmith, BC V0R 2E0
(250) 245-8092 Fax: (250) 245-8092
(area code 604 before October 1996)

- In Saltair, on the old Chemainus Road, midway between Ladysmith and Chemainus. Seventy-five minutes from Victoria. Thirty minutes from Duncan and Nanaimo.
- Two rooms. One person $65; two people $75. Queen-sized bed; queen-sized bed and twin bed. Ensuite bathrooms. Additional person $15.
- A new oceanside house on two acres, a few steps from a pebble beach. Guest lounge with wood stove and books. Seals, herons, ducks, loons, eagles, and other birds can be seen from a patio. Seven minutes from golfing and Chemainus's murals. Thirty minutes from a forest museum and a Native heritage centre in Duncan. Morning coffee or tea is delivered to guests' rooms before breakfast. Hosts' orchard provides fresh juice, syrups, jams, and jellies for breakfast served on an oceanside deck or in a formal dining room. No children. No pets. No smoking. **In the hosts' own words:** "We invite you to discover the treasures that await you."

Mañana Lodge and Marina

Jim and Ruth Bangay and Don and Gail Kanelakos
4760 Brenton Page Road
Mail: RR 1
Ladysmith, BC V0R 2E0
(250) 245-2312 Fax: (250) 245-7546
(area code 604 before October 1996)

• Ten kilometres from downtown Ladysmith.
• Five rooms. Two people $59–99. Queen-sized bed; double bed; queen-sized
bed and single bed. Ensuite bathrooms and half bathroom.
Two cabins. Two people $89. Queen-sized bed, double bed, and hide-a-bed.
Private bathrooms. Additional person $10.
• A waterfront lodge built in the 1940s, with a licensed dining room and a marina. Ten kilometres from downtown Ladysmith. Guest rooms have ocean views. Three of the guest rooms have ensuite bathrooms with Jacuzzi tubs. Cabins have kitchens and TVs. Bicycles, canoe, and rowboat. Gift shop, marine store, laundry facilities, fuel, and overnight moorage and power. Hosts arrange car rentals. Near hiking, golfing, fishing, biking, canoeing, scuba diving, mill tours, museums, waterfront parks, and Native heritage sites. Full breakfast is served in the dining room, which has a view of the ocean and mountains. Visa, MasterCard. **In the hosts' own words:** "We're a bed and breakfast inn with waterfront dining and spectacular views. A special place for special people."

Carey House

Catherine Molnar
750 Arbutus Avenue
Nanaimo, BC V9S 5E5
(250) 753-3601
(area code 604 before October 1996)

• From Nanaimo, go north on Highway 1. Turn
left onto Townsite Road and right onto Arbutus
Avenue. The B&B is the last house on the right.
• Two rooms. One person $30; two people $45.
Double bed. Shared guest bathroom.
Self-contained suite. Two people $50. Queen-sized bed. Bathroom in suite.
Ten percent discount on stays of one week or longer.
• A B&B in a quiet residential area, fifteen minutes' walk from downtown Nanaimo and the
downtown harbour walkway. Fifteen minutes' drive from Chemainus's murals. Thirty minutes' drive from Cathedral Grove's Douglas fir trees. Hourly ferries to Gabriola Island,
Protection Island, and Newcastle Island are 1.5 kilometres away. Guest TV room and guest
library/study. Self-contained suite with private entrance, small fridge, microwave, sink,
dishes, cutlery, and linen. The hosts provide local travel information. Pickup from ferry,
train, and bus. Coffee or tea with a snack in the evening. Breakfast includes homemade
bread, jam, and marmalade and is served in a dining room furnished with antiques. Deposit
of one night's rate required to hold reservation. Check-in time flexible. Cash, traveller's
cheques. No pets; dog and three cats in residence. No smoking.

Annabelle's Upper Deck B&B

Annabelle Mackintosh
3959 Hammond Bay Road
Nanaimo, BC V9T 1G4
(250) 758-0036
(area code 604 before October 1996)

• From the Departure Bay ferry terminal, turn
right onto Brechin Road. At the first traffic
lights, turn right onto Departure Bay Road. Turn
right onto Hammond Bay Road and continue
past Piper's Lagoon Beach. The B&B is on the
left side of the road, overlooking the water.
• Suite. Queen-sized bed and roll-away bed. Private bathroom with separate shower room.
Infant cot available. Call for rates.
• A quiet B&B with a view of Georgia Strait from the dining table. Two minutes' walk from
a beach, five minutes' drive from a shopping centre, and ten minutes' drive from the
Nanaimo ferry terminal. Within walking distance of a neighbourhood pub. On bus route.
Suite is on the ground floor, with no stairs to climb, and has a lounge with a TV, a VCR, and
books. Full or light breakfast. Cash, traveller's cheques. Children welcome. No pets. No
smoking. **In the hosts' own words:** "Relax in comfort."

Jake and the Weaver's B&B

Carol and Jack Craig
4111 Salal Drive
Nanaimo, BC V9T 5L2
(250) 756-1223
(area code 604 before October 1996)

• Seven kilometres from the Departure Bay ferry terminal. Go north on the Island Highway (19). Turn right onto Rutherford Road, right onto Uplands Drive, right onto Collishaw Road, right onto Ross Road, and right onto Salal Drive.
• Two rooms. One person $45; two people $55. Queen-sized bed; twin beds. Shared guest bathroom.
• A custom-designed house surrounded by trees, shrubs, and flower beds, in a quiet residential area close to shopping, restaurants, and parks with trails. A deck overlooks a green belt bordering a golf course. A base for trips south to Chemainus and Victoria; north to Courtenay, Comox, and Campbell River; and west to Coombs, Cathedral Grove old-growth forest, Port Alberni, and the island's west coast beaches. The second floor of the house is for guest use only. One of the guest rooms has a queen-sized bed and a TV. One host spins various fibres and weaves and knits clothing. Pickup from ferry, bus, and train. Full breakfast includes homemade breads, muffins, jams, and jellies and locally produced honey, bacon, and farm-fresh eggs. Cash, cheques. Adults only. No pets. No smoking. **In the hosts' own words:** "Our name means hospitality. Our location exudes peace and quiet. Our service is superior quality."

The Island View B&B

Darlene and Russ Dillon
5391 Entwhistle Drive
Nanaimo, BC V9V 1H2
(250) 758-5536 Fax: (250) 758-5536
(area code 604 before October 1996)

• Fifteen minutes north of the Departure Bay ferry terminal.
• Room. Two people $50. Twin beds. Private bathroom.
Suite. Two people $75. Queen-sized bed.
Bathroom in suite.
Additional person $15.
• A B&B on one-half acre in a garden setting. Four kilometres from a shopping centre, ten kilometres from the ferry terminal, and thirteen kilometres from downtown. Hosts pick up and drop off guests in Nanaimo. Newly renovated eight-hundred-square-foot suite with view, private entrance, kitchen, living room with queen-sized sofa bed, gas fireplace, TV, VCR, and collection of videos. Guests watch sunsets from the patio and walk on the rocky shoreline one-half block away. Fruit bowl, snacks, and drinks. Laundry facilities. Full breakfast is served at guests' convenience in the main-floor dining room. Children welcome. No pets. Smoke-free environment. **In the hosts' own words:** "Lots of fresh flowers and hospitality. Enjoy tastefully served breakfasts and magnificent sunsets in our garden paradise."

The Tudor Cottage

Freddie Vernon
7168 Lancrest Terrace
Mail: Box 344
Lantzville, BC V0R 2H0
(250) 390-3117
(area code 604 before October 1996)

• Two rooms. Two people $70, double bed, private bathroom; two people $85,
queen-sized bed, ensuite bathroom.

• A B&B with a view of the Winchelsea Islands and the Strait of Georgia, with hardwood
floors, leaded glass windows, antiques, and collectibles. Guest lounge with fireplace, stereo,
TV, and VCR. Guests walk by the ocean and watch cruise ships, eagles, seals, and sea lions.
Twenty minutes from the Departure Bay ferry terminal. Ten minutes from shopping malls,
golf, and theatres. Within walking distance of beach, restaurants, a pub, and village shops.
Mid-island location provides a base for day trips. A guest room with a queen-sized bed overlooks the sea; a guest room with a double bed overlooks the garden. Beds have down duvets.
A glass of wine or another beverage is served in the afternoon in the solarium, which has a
view of the ocean. Coffee is served in guest rooms before breakfast if guests wish. Full
breakfast, including homemade baked goods, is served in the dining room. Diets are accommodated by arrangement. Deposit of one night's rate required to hold reservation. Visa.
Adult oriented. No pets; cat and dog in residence. Non-smoking house. **In the hosts' own
words:** "We invite our guests to delight in our home and hospitality."

Warwick Manor B&B

John and Bea Weber
517 Pym Street
Parksville, BC V9P 1B6
(250) 248-8645 Fax: (250) 248-1260
(area code 604 before October 1996)

• Half a kilometre from the intersection of Highway 19 and Pym Street.
• One person $45–49; two people $65–75. King-sized bed; queen-sized bed; twin beds. Private bathrooms. Additional person $10–20. Off-season rates.

• A Tudor-style house with a garden, close to shopping, golf, tennis, fishing, boating, and beaches. Two guest lounges. Guest hot tub and patio. Off-street parking. Full breakfast. Adult oriented. No pets. Non-smoking rooms available. **In the hosts' own words:** "Relax at our traditional English Tudor-style manor amidst beautiful lawns and gardens, and enjoy the comfort of your large bedroom."

Vista del Mar B&B

Anita and Roger Marion
343 Poplar Avenue
Qualicum Beach, BC V9K 1J7
(250) 752-1795 Fax: (250) 752-1078
(area code 604 before October 1996)

• From Qualicum Beach, go north on the Island Highway (19). Turn left onto Memorial, right onto Crescent Road, right onto Bay, and left onto Poplar.
• Two rooms. $80–90. Queen-sized bed, private bathroom; twin beds, ensuite bathroom. Extended stay and off-season rates.

• A new Mediterranean-style house in a quiet residential area, on a bluff overlooking the Strait of Georgia, forty-five minutes north of Nanaimo. Panoramic view from guest rooms and patio. Ten minutes' walk from the village. Five minutes' walk from the beach, a golf course, and restaurants. Guest rooms have sitting areas with TVs and VCRs. One of the guest rooms has a fireplace. Guest entrance. Guest patio and hot tub. Robes provided. Full breakfast is served in a dining area with a view. Reservations recommended. Cancellation notice three days. Check-in 3:00 to 6:00 p.m.; check-out 11:00 a.m. Cash, cheques, MasterCard. French spoken. Adult oriented. No pets; dog in residence. No smoking. **In the hosts' own words:** "We offer warm hospitality, breathtaking scenery, and luxurious guest rooms that make for a memorable experience."

Surf Winds B&B

Ron and Kate Mitchell
542 Rye Road
Qualicum Beach, BC V9K 1K5
(250) 752-1741
(area code 604 before October 1996)

• From the Island Highway, turn onto Memorial (Payless gas station on corner). At the golf club, turn right onto Crescent Road West. Continue for two blocks to Rye Road and turn left. The B&B is the second house on the left.

• One person $45; two people $60–65. Queen-sized bed; twin beds.

• A B&B with views of the ocean, islands, and mainland mountains. Five minutes' walk from beach, village centre, restaurants, and golf course. Within eight kilometres of five golf courses. Forty-five minutes' drive from the Nanaimo ferry terminal. Downstairs patio and family room, upstairs sunroom and deck, and garden. Full or Continental breakfast includes homemade jams and Irish-style breads. Cancellation notice two days. Visa, MasterCard. **In the hosts' own words:** "After a three-year layoff, in which we travelled extensively, we are now open for business again at a new location. We look forward to meeting new and old friends."

Bahari B&B

Len and Yvonne Hooper
5101 Island Highway West
Qualicum Beach, BC V9K 1Z1
(250) 752-9278 Fax: (250) 752-9038
(area code 604 before October 1996)

• On Highway 19, 8 kilometres west of Little Qualicum River Bridge.

• Four rooms. One person $75; two people $85, double bed, queen-sized bed, or king-sized bed; two people $90, twin beds. Ensuite bathrooms. Two-bedroom apartment. $120–150 per day; $750 per week. Ensuite bathrooms. Breakfast ingredients supplied. Minimum stay two days.

• A waterfront B&B on seven acres of high bluff overlooking Georgia Strait, with a switch-back trail to a rocky beach. The house is Craftsman style with Asian influence. Apartment has kitchen and private entrance. Fifteen minutes' drive from the village of Qualicum Beach; forty-five minutes from Nanaimo, Courtenay, and Port Alberni. Full breakfast. Breakfast ingredients are supplied for guests in the apartment. Cancellation notice seven days for rooms, thirty days for apartment. Non-refundable deposit of 10 percent on apartment. Visa. Adult oriented. No pets. **In the hosts' own words:** "Tranquil elegance."

Blue Willow B&B

Arlene and John England
524 Quatna Road
Qualicum Beach, BC V9K 1B4
(250) 752-9052 Fax: (250) 752-9039
(area code 604 before October 1996)
E-mail: bwillow@qb.island.net

• From the Island Highway, turn west onto Qualicum Road and then right onto Quatna Road.

• Rooms. One person $65–70; two people $80–85. Additional person $25. Suite. Two people $95. Queen-sized bed and three twin beds. Additional person $25.

Off-season rates November 1 to March 31.

• A Tudor-style house with beamed ceilings, leaded windows, and garden views, surrounded by evergreens. Five minutes' walk from an ocean beach. Fifteen minutes' walk from the village of Qualicum Beach. Suite has a separate entrance. Garden, patio, and guest lounge with TV. Full breakfast. Visa, MasterCard. French and German spoken. Children welcome in the suite. Pets welcome by arrangement. Dachshund in residence. A non-smoking house. **In the hosts' own words:** "We offer hospitality, comfort, quiet, and relaxation. Breakfast is a very special event."

Quatna Manor

Bill and Betty Ross
512 Quatna Road
Qualicum Beach, BC V9K 1B4
(250) 752-6685
(area code 604 before October 1996)

● From the Island Highway (19), turn west onto Hall Road. Take the first left onto Quatna Road. Brochure with map is available at the Qualicum travel information centre.

● One person $60; two people $65–85. Queen-sized bed; king-sized bed; twin beds. Private and shared guest bathrooms. Two-bedroom suite. $120–130. Queen-sized bed and twin beds. Ensuite bathroom.

● A Tudor-style house with European and English antiques, down duvets, and crystal chandeliers. Guest rooms and suite are on the second storey. Guest entrance. Guest patio and TV room with fireplace. Hosts arrange tee times at four local all-season golf courses, some of which provide reduced rates for guests of the B&B. Full or Continental breakfast is served in the dining room. Dachshund in residence. A smoke-free environment. **In the hosts' own words:** "Enjoy the peaceful luxury of our charming house. We offer exceptional privacy."

Falcon Crest B&B

Kurt and Lisa Zurbuchen
4265 Island Highway West
Qualicum Beach, BC V9K 2B1
(250) 752-1989 Fax: (250) 752-1969
(area code 604 before October 1996)

● Forty-five minutes north of Nanaimo; 14 kilometres from Parksville; 55 kilometres from the Nanaimo ferry terminal; 168 kilometres from Victoria.

● Six rooms. Two people $65–80. Queen-sized bed, ensuite bathroom; king-sized bed, ensuite bathroom; two double beds, ensuite or private bathroom. Additional person $20. Child $10–15. Off-season rates.

● A B&B on six and a half acres on a bluff, with a private trail to a beach. The trail leads through a forest with four-hundred-year-old trees. Sea lions, seals, eagles, deer, and birds can be seen. Swimming at the beach by the property or three kilometres away at Qualicum Beach. Close to shopping mall, golf, salmon-fishing charters, and boating. Three of the guest rooms have views of the ocean. Guest dining/recreation room has a fireplace, a TV, and games. Full breakfast is served in the guest dining/recreation room, which has an individual table for each guest room. Reservations recommended in summer, mid-June to mid-September. Cancellation notice seven days. Swiss, German, Chinese, and French spoken. Children welcome under parents' supervision. A non-smoking house. **In the hosts' own words:** "Enjoy the ocean view, privacy, swimming, and relaxation."

Grauer's Getaway Destination B&B

Brenda and Steven Grauer
395 Burnham Road
Qualicum Beach, BC V9K 1G5
(250) 752-5851
(area code 604 before October 1996)

• From Nanaimo, go north on the Island Highway (19). Approaching Qualicum Beach, turn right onto Hemsworth Road. Continue under the trees for one block. Turn right onto Burham Road. The B&B is the first house on the right, behind a cedar hedge.

• Three rooms. $95. Queen-sized bed; twin beds. Ensuite bathrooms. Cottage. $800 weekly.
Extended stay and off-season rates.
Golf, tennis, and fishing packages.

• A B&B in a traditional house on one acre, with a panoramic view of Georgia Strait and a private pathway to a beach below. Each guest room has a sitting area. A self-contained cottage with one bedroom and a loft is available by the week during July and August. Rose gardens, tennis court, ball machine, swimming pool, hot tub, enclosed children's garden, and private patios for picnics. Five minutes' drive from four golf courses. The hosts share their knowledge of the area's attractions, shops, and restaurants. Continental breakfast, including fresh fruit and homemade baked goods, is served in the living room, which overlooks the ocean. Children welcome. No pets; dog and cat in residence. No smoking in guest rooms.

Qualicum Bay B&B

Jillian and Len Ralph
6253 Island Highway West
Qualicum Beach, BC V9K 4E2
(250) 757-8802 Fax: (250) 757-8802
(area code 604 before October 1996)

• Forty-five minutes north of Nanaimo, on the Island Highway (19). Fifteen minutes north of Qualicum Beach.

• Three rooms. In summer (April to September), two people $85, queen-sized bed, ensuite bathroom; two people $75, double bed, ensuite bathroom; two people $75, twin beds (or a king-sized bed), private bathroom. Additional person $20. Off-season rates October to March.

Self-contained cottage. Double bed and bunk beds. In summer (June to September), seven days $500; minimum stay seven days. Breakfast not included. Off-season rates October to May.

• A B&B on a beach, near golfing, fishing, hiking, and skiing. A base for day trips to Long Beach in Pacific Rim National Park. Secluded bay for swimming, beachcombing, clam digging, and bonfires. Guest rooms have coffeemakers and private oceanfront balconies with panoramic views. One of the guest rooms has a queen-sized bed and a TV. The house's top floor is for guest use only and has games, a TV, a VCR, a billiard table, a piano, a chess set, books, and a small fridge. Self-contained waterfront cottage has a kitchen, a TV, and a stereo. Full breakfast for guests staying in the rooms is served in a sunroom overlooking the beach or on the patio. Cancellation notice for rooms in house and for winter rental of cottage, forty-eight hours; for summer rental of cottage, fourteen days. Visa, MasterCard. Children and pets welcome in the cottage; dog in residence in the hosts' house. Smoking outside. **In the hosts' own words:** "Let us show you what true hospitality is all about."

Ships Point Beach House

Lorinda and David Rawlings
7584 Ships Point Road
Mail: Site 39 C–76
Fanny Bay, BC V0R 1W0
(250) 335-2200 Fax: (250) 335-2214
(area code 604 before October 1996)
Toll-free: 1-800-925-1595

• Seventy kilometres north of Nanaimo. Turn right onto Ships Point Road.
• Five rooms. In summer (May 15 to October 15), two people $145–195. In winter, two people $100–150. Queen-sized bed; two extra-long twin beds. Ensuite bathrooms. One-person rates.
Guided boat charters and kayak rentals.
• A waterfront house with a panoramic view of the ocean. Bald eagles, blue herons, sea lions, and other marine wildlife can be seen. Guests beachcomb at low tide for oysters and clams, walk along paths surrounding a bird sanctuary, and walk in a protected forest to a local artist's gallery. Guided charters on 21-foot and 16-foot fully equipped salmon fishing boats. Single and double kayak rentals. Near skiing, golfing, and restaurants. Guest rooms have down duvets, bathrobes, and ocean views. Living room with stone fireplace, TV, and VCR. Meals are served on a veranda with heat lamps, weather permitting. Guest outdoor Jacuzzi surrounded by a rose garden, with a view of the ocean. Conference room available for seminars and workshops. Suitable for weddings and receptions. Full breakfast includes coffee, teas, homemade breads, and muffins. Evening meals available on request. Reservations recommended. Cancellation notice seven days. Credit cards. Adult oriented. No pets. Smoking outdoors. **In the hosts' own words:** "We welcome you to enjoy pampered hospitality in our luxury seaside inn—a beautiful waterfront setting that invites a state of relaxation and peaceful tranquillity."

Gull Cottage B&B

Bruce and Mary Jaffary
6634 South Island Highway
Mail: RR 1 Site 3 C–5
Fanny Bay, BC V0R 1W0
(250) 335-1932
(area code 604 before October 1996)

• Seventy-five minutes north of Nanaimo. One kilometre north of Denman Island ferries.
• Three rooms. One person $40–50; two people $50–65. Queen-sized bed and twin beds, ensuite bathroom; queen-sized bed, ensuite bathroom; twin beds, private bathroom. Additional person $10–20. Off-season rates.
• A beach house on two hundred feet of waterfront. An enclosed porch is twenty-five feet from the sea. Sunrises above Denman Island, Baynes Sound, and the mainland mountains. Birds can be seen eating oysters along a mile of undeveloped beach. Garden, bonfires, and beachside hot tub. In the area are golf, hiking, swimming, beachcombing, boating, skiing at Mount Washington, and hiking at Strathcona Park. Full breakfast, including homemade bread and jams, farm-fresh eggs, and, in season, fruit from the hosts' orchard, is served by a wood stove in the dining area or on the porch overlooking the water. Visa, MasterCard. Two cats and a cocker spaniel in residence. Smoking outdoors. **In the hosts' own words:** "We are the former operators of the Cedars B&B. We welcome you—our home is your home to enjoy."

Standing People Farm B&B

Susan Hughes and Paul Schleicher
4600 Northwest Road
Denman Island, BC V0R 1T0
(250) 335-0542
(area code 604 before October 1996)

• Take the ferry to Denman from Buckley Bay, 1¼ hours north of Nanaimo. Call for directions.
• Two rooms. One person $45–55; two people $55–75. Queen-sized bed; queen-sized bed and two single beds. Private and shared bathrooms. Additional person $10–15. Space available for retreats and small workshops. Extended stay rates.
• An open-plan solar house on a forty-two-acre Christmas-tree farm surrounded by fields, forest, sea, and mountains. Organic orchard, flower and vegetable gardens, and several ponds. Woodland trails from the B&B. Five minutes' walk from a private beach. Small dome for meditation. Space available for retreats and small workshops. Hot tub with a view. Guest rooms are decorated in spring colours and have cotton bed linen and down comforters. Living space with paintings, music, and wood stove. Full breakfast of organic food; free-range ducks and chickens can be seen from the breakfast table. Cash, traveller's cheques. Children and dogs welcome by arrangement. **In the hosts' own words:** "We live simply here, treading gently on the land. Our life is rich beyond measure, and we love to share this with those who visit."

Eagledown B&B

Diane Edgar and Michael Stanton
6521 Reginald Road
Denman Island, BC V0R 1T0
(250) 335-2889 Fax: (250) 335-2757
(area code 604 before October 1996)

• From Nanaimo, go north for seventy-five minutes to Buckley Bay. At the
Buckley Bay ferry terminal ticket booth, ask for a Denman Island brochure;
the B&B is on the map in the brochure. Take the ferry to Denman Island.
Turn off McFarlane Road onto Reginald Road and continue for 1.8 kilometres
to the driveway marked by the B&B's sign.

• Three rooms in a separate guest house. $90–100. Queen-sized bed; double
bed; twin beds. Private and shared guest bathrooms.
Extended stay rates.

• A B&B on a rural five-acre wooded lot with two lily ponds and flower and vegetable gardens. A main house, a separate guest house, and an outdoor hot tub are on the waterfront
with a view over Baynes Sound to Mount Arrowsmith on Vancouver Island. Guest house living room with airtight fireplace and wet bar area with fridge, sink, dishes, cutlery, and kettle. Barbecue. Two downstairs guest rooms have separate guest entrances through sliding
glass doors from a seaside porch. Main house with living room, fireplace, glass-enclosed
den with airtight fireplace and forest views, and dining room. Magazines, games, and books.
Guests swim, cycle, walk, and watch birds, eagles, seals, and deer. Near parks and artisans'
studios. Diets are accommodated. Not suitable for children under thirteen. No pets. No
smoking. **In the hosts' own words:** "The Natives use eagle down as a symbol of peace,
friendship, and welcome. We would like to have you visit with us so that we may share that
spirit."

Good Morning B&B

Marian Sieg
7845 Central Road
Hornby Island, BC V0R 1Z0
(250) 335-1094 Fax: (250) 335-1094
(area code 604 before October 1996)

• On the corner of Central and Sandpiper.
• Three rooms. In summer, one person $60, two people $75. In winter, one person $55, two people $60. Queen-sized bed; double bed and single bed. Shared guest bathroom.
• A B&B on Hornby Island with a guest living room with fireplace. Guest entrance and deck. On Hornby are eagles' nesting grounds at Helliwell Park, fossils on Fossil Beach, three sandy swimming beaches, boating, and hiking trails. Kayaks, bikes, and charter boats for fishing are available on the island. Bike storage available. Breakfast of homemade bread, muffins, jams, and a choice of pancakes or bacon and free-range eggs is served in the dining room. German spoken. No pets. Smoking on the patio. **In the hosts' own words:** "Enjoy European hospitality. Wir sprechen deutsch."

Wellington House B&B

Shelagh Davis and Doug Jackson
2593 Derwent Avenue
Mail: Box 689
Cumberland, BC V0R 1S0
(250) 336-8809 Fax: (250) 336-2455
(area code 604 before October 1996)

• Take Highway 19 to Royston. Follow signs to Cumberland, 7 kilometres. Go through the village and turn left, towards Comox Lake. Take the first right onto Derwent Avenue.
• Two rooms. One person $45; two people $60–90. Queen-sized bed; double bed. Ensuite and private bathrooms.
Suite with kitchen. $90–110. Additional person $20.
• A modern house in the foothills of the Beaufort Mountains, in the historical mining village of Cumberland. Garden-level guest entrance. Each guest room has its own sitting room with a TV. Deck, covered patio, and parklike garden. Five to forty-five minutes' drive from golf courses, skiing, sport fishing, fresh and saltwater activities, and nature parks for biking and hiking. Full breakfast with homemade preserves. Visa. No pets. Smoking on patio. **In the hosts' own words:** "This is one area where you can golf and ski on the same day. We look forward to sharing our peaceful surroundings and hospitality with you."

The Beach House B&B

Anke Burkhardt
3614 South Island Highway
Mail: RR 6 Site 688 C–28
Courtenay, BC V9N 8H9
(250) 338-8990 Fax: (250) 338-5651
(area code 604 before October 1996)

• Two kilometres north of Royston; 2 kilometres south of Courtenay on Highway 19.
• Four rooms. One person $35; two people $45, shared bathroom; two people $65, ensuite bathroom. Additional person $10.
• A waterfront cedar house with its own path along a beach, where trumpeter swans, seals, and ducks can be seen. Forty-five minutes' drive from cross-country and downhill skiing and hiking at Strathcona Park (Mount Washington). Ten minutes' drive from a golf course; several other golf courses in the area. Deck, pool table, darts area, and upright piano. Guest sitting room on the second floor. Breakfast, available until 9:00 a.m., includes eggs from the hosts' hens, fresh yogurt and fruit, oven-baked granola, scones, muffins, and sourdough rye bread. Kitchen facilities and barbecue available for guests to prepare additional meals. Visa, MasterCard. German spoken. Not suitable for small children or for pets; cats and chickens on the property. A non-smoking house. **In the hosts' own words:** "Relax in our unique waterfront house."

Forest Glen B&B

Art and Lois Enns
5760 Sea Terrace Road
Mail: RR 2 Site 280 C–37
Courtenay, BC V9N 5M9
(250) 334-4374

(area code 604 before October 1996.)

• Fifteen minutes north of Courtenay. Ten minutes north of the Powell River ferry. From Courtenay, go north on Highway 19 for 6 kilometres. Turn right onto Hardy Road and continue to Coleman Road. Turn right onto Coleman. Turn right onto Loxley and continue to the end, go down Avonlea, and turn right onto Sea Terrace.
• Two rooms. One person $45; two people $60. Queen-sized bed, ensuite bathroom; twin beds, private bathroom. Additional person $10. Roll-away cot available. Winter rates November 1 to April 30.
• A new country-style house near Bates Beach in the Seal Bay Forest. Easy walking trails from the B&B, in the Seal Bay Forest, which extends through Seal Bay Park to Seal Bay. Thirty-five minutes' drive from skiing and hiking on Mount Washington and Forbidden Plateau, five minutes' drive from fishing at Bates Beach, and fifteen minutes' drive from beaches. Living room with fireplace and high ceilings. Lower level lounge with TV overlooks the garden and opens onto a guest outdoor hot tub. Morning coffee is served on the front porch. Full breakfast, including fruit, juice, and homemade baked goods, is served on the back deck; during breakfast, deer may be seen on the lawn. No smoking. **In the hosts' own words:** "We've built our dream house, and now we invite you to come and enjoy it with us."

Greystone Manor B&B

Mike and Maureen Shipton
4014 Haas Road
Mail: RR 6 Site 684 C–2
Courtenay, BC V9N 8H9
(250) 338-1422
(area code 604 before October 1996)

• From Courtenay, take Highway 19 south for 3 kilometres. Look for the B&B's signs.

• Three rooms. One person $55; two people $70. Queen-sized bed; double bed; twin beds. Ensuite and private bathrooms. Additional person $20.

• A waterfront house built in 1918, on one and a half acres of English flower gardens, surrounded by maples and firs. Views across Comox Bay to the Coast Mountains. Seals, herons, sea birds, and eagles can be seen. Guests walk through the gardens to the beach. Guest sitting room has a fireplace. In the area are Denman and Hornby islands and hiking and skiing at Mount Washington, Forbidden Plateau, and Strathcona Park. The hosts came to Canada from Bath, England, in 1990. Full breakfast. Visa, MasterCard. Children over twelve welcome. No pets. No smoking. **In the hosts' own words:** "A friendly welcome awaits you. Relax in our lovely old house and spectacular gardens."

Heatherwood House B&B

Vivian and John Webb
2762 O'Brien Road
Mail: RR 2 Site 205 C–7
Courtenay, BC V9N 5M9
(250) 334-4770
(area code 604 before October 1996)

• From Courtenay, go for 3 kilometres north on
the Island Highway. Turn left onto O'Brien,
which is the third road past the Petro-Canada gas
station.

• Three rooms. One person $35; two people $45. Shared guest bathroom.
Three-night rate, without breakfast, one person or two people $75.

• A two-and-a-half-acre hobby farm in the country, with views of Forbidden Plateau and
Mount Washington. A sunroom overlooks the mountains and a golf course. Guest rooms are
on the main floor and have TVs. Sunroom, kitchen, dining room, and living room with fireplace. One of the hosts spins and weaves undyed wool from the farm's sheep in a studio on
the main floor. Guests are invited to try spinning. Tours of the sheep farm are available on
request. Half an hour's drive from downhill and cross-country skiing. Twenty minutes' drive
from ocean fishing. Breakfast is served in the sunroom or the dining room. Not suitable for
pets; canaries and a Persian cat in residence. Smoking on decks and grounds. **In the hosts'
own words:** "Enjoy beautiful sunsets over Forbidden Plateau and Mount Washington."

Foskett House B&B

Dove and Michael Hendren
484 Lazo Road
Comox, BC V9M 3V1
(250) 339-4272 Fax: (250) 339-4272
(area code 604 before October 1996)

• Five kilometres east of Comox, at Point
Holmes.

• Room. One person $55; two people $70.
Queen-sized bed and single hide-a-bed. Ensuite
bathroom. Additional person $15.

• A 1920 South African–style ranch house with wrap-around verandas and wind-sculpted
trees, with oceanfront at the end of the driveway. Finished inside with cedar and a beach-
stone fireplace and furnished with antiques and collectibles. Garden-level guest room has a
private entrance. In the Comox Valley are skiing, fishing, golfing, and craft and music festivals. Folk artist in residence. Five minutes from the Powell River ferry. Dog and cat in residence. Smoking outdoors. **In the hosts' own words:** "After the sound of the ocean has
lulled you to sleep, awake from a wonderful night's rest to be pampered with a gourmet
breakfast."

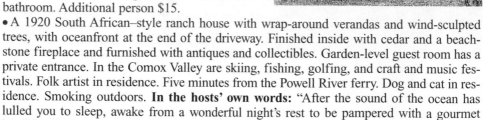

Levenvale B&B

Shirley and Alan Robb
2081 Murphy Avenue
Comox, BC V9M 1V4
(250) 339-3307
(area code 604 before October 1996)

• In Comox, near the hospital.
• Two rooms. One person $30; two people $45.
Queen-sized bed; twin beds. Private bathrooms.
Family rates.
• A B&B centrally located in a quiet residential
district, within walking distance of restaurants, a beach, and a marina. Near golf courses. Sun deck, living room, and recreation room with TV. Pickup from bus, train, and plane. Full breakfast is served on the sun deck, which has a view of the water and mountains, or in the formal, antique-furnished dining room, which also has a view. Children welcome. **In the hosts' own words:** "We look forward to meeting our guests and sharing our hospitality and travel experiences with you."

Tudor Acres

Betty and Peter Cartwright
2065 Endall Road
Black Creek, BC V9J 1G8
(250) 337-5764 Fax: (250) 337-5764
(area code 604 before October 1996)

• Fifteen minutes north of Courtenay, on the corner of the Island Highway (19) and Endall Road.

• Two rooms. One person $45; two people $55. Queen-sized bed; two double beds. Ensuite half bathrooms and shared guest bathroom. Additional person $10.
Self-contained suite. Two people $65. Queen-sized bed and day bed. Bathroom in suite.
Additional person $10.
• A Tudor-style house on a twelve-acre sheep farm with trees and meadows, a half-hour drive from Mount Washington. Guest lounge with TV, VCR, and open brick fireplace. The hosts' farm dog plays frisbee with guests but is not allowed in the guest area. Two guest rooms have ensuite half bathrooms and share a guest bathroom. Self-contained suite has a private entrance, a sitting room, and a kitchen. Breakfast includes an entrée, fruit from the hosts' garden, and homemade breads and preserves. Picnic breakfast is provided for guests who leave for the ski slopes early in the morning. No pets. No smoking. **In the hosts' own words:** "Welcome to our home."

Country Comfort B&B

Elaine and Ron Bohn
8214 Island Highway
Black Creek, BC V9J 1H6
(250) 337-5273
(area code 604 before October 1996)

• On Highway 19. Fifteen minutes north of Courtenay; look for sign 2 kilometres north of small Black Creek bridge. Twenty minutes south of Campbell River, one block south of Black Creek country market.

• Three rooms. One person $30; two people $45. Queen-sized bed; double bed. Shared guest bathroom.

Family and extended stay rates.

• A split-level house with hand-crafted décor on a fifty-acre hobby farm with lawns, orchards, and vegetable and flower gardens. A few minutes' drive from golfing, hiking, trail riding, fishing, a provincial park, beaches, and fine dining restaurants. Hosts help guests with arrangements for guided whale watching and helicopter tours and visits to mines, a pulp mill, and timber operations. Forty minutes' drive from Mount Washington ski resort; close to daily ski bus stop. Mount Washington's hiking trails, chairlift, and restaurant are also open in the summer months. A stopover point on the way to Strathcona Park and the ferry from Port Hardy to Prince Rupert. Solarium and family room with TV, VCR, and books. Small gift shop. Full or light breakfast is served at flexible hours. **In the hosts' own words:** "After a long day's travel, take this opportunity to stop and smell the flowers. Please let us pamper you on your holiday."

Bishops of Black Creek B&B

Susan and Hector Bishop
2004 and 2010 Wilfred Road
Black Creek, BC V9J 1J8
(250) 337-5187
(area code 604 before October 1996)

• Halfway between Courtenay and Campbell River. From the Island Highway (19), turn at the Payless gas station onto Miracle Beach Drive and continue for .75 kilometre. Turn left onto Paulson and continue for half a block to Wilfred Road.

• Three rooms. One person $40, one twin bed, shared guest bathroom; two people $50, double bed, shared guest bathroom; two people $60, queen-sized bed, ensuite bathroom. Rollaway cot and extra twin bed available. Additional person $10.

• A five-thousand-square-foot house five minutes from Miracle Beach, mini golf, a grocery store, a post office, and a park. Ten minutes from a liquor store. Twenty minutes from an eighteen-hole golf course and a boat launch. Forty-five minutes from Mount Washington and skiing at Forbidden Plateau. Twenty minutes from salmon fishing at Campbell River. Three kilometres from Saratoga Speedway. Guest rooms have TVs. Living room is sixteen feet by forty feet and has two fireplaces, a TV, and antique furniture. Pickup from bus and plane. Light lunch is served when guests arrive. Breakfast of guests' choice is served. Early breakfast by arrangement. Deposit required. Cheques, Visa. Children welcome by arrangement. Pets welcome by arrangement. **In the hosts' own words:** "There are no strangers here—only friends we have yet to meet."

The Grey Mouse B&B

Hanayo and John Oughtred
2012 Eyre Road
Black Creek, BC V9J 1B2
(250) 337-5795 Fax: (250) 337-2036
(area code 604 before October 1996)

• Twenty-two kilometres north of Courtenay. Twenty kilometres south of Campbell River. From Highway 19, follow signs to Saratoga Beach resort area.

• Three rooms. One person $40–50; two people $60–70. Queen-sized bed; double bed; twin beds. Shared guest bathroom. Additional person $20.

• A beachfront house with views of the Strait of Georgia and the Coast Mountains from the guest rooms. Guests walk on the sandy beach. Court for tennis, basketball, volleyball, and shuffleboard. Ten minutes' walk from golf, fishing, and hiking. Forty minutes' drive from Mount Washington ski resort and Strathcona Provincial Park. Guest rooms, guest lounge with TV, and shared guest bathroom are on one floor of the house, with a separate entrance. Full breakfast is served in the dining room, which has a view of the ocean. Japanese spoken. No pets. No smoking indoors. **In the hosts' own words:** "Wake to a magnificent sunrise and enjoy a hearty breakfast."

Bright's Willow Point Guest House B&B

Valerie and George Bright
2460 South Island Highway
Campbell River, BC V9W 1C6
(250) 923-1086 Fax: (250) 923-5121
(area code 604 before October 1996)

• Four kilometres south of Campbell River. Two hundred metres north of Erickson Road (Airport Road), at Willow Point. The B&B is on the west side of the road.

• Two rooms. One person $55; two people $75. King-sized bed; twin beds. Ensuite and private bathrooms.

• A B&B with guest room views of mountains and Discovery Passage. Guest lounge with a bay window seat from which cruise ships can be seen. Within driving distance of a beach, golfing, whale watching, and cruises through the inlets. Within an hour's drive of skiing at Mount Washington and Forbidden Plateau. Fishing at Campbell River's saltwater sport fishing pier. Hosts arrange private fishing guides. A stopover point on the way to Port Hardy. Full English breakfast or light breakfast, including homemade bread, muffins, granola, scones, and preserves, is served from 7:00 to 9:00 a.m. Breakfast is served at 4:00 a.m. for guests who are going fishing. Cancellation notice twenty-four hours. Check-in from 2:00 to 7:00 p.m. or by arrangement; check-out by 10:30 a.m. Visa. Adult oriented; not suitable for children under twelve. No pets; cat in residence. No smoking. **In the hosts' own words:** "We are widely travelled, and we invite you to join us for conversation by the fireplace. A warm welcome awaits you at our attractive contemporary house in the salmon capital of the world."

Sea Tangles on the Beach B&B

Ron and Monica Hempell
583 Island Highway
Campbell River, BC V9W 2B9
(250) 286-6886 Fax: (250) 286-6666
(area code 604 before October 1996)

• One block from downtown Campbell River and
Discovery Fishing Pier.
• Rooms and suite. In summer (May 1 to
October 31), one person $45–50, two people
$55–65. In winter (November 1 to April 30), one
person $40–45, two people $50–55. Private and shared guest bathrooms.
• A beachfront B&B with views of Discovery Passage, passing cruise ships, sailing and fishing boats, and other marine traffic. Scuba diving and fishing in Discovery Passage. In the area are hiking, canoeing, kayaking, and skiing. Suite has a private entrance, kitchen facilities, a TV, a private deck overlooking the ocean and can accommodate up to four guests. Guest refrigerator and freezer. Sitting room with fireplace and TV. Living room with TV. Breakfast is served in the dining area or delivered to guests' rooms. No pets. No smoking. **In the hosts' own words:** "Enjoy the unique atmosphere of our beachfront home. Herons can be seen fishing in the tidal pools in front of the house, eagles fly overhead, and sea lions frolic in the kelp beds."

Arbour's Guest House

Sharon and Ted Arbour
375 South Murphy Street
Campbell River, BC V9W 1Y8
(250) 287-9873 Fax: c/o (250) 287-2353
(area code 604 before October 1996)

• Five minutes' drive from downtown.
• Two rooms. One person $55–80; two people
$70–95. Queen-sized bed; twin beds. Ensuite
and private bathrooms. Additional person $20.
Open seasonally. Weekly rates.
• A B&B with antique décor, on treed property with a view of the mountains, ocean, and fishing grounds. Glass of wine on arrival. Close to golf courses. Bicycle rentals available. Boat rentals arranged. Experienced fishing guides available for saltwater salmon fishing. One of the guest rooms has a kitchen and a TV and accommodates up to four people; the other has a living room with a TV. Reservations recommended. Visa, MasterCard. Adult oriented. No pets. No smoking. **In the hosts' own words:** "Hospitality is our business. We are in the sport fishing capital of the world."

Bonnie Belle B&B

John and Trudy Parkyn
1015–1017 West Road
Quadra Island, BC
Mail: Box 331
Campbell River, BC V9W 5B6
(250) 285-3578 or 287-7775
(area code 604 before October 1996)

• Four kilometres from the Quathiaski Cove
ferry terminal. Call for directions.
• Two rooms. One person $40; two people
$60. Double bed; twin beds. Shared guest bathroom.
Charters on the hosts' boat.
• A B&B in a woodland overlooking Gowland Harbour, entirely hidden from other houses
and the road. Fifteen minutes by ferry from Campbell River. Ten minutes' drive from
beaches. Five minutes' walk from tennis court, hiking trails, and community hall. Guests
charter the hosts' boat for sightseeing and fishing. Two upstairs guest rooms have access to
an outside covered porch and a reading nook. Full breakfast is served. Evening meals on
request. Diets are accommodated. Dog in residence. Smoking on the porch. **In the hosts'
own words:** "For guests who wish to charter a boat, we offer our classic wooden heritage
vessel, the *Bonnie Belle*. Hope you enjoy Quadra Island as much as we do."

Joha's Eagleview

Joyce and Harold Johnson
849 Pidcock
Mail: Box 668
Quathiaski Cove
Quadra Island, BC V0P 1N0
(250) 285-2247
(area code 604 before October 1996)

• Fifteen-minute ferry ride from Campbell River
to Quadra Island. From the ferry terminal, turn
left at the first intersection and continue to the
stop sign. Continue in the same direction; the road parallels the ocean. Look for the B&B's
sign at the top of the driveway. Park on blacktop at bottom of driveway.
• Two rooms. One person $45–55; two people $55–65. Queen-sized bed; double bed.
Shared guest bathroom and shared guest half bathroom.
Self-contained suite. Two people $80. Queen-sized bed and sofa bed. Bathroom in suite.
Breakfast included. Additional person $12. Minimum stay three days. Weekly rate of $450
for one to four people, with breakfast included on last morning only.
• A waterfront house overlooking Discovery Passage, with a deck from which sunsets,
eagles, seals, salmon, and commercial fishing boats can be seen. Guest living room. One of
the guest rooms faces the water. The other guest room has a view of a wooded hillside. Both
guest rooms have handmade quilts. Self-contained suite has a private entrance, a kitchen, a
dining area, and a living room with sofa bed. The hosts share information on local activities.
Near canoeing, kayaking, fishing, swimming, sailing, horseback riding, and well-developed
trails of various levels of difficulty for walking and hiking. Dock space for boats. Choice of
full or light breakfast with homemade breads and jams. Not suitable for young children. No
pets. Smoking outdoors.

The Yum Yum Tree

Mitch and Rosemary Lukinuk
660 Heriot Road
Mail: Box 387
Heriot Bay, Quadra Island, BC V0P 1H0
(250) 285-2491
(area code 604 before October 1996)

• From Quadra ferry landing, follow signs to Heriot Bay (turn left after school), a ten-minute drive. A sign for the B&B is immediately to the right of the Cortes ferry line-up.

• Three rooms. Two people $60–95. Queen-sized bed; king-sized bed; twin beds. Breakfast ingredients supplied. Additional person $15.
Fishing and sightseeing charters on hosts' 22-foot cabin cruiser.

• A four-level contemporary house that overlooks Heriot Bay, one block from a marina, a store, and restaurants. Four kilometres' walk along Drew Harbour from Rebecca Spit Provincial Park. In the area are fishing, water sports, and hiking. One of the guest rooms has a loft for children. Another guest room and bathroom are wheelchair accessible. Each guest room has a private entrance, a sitting area, a kitchen, and a deck. Breakfast ingredients are supplied in the rooms. Smoking on deck and balconies. **In the hosts' own words:** "Our home has a candy kitchen, and there are treats for guests. Our top-floor loft is a honeymooners' delight."

Blue Heron B&B

Gunnar and Emilia Hansen
Potlatch Road
Mail: Box 23
Manson's Landing
Cortes Island, BC V0P 1K0
(250) 935-6584
(area code 604 before October 1996)

• Twenty kilometres from the Whaletown ferry landing; 1 kilometre from Smelt Bay Provincial Park.

• Two rooms. One person $40–65; two people $45–70. King-sized bed; twin beds. Ensuite and shared bathrooms. Additional person $15.

• A country house with a garden, looking over Sutil Channel toward Vancouver Island, a few steps from a beach. Guests walk along the beach, explore tide pools, and watch sunsets. Living room and view deck. Wood-fired sauna available for a fee. Full breakfast includes fresh fruit, free-range eggs, and homemade preserves. Cancellation notice seven days. Danish spoken. No pets; dog and cat in residence. No smoking in guest rooms. **In the hosts' own words:** "We invite guests to relax and read in the pleasant living room and enjoy the view deck."

Fairhaven Farm and B&B

David and Margaret Hansen
Mail: Box 141
Manson's Landing
Cortes Island, BC V0P 1K0
(250) 935-6501
(area code 604 before October 1996)

• Two and a half kilometres from the centre of
Manson's Landing.
• Three rooms. One person $55; two people $65.
Queen-sized bed; twin beds. Ensuite and private
bathrooms. Additional person $15.
• A modernized turn-of-the-century log house on a seventeen-acre farm, with views of an
orchard and a pasture with grazing sheep. Twenty minutes' walk from a gravel beach on the
ocean. Within five minutes' drive of two sandy beaches, one on the ocean and the other on
Hague Lake. Near kayak rentals. Full breakfast is served between 8:00 and 10:00 a.m. Lunch
and dinner and the hosts' own produce available on request. MasterCard. Children welcome.
No pets; cat in residence. No smoking indoors. **In the hosts' own words:** "Come and enjoy
the quiet pleasures of life down on the farm."

Picard's B&B

Bevann and Fred Picard
Mail: Box 165
Manson's Landing
Cortes Island, BC V0P 1K0
(250) 935-6683
(area code 604 before October 1996)

• From the Cortes ferry terminal, go towards
Manson's Landing for 8 kilometres. Turn right
onto Thunder Road and continue for 90 metres.
• Two rooms. Two people $75. Queen-sized bed.
Ensuite bathrooms. Additional person $20. Twin-sized hide-a-bed available.
Self-contained two-bedroom cottage. $700 per week. Double bed and twin beds. Breakfast
not included in cottage.
• A new Mediterranean-style house on three parklike acres on a peninsula, surrounded on
three sides by the ocean. Guest rooms overlook the water and have private entrances. Guest
patio. Guests play basketball and tennis, swim on the hosts' private beaches, and row in the
harbour. Near kayaking, bicycling, hiking, birdwatching, and scooters. Full breakfast is
served on a covered deck, in the kitchen, or in guests' rooms. Visa. No pets. Smoking outdoors. **In the hosts' own words:** "Enjoy a luxurious waterfront retreat."

Roseberry Manor B&B

Diane and Bob Hitchcox
810 Nimpkish Heights Drive
Port McNeill, BC V0N 2R0
(250) 956-4788 or (250) 956-4596
(area code 604 before October 1996)

• Seven kilometres south of Port McNeill off
Highway 19. Turn onto Nimpkish Heights Drive.
The B&B is on the left side of the road, a short
distance from the highway turnoff.

• Three rooms. Two people $60–70. Queen-sized
bed; double bed; twin beds. Shared guest bathrooms.

• A house on two acres in a quiet rural setting decorated in country Victorian style with
family heirlooms, antiques, collectibles, dolls, and teddy bears. Guest living room with fireplace. Guest entrance. Dining room, sunrooms, and porch. Collection of books, magazines,
and local tourist information. Guest rooms have feather pillows, fresh flowers, chocolates,
toiletries, hair dryers, and curling irons. Thirty minutes' drive from killer whale and forestry
tours, Native culture, caving, scuba diving, kayaking, wind surfing, golfing, and ferry to
Prince Rupert. Thirty minutes' drive from fishing in lake, stream, and ocean. Afternoon tea
and evening cappuccino and hot chocolate are served in the guest living room. Breakfast is
served from 7:30 to 10:00 a.m., by candlelight with music and fresh flowers, on china, silver, and crystal, in a Victorian-style dining room. Breakfast includes fresh-ground coffee,
regular and herbal teas, fresh fruit, baked goods with homemade preserves, and a choice of
sausages, bacon, and eggs; French toast; or eggs Benedict. Laundry facilities. Reservations
recommended. Check-in 3:00 p.m.; check-out 11:00 a.m. or by arrangement. Cash, traveller's cheques. Adult oriented. No pets; two small dogs in residence. Smoking in designated area.

Barbara Bruner's B&B

Larry and Barbara Bruner
8835 Seaview Drive
Mail: Box 193
Port Hardy, BC V0N 2P0
(250) 949-2306
(area code 604 before October 1996)

• Two rooms. One person $40, one twin bed; two
people $60, two twin beds. Shared guest bath-
room.

• A quiet house within walking distance of bus depot, restaurants, stores, recreation facilities, and Port Hardy's seawall walkway. Guest rooms share a sitting room with fireplace,
piano, TV, pool table, and telephone. Tea, coffee, and hot chocolate available in the sitting
room. Pickup from the ferry terminal. Full breakfast includes fresh fruit, eggs, homemade
baked goods homemade preserves. **In the hosts' own words:** "We invite you to spend a
night or a few days enjoying the North Island attractions and our hospitality."

Lakewoods B&B

Dick and Jane Visee
9778 Stirling Arm Crescent
Mail: RR 3 Site 339 C–5
Port Alberni, BC V9Y 7L7
(250) 723-2310
(area code 604 before October 1996)

• Twenty minutes from Port Alberni. From Highway 4, west of Port Alberni, turn left onto Faber Road and continue for 4.8 kilometres. At the stop sign, turn right onto Stirling Arm Crescent.

• Three rooms. One person $40–50; two people $55–75. King-sized bed; queen-sized bed. Private bathroom and shared guest bathroom.

• A waterfront house in a garden setting, overlooking Sproat Lake. Guests make day trips to Long Beach in Pacific Rim National Park, ninety kilometres away, and take cruises on the *Lady Rose* passenger boat down the Alberni Inlet. Swimming in Sproat Lake from the B&B. Garden. Living room with TV. Homemade breakfast. Dutch spoken. Adult oriented. No pets. No smoking. **In the hosts' own words:** "We welcome travellers to our peaceful waterfront house overlooking beautiful Sproat Lake."

The Garner House B&B

Pete and Cori Knott
4927 Redford Street
Port Alberni, BC V9Y 3N9
(250) 723-4329
(area code 604 before October 1996)

• In the centre of Port Alberni.

• Two rooms. One person $50; two people $70. Double bed. Ensuite bathrooms.

• A B&B with hardwood floors throughout, a covered porch overlooking Port Alberni, and a fish pond in the back yard. Living room with fireplace. Guest rooms have TVs and coffeemakers and a separate entrance. Three minutes from the *Lady Rose* passenger boat, an hour and a half from Tofino, and two hours from the Carmanah Valley. Full breakfast is served in the dining room or on the covered porch. Visa. No smoking. **In the hosts' own words:** "Welcome to our classic heritage house centrally located in Port Alberni."

Water's Edge B&B

Peter and Kathy Sevigny
9606 Stirling Arm Crescent
Mail: Site 340 C–9
Port Alberni, BC V9Y 7L7
(250) 724-5354 Fax: (250) 724-5308
(area code 604 before October 1996)

• From Highway 4, west of Port Alberni, turn left onto Faber Road and continue for 4.8 kilometres. At the stop sign, turn right onto Stirling Arm Crescent. The B&B is the second house on the left.

• Three rooms. One person $40–45; two people $50–60. Queen-sized bed and a single bed; double bed; queen-sized bed. Ensuite bathroom and shared guest bathroom. Additional person $15. Child 7 to 12 $10. Children under 7 free. Off-season rates October 15 to May 15.

• A B&B on a pebble beach on the shore of Sproat Lake, fifteen kilometres from Port Alberni and en route to Pacific Rim National Park (ninety kilometres away). Swimming in the lake and evening bonfires on the beach. TV sitting room, sun deck with lake view, lawns, and beach. Day trips on the *Lady Rose* passenger boat. Full breakfast is served in the dining room or on the sun deck. Visa. No pets; two dogs and a cat in residence. **In the hosts' own words:** "We're family oriented and can accommodate both tourists and business travellers."

The Octagon Retreat B&B

Jill Lightheart and Laara Daniel
1364 Chesterman Beach Road
Mail: Box 616
Tofino, BC V0R 2Z0
(250) 725-3737
(area code 604 before October 1996)

• Four kilometres past Pacific Rim National Park, turn left onto Chesterman Beach Road. Continue past a large gravel parking area on the right. The B&B is the second driveway on the right.

• Suite. Two people $160. Queen-sized bed. Ensuite bathroom. Breakfast ingredients supplied. Minimum stay two nights; preferred maximum stay four nights. Off-season rates. Open March 21 to November 30.

• A B&B with an octagonal guest room with a private entrance and a private indoor hot tub. Floor-to-ceiling rock fireplace, chairs, leather sofa, TV, VCR, skylights, Native art, local watercolours, and plants. A twenty-three-foot yellow cedar pole supports the ceiling. Local wood and mica slate on the floors and walls. Private covered deck with steps that lead to an open deck surrounded by gardens and a fish pond. One hundred yards from caves and sea life at mile-long Chesterman Beach. Cereal, fresh fruit, homemade baked goods, juice, coffee, tea, and condiments are provided in a small fridge. Small microwave for warming baked goods. No cooking facilities. Reservations recommended. Deposit required to hold reservation. Cancellation notice thirty days in summer (June 15 to September 15), seven days the rest of the year. Visa. Adults only. No pets. Smoke-free environment. **In the hosts' own words:** "Experience the ultimate in West Coast comfort."

Christa's B&B

Christa Kirste
1367 Chesterman Beach Road
Mail: Box 517
Tofino, BC V0R 2Z0
(250) 725-2827 Fax: (250) 725-4416
(area code 604 before October 1996)

● On the way to Tofino, 4.5 kilometres past Pacific Rim National Park, one block off the highway.

● Self-contained suite. Two people $85. Queensized bed. Ensuite bathroom. Additional person $15.

● A waterfront B&B on Chesterman Beach, with access to the beach via a garden path. Suite has a private entrance, a bedroom with a queen-sized bed, an ensuite bathroom, a living/dining area with ocean view, and a kitchen with stove, sink, and fridge. Guests take long walks on the beach. Pickup from plane and bus. Breakfast, which includes homemade bread, is served on a service cart to the suite at a time specified by guests. Cancellation notice seven days. No pets. No smoking. **In the hosts' own words:** "Come and experience the extraordinary beauty of the west coast at any time of the year."

Midori's Place B&B

Midori and Peter Matley
370 Gibson Street
Mail: Box 582
Tofino, BC V0R 2Z0
(250) 725-2203 Fax: (250) 725-2204
(area code 604 before October 1996)

● Three rooms. One person $45–50; two people $55–60; three people $75. In winter, one person $40, two people $45. Queen-sized bed; twin beds. Private and ensuite bathrooms.

● A quiet B&B, two blocks from the centre of Tofino. Within ten minutes' walk of Tonquin Park's hiking trails and Tonquin Beach. Full breakfast is served. No pets. Non-smokers.

The Tide's Inn on Duffin Cove B&B

Val and James Sloman
160 Arnet Road
Mail: Box 325
Tofino, BC V0R 2Z0
(250) 725-3765 Fax: (250) 725-3325
(area code 604 before October 1996)

• In Tofino, turn left onto First Street. Turn right onto Arnet Road. The B&B is a brown house, the first house after the Y in the road.

• Rooms. In summer (June 15 to October 15) and on long weekends, one person $80, two people $85–90. Off-season, one person $65, two people $75–85. Queen-sized bed. Ensuite bathrooms.

Two-bedroom suite. In summer (June 15 to October 15) and on long weekends, two people $90. In winter, two people $70. In spring and fall, two people $80. Queen-sized bed, twin beds, and pull-out couch. Additional person $20. In summer and on long weekends, minimum stay two days.

• A waterfront house on Duffin Cove, with views of the cove, Duffin Passage, and the mountains and islands of Clayoquot Sound. Shoreline with tidal pools. Ten minutes' walk from the beach at Tonquin Park, a sandy beach protected from the open ocean by Wickaninnish Island. Five to fifteen minutes' drive from other beaches in Tofino and Pacific Rim National Park and Long Beach. Ten minutes' walk from the village centre's galleries, restaurants, and charters and tours including whale watching, kayaking, hot springs, Clayoquot Sound harbour, and Meares Island hiking. Guest rooms face the ocean and have private entrances, fridges, and facilities for making coffee and tea. One of the guest rooms has a Jacuzzi. Another guest room has a private balcony. Two-bedroom suite has a sitting room with fireplace, pool table, TV, coffee bar, and fridge. Decks and guest hot tub. Full breakfast includes baking, hot entrée, fruit, juice, and fresh-ground coffee. Cancellation notice three days. Children over ten welcome. No pets; cat in residence. Smoking on decks. **In the hosts' own words:** "We welcome you to Tofino and our home. We'll help in any way we can to make sure your visit to Clayoquot Sound is a comfortable and memorable one."

Wilp Gybuu (Wolf House) B&B

311 Leighton Way
Mail: Box 396
Tofino, BC V0R 2Z0
(250) 725-2330
(area code 604 before October 1996)

• In Tofino, turn left onto First Street. Turn right onto Arnet Road. Turn left onto Leighton Way. The B&B is the first driveway on the right.
• Three rooms. One person $70; two people $75–80. Queen-sized bed; twin beds. Ensuite bathrooms. Off-season rates and extended stay rates.
• A West Coast contemporary cedar house with a view of Duffin Passage and islands in Clayoquot Sound. Within walking distance of restaurants, galleries, kayaking, whale watching, sea plane tours, hot springs tours, and Tonquin Park beach. Within fifteen minutes' drive of golfing and Pacific Rim National Park's beaches and trails. Guest lounge with view. Two of the guest rooms have fireplaces. Each of the guest rooms has a private entrance. Pickup from bus and plane. One host is a Native artist who makes Native-design jewellery. Coffee or tea is delivered to guests' rooms before breakfast. Full breakfast is served in the dining room, which has a view of the inside waters of Duffin Passage. Reservations recommended. Cancellation notice seventy-two hours. Visa, MasterCard. Adult oriented. No pets; cat in residence. Smoking outdoors. **In the hosts' own words:** "We welcome guests to our home with warm western hospitality."

Pacific Rim Accommodations

Louise McIntosh
1316 Lynn Road
Mail: Box 498
Tofino, BC V0R 2Z0
(250) 725-1248
(area code 604 before October 1996)

• Two cottages (each sleeps four). $115–145.
Double bed and futon sofa bed; two double beds.
Breakfast not included. Minimum stay four days.
Weekly rates.
• Two cottages on acreage surrounded by gardens and wild flowers. The self-contained cottage has a double bed and a futon sofa bed and is on one and a half acres in a cedar forest. The one-bedroom cottage has two doubled beds, has beach access, is four hundred feet from Chesterman's Beach, and is decorated in West Coast style with seaweed basketry, driftwood, and whale bones. Cottages have dishes, towels, linen, and bedding. Near kayaking, golfing, fishing, surfing, and Pacific Rim National Park. Tea and coffee supplies provided in self-contained cottage. Tea and coffee supplies and granola provided in one-bedroom cottage. Reservations recommended. Cancellation notice fourteen days. No pets.
In the hosts' own words: "Our charming character cottages offer an enchanting and memorable experience. Soothe your soul with the sounds of the surf, the smell of the sea air, and the spirit of the ancient rainforests."

Silver Cloud B&B

Olivia A. Mae
Campbell Street
Mail: Box 188
Tofino, BC V0R 2Z0
(250) 725-3998
(area code 604 before October 1996)

• Three rooms and one suite. Easter to October 15, $85–$195. Queen-sized
bed; queen-sized bed and one single bed; two double beds and one twin bed. Ensuite bathrooms. Minimum stay three days. Off-season rates.

• A quiet waterfront B&B on three acres, with flower gardens. Heavily wooded in the back
with mature cedar, Sitka spruce, and Douglas fir trees. Gardens with over five hundred flowering shrubs. Brick terrace and glass solarium overlooking the water. Furnished gazebo
incorporates a section of three-thousand-year-old Sitka spruce as its back wall and has a
three-hundred-square-foot deck with a propane barbecue and a ramp to the beach. Guest
rooms have views. One of the guest rooms has an ensuite bathroom with a hot tub. Suite has
a kitchen. Continental breakfast is served from 8:00 to 10:00 a.m. in the solarium or on the
terrace. Breakfast includes tea or coffee, fresh fruit, cheeses, smoked salmon, specialty
spreads, homemade jams, and homemade baking such as scones, muffins, quiche, and
sausage rolls. Reservations required. Cancellation notice thirty days. Visa. Children welcome in the suite. No pets. **In the hosts' own words:** "Last year, people from thirty-two
countries visited with me. I invite you to come and share in the romance of my B&B; you'll
find it as unique and delightfully surprising as the sea itself."

Ocean on the Beach Retreat

Sandra Snetsinger
1377 Thornberg
Mail: Box 629
Tofino, BC V0R 2Z0
(250) 725-2710
(area code 604 before October 1996)

• House. $145. Queen-sized bed, twin beds, and a sofa bed. Private bathroom.
Three-bedroom house. $200. One and a half bathrooms.
Breakfast not included.
• Two two-storey houses joined by a covered walkway. Both houses have ocean views, kitchens, wood stoves, laundry rooms, and outside deck showers. One house is steps from a beach and has a bath and an indoor shower. The other house sleeps six and has a Jacuzzi tub. Five minutes' walk from a restaurant. **In the hosts' own words:** "Cedar walls inside both houses bring the West Coast experience into the comfort of the restful interiors. Our accommodation on beautiful Chesterman Beach is ideal for weddings on the beach and surfers' holidays."

Water's Edge B&B

Ed and Mary Ellen Ironside
331 Park Street
Mail: General Delivery
Tofino, BC V0R 2Z0
(250) 725-1218
(area code 604 before October 1996)

• One kilometre from the centre of Tofino.
• Three rooms. Two people $90, queen-sized bed,
ensuite bathroom. Two people $70, queen-sized
bed or twin beds, shared guest bathroom.
Additional person $15. Off-season rates.
• A house on a cliff, with a view of the Pacific Ocean and several islands, a few minutes'
drive from Pacific Rim National Park. During the spring migration, grey whales are occasionally seen from the deck. Stairs lead down to rocks and tidal pools. A boardwalk through
the forest leads to Tonquin Park's beach. One kilometre from restaurants and galleries in the
centre of Tofino. Guest room with a queen-sized bed has an ensuite bathroom with Jacuzzi.
Full breakfast is served in the dining room, which has a view of passing boats. Suitable for
families. No pets. No smoking. **In the hosts' own words:** "Come and experience the west
coast's many moods—summer's beautiful sunsets and winter's crashing waves."

L'Auberge on the Island

Louise Picard
Nielson Island, Tofino District
Mail: Box 594
Tofino, BC V0R 2Z0
Telephone 0 and ask for Marine Operator,
Channel 24, Tofino for Sea Sip N11 1658.
Telephone line is open 9:00 to 10:30 a.m. and
5:00 to 8:00 p.m.

• In Tofino, go down Olsen Road to Crab Dock.
The B&B, on an island, is the white house seen
looking straight across from the top of the ramp. Call in advance; a boat from the island
picks guests up at the dock. The boat ride takes five minutes.
• Four rooms. One person $40; two people $65. Double bed. Additional person $10. Two-
day stay rate. Open April 1 to October 15.
• A two-storey house with a sun deck overlooking the tidal waters of Clayoquot Sound, on a
twenty-acre private island opposite Tofino's Crab Dock. Reached by a five-minute boat ride;
boat rides to and from the dock once per day are included in rates. Return boat ride to the
dock between 8:00 and 11:00 a.m. Large yard with picnic table and raised-bed vegetable and
flower gardens. Walking trails lead through a forest of first- and second-growth cedar trees
to pebble beaches and sandy flats. Guests fish for salmon at a dock. Guest rooms have
feather pillows and cotton sheets. Cruise boats for whale watching, hot springs day trips, and
sunset cruises stop at the B&B's dock. Packed lunch is provided for guests taking boat cruises. Full breakfast is served at a hand-crafted cedar table. Cash, traveller's cheques. **In the
hosts' own words:** "An absolutely unique and comfortable place to be. Looking forward to
sharing its peace with you."

Sea Star Beach Retreat

Rod and Kelly Cameron
1294 Lynn Road
Mail: Box 2
Tofino, BC V0R 2Z0
(250) 725-2041 Fax: (250) 725-3207
(area code 604 before October 1996)

• Five minutes from the centre of Tofino.
• Studio suite. In summer (March 15 to October 15), $115. In winter, $90. Queen-sized bed. Bathroom in suite.
Lower two-bedroom suite. In summer (March 15 to October 15), $140. In winter, $120. Two queen-sized beds and one queen-sized sofa bed. Ensuite and private bathrooms.
Upper two-bedroom suite. In summer (March 15 to October 15), $115. In winter, $90. Queen-sized bed, bunk beds, and queen-sized sofa bed. Private bathroom.
Breakfast ingredients supplied. Minimum stay three nights. Off-season weekly and monthly rates.
• A B&B with three suites, in a forested residential area, across the road from the open ocean. The suites—one studio and two two-bedroom suites—have kitchens, laundry facilities, and private entrances. The open-design West Coast–style studio suite has a Jacuzzi and a TV. The lower-level two-bedroom suite occupies the main floor of the house and has a fireplace, a TV, a VCR, and a private deck. The upper-level two bedroom suite has a TV and access to a deck. Outdoor hot tub with cedar decks and a shower area. Near old-growth forests, sandy beaches, whale watching, kayaking, hiking, canoeing, diving, and surfing. Fifteen kilometres from Pacific Rim National Park. Near fine dining restaurants. Coffee, tea, and ingredients for self-serve breakfast are provided. Deposit of one night's rate required to hold reservation. Cancellation notice fourteen days. Cheques, credit cards. Children welcome. No smoking in the suites. **In the hosts' own words:** "Clayoquot Sound is world famous for its beauty, pristine beaches, and old-growth forests. Miles of white sandy beaches with driftwood, seashells, and the occasional glass ball all the way from Japan are there for you to enjoy and explore. A restless sea and ever-changing shoreline offer storms, surf, and tranquillity. Bask in the awesome power of nature and then settle into a room by the sea."

"O Canada" House B&B

Jim Britten and Mike Browne
1114 Barclay Street
Vancouver, BC V6E 1H1
(604) 688-0555
Cellular: (604) 313-1233 after 6:00 p.m. and on weekends

• Four rooms. From $150–225. King-sized bed; queen-sized bed; two queen-sized beds. Ensuite bathrooms. Off-season and extended stay rates.

• A B&B in a restored 1897 house, where the national anthem was written in 1909. Each guest room is decorated in late Victorian style and has a sitting area, a TV, a VCR, a fridge, and a telephone. The main floor of the house has an entry hall with open staircase, two sitting rooms with fireplaces, a dining room, and a wrap-around porch. Garden. Parking and luggage storage. Sherry is served in the sitting room at 5:00 p.m. Full breakfast is served in the dining room, in guest rooms, or on a front porch. Deposit of one night's rate required to hold reservation. Visa, MasterCard. Adult oriented. No children under twelve. No pets. Smoking on front porch and in garden. **In the hosts' own words:** "We offer a quiet oasis of Victorian tranquillity just steps away from Vancouver's finest restaurants, shopping, and entertainment."

Shaughnessy Village B&B Guest House

Jan Floody
1125 West Twelfth Avenue
Vancouver, BC V6H 3Z3
(604) 736-5511 Fax: (604) 737-1321

• Between Granville and Oak streets, 5 minutes from downtown Vancouver.
• Two hundred forty rooms. One person $47.95–65.95, one-room studio; one person $69.95–88.95, two-room suite. Ensuite and private bathrooms. Additional person $15. Rates include twelve video movies per day and health club membership. Weekly rates. Monthly rate of $585.
• A resort-style B&B with gardens, a heated swimming pool, a Jacuzzi, crazy-putt golf, a shuffleboard, and outdoor barbecues. Two blocks from shopping and buses. Five minutes' drive from downtown Vancouver. On direct route to the airport. Rooms and suites have Victorian décor. Most have views of Vancouver and False Creek or trees and Mount Baker. Each has a private balcony, a microwave, a fridge, a TV, a clock radio, and a thermostat for individually controlled heat. A health club has a TV lounge, a reading lounge, a billiard room, an exercise room, a sauna, an indoor swirlpool, a suntanning bed, and an acumassage couch. Licensed restaurant, hair salon, full and coin-operated laundry, housekeeping service, dry-cleaning service, and secretarial service. On-camera security and twenty-four-hour front desk security/medicalert response system. Full breakfast is served all day. Visa, MasterCard.
In the hosts' own words: "Our resort-style residence is designed to accommodate B&B visitors to Vancouver who require affordable, well-equipped, comfortable, furnished facilities. There is lots for the visitor to do in a friendly city-country atmosphere."

Lillian Feist

896 West Thirteenth Avenue
Vancouver, BC V5Z 1P2
(604) 873-0842

• Near Oak Street and West Twelfth Avenue.
• One room and four suites. One person $40–50;
two people $50–65. Shared guest bathrooms.
Additional person $10. Off-season and weekly
rates.
• A centrally located B&B near Oak Street and
Twelfth Avenue, one block from Vancouver
General Hospital and public transportation. Ten minutes' drive from downtown. Near shops,
restaurants, Granville Island, Queen Elizabeth Park, the VanDusen Gardens, Gastown, and
Chinatown. Room and suites have TVs. Suites have bed-sitting rooms and kitchens and
accommodate up to four people. Controlled pets welcome. **In the hosts' own words:** "Enjoy
this large older house in the heart of the city."

Columbia Cottage B&B

Susanne Sulzberger and Alisdair Smith
205 West Fourteenth Avenue
Vancouver, BC V5Y 1X2
(604) 874-5327 Fax: (604) 879-4547

• Twenty minutes' drive from the airport. Ten
minutes from downtown.
• Four rooms. Call for rates. Queen-sized bed;
king-sized bed; twin beds; double bed. Ensuite
bathrooms.
One suite. Call for rates. Queen-sized bed and
pull-out sofa. Ensuite bathroom.
• A 1920s Tudor-style cottage in the Mount Pleasant area of Vancouver, five minutes' drive
from Queen Elizabeth Park and Science World and ten minutes' drive from Granville Island,
downtown, Stanley Park, the waterfront, and the cruise liners at Canada Place. Guest lounge
with fireplace. Suite with a lounge and a kitchen accommodates four people. Chocolates,
cookies, and sherry provided. Full breakfast is served in the dining room. No smoking. **In
the hosts' own words:** "You will enjoy our elegant accommodation and gracious hospitality. We look forward to meeting you."

Paul's Guest House International

Paul Ordelt
345 West Fourteenth Avenue
Vancouver, BC V5Y 1X3
(604) 872-4753

• Near city hall; two blocks east of Cambie Street, between Yukon and Alberta streets.

• One person $40–50, two people $50–65, shared guest bathrooms; additional person $15. One person or two people $90, private bathrooms; additional person $20.

• A centrally located B&B in a quiet residential area, a few minutes' walk from Queen Elizabeth Park, City Square shopping mall, and Vancouver General Hospital. On a direct bus route to the airport and downtown. Sightseeing tour buses pick up daily at the B&B's door. The hosts provide free luggage storage and hold mail for guests making side trips and also arrange car rentals. Reservations recommended, May to October. Cash, traveller's cheques (U.S., German, Swiss, French, and other major currencies accepted). The hosts speak ten European languages and Japanese. Children welcome. No pets. Smoking in designated areas. **In the hosts' own words:** "Come as a tourist, leave as a friend. We speak English, French, Spanish, Italian, German, Swedish, Danish, Russian, Czech, Polish, and Japanese. Come and help us to learn others."

Pillow 'n Porridge Guest House

Dianne Reader Haag
2859 Manitoba Street
Vancouver, BC V5Y 3B3
(604) 879-8977 Fax: (604) 879-8966

• From Cambie Street and Twelfth Avenue (Vancouver City Hall), go east on
Twelfth for four blocks and turn right onto Manitoba Street. The B&B is the
third house south of Twelfth Avenue.

• Rooms. One person $75–110; two people $85–135. King-sized bed; queen-
sized bed; double bed; twin beds. Ensuite and shared guest bathrooms.
Three self-contained suites. One person $115–135; two people $145–165.
King-sized bed; queen-sized bed; twin beds. Additional person $10.
Off-season and extended stay rates.
Minimum stay three days in suites. Breakfast not included when more than
two people occupy a suite.

• Three residences side by side, constructed between 1906 and 1910, in the city hall area,
within walking distance of fine dining restaurants, ethnic restaurants, Queen Elizabeth Park,
Granville Island, Science World, the Ford Centre for the Performing Arts, Queen Elizabeth
Theatre, General Motors Place, Vancouver General Hospital, and B.C. Place Stadium.
Within five minutes' drive of downtown. Three blocks from bus and rapid transit routes.
Twenty minutes' drive from the airport. Ten minutes' drive from bus and train. Some rooms
have living rooms, TVs, clock radios, fridges, and facilities for making tea and coffee. Each
suite has a bedroom, a kitchen, a living room, a dining area, an ensuite bathroom, a private
entrance, a clock radio, a TV, and a fireplace. One of the suites has a terrace. Robes provided.
Full breakfast, including wild oat porridge, topped with fresh fruit, almonds, pumpkin seeds,
sunflower seeds, and brown sugar, and a choice of fruit pancakes, frittatas, smoked salmon
and eggs, or peach and Grand Marnier french toast, is served in two dining rooms in the
hosts' house. **In the hosts' own words:** "We offer a warm smile to greet you in the beautiful city of Vancouver."

Kitsilano Point B&B

Jennifer and Larry Barr
1936 McNicoll Avenue
Vancouver, BC V6J 1A6
(604) 738-9576

• Near Cornwall Avenue and Burrard Street.
• Two rooms. One person $65–70; two people $75–80. Twin beds. Ensuite washbasins and showers and shared guest toilet. Additional person $35.
$10 less October 1 to March 31.
• A 1911 house within walking distance of a beach and pool at Kitsilano Beach Park and Vanier Park's museums, planetarium, and observatory. The Vancouver Aquatic Centre and Granville Island market can be reached by a pedestrian ferry a couple of blocks from the B&B. Three to seven blocks from a store and restaurants. Three blocks from a bus stop. Five minutes' drive from downtown Vancouver. One of the guest rooms has a fireplace. The other guest room has an extra-long twin bed. Living room with TV and a garden. Cooked breakfast is served from 7:30 to 8:30 a.m. Check-in after 4:00 p.m. or earlier by arrangement; check-out by 10:30 a.m. Some French spoken. Not suitable for pre-school children or for pets. Non-smokers preferred. **In the hosts' own words:** "A friendly home, convenient to the annual children's festival and the Bard on the Beach Shakespeare festival."

Jolie Maison

Dimka and Louis Gheyle
1888 West Third Avenue
Vancouver, BC V6J 1K8
(604) 730-8010 Fax: (604) 730-8045

• One block west of Burrard Street. One block north of Fourth Avenue.
• Four rooms. One person $70–80; two people $85–95, queen-sized bed, shared guest bathroom; two people $85–95, queen-sized bed, private bathroom; two people $105–125, king-sized bed, ensuite bathroom. Additional person $20.
Off-season and extended stay rates.
• A restored 1901 house in Kitsilano, four blocks from Kitsilano Beach Park and one block from shops and restaurants. Ten minutes' drive from downtown, Stanley Park, and Granville Island. Fifteen minutes' drive from the University of British Columbia. Around the corner from a bus stop. Sitting room with fireplace and TV. One of the guest rooms has a Jacuzzi tub and a walk-in shower. Other guest rooms have views of mountains. Breakfast is served in the dining room. Deposit of one night's rate required to hold reservation. Cancellation notice three days. French, Dutch, and German spoken. Smoking on the porch. **In the hosts' own words:** "We are located in Kitsilano, Vancouver's truly original and trendy neighbourhood. Put your feet up in front of the fire to read a book, watch TV, or visit with other guests. The relaxed and tranquil atmosphere of our charming B&B will make you feel right at home."

Heritage Harbour B&B

Debra Horner
1838 Ogden Avenue
Vancouver, BC V6J 1A1
(604) 736-0809 Fax: (604) 736-0074
E-mail: dhorner@direct.ca

• Five minutes from downtown Vancouver.

• Two rooms. Two people $135–200. Queen-sized bed. Private bathrooms.

• A new traditional-style house in Kitsilano Point across the street from a beach, with views of the ocean, heritage boats, mountains, and downtown. Five minutes' walk along the waterfront from tennis courts and a heated outdoor swimming pool. Two minutes' walk along the waterfront from Vanier Park's museum, planetarium, observatory, and moorage for heritage boats. Fifteen minutes' walk from Granville Island, boutique shopping, and fine dining restaurants on Fourth Avenue. Five minutes by bus, or fifteen minutes by aquabus, or thirty minutes by foot from downtown, Stanley Park, and English Bay beaches. Fifteen minutes' drive from the University of British Columbia. One of the guest rooms has a view of the ocean, mountains, and downtown. The other guest room has French doors that lead to a private veranda overlooking a garden. Guest living room with oak wainscoting, TV, VCR, stereo, marble fireplace, and views of the city and the ocean. Full breakfast is served in the dining room, which has a harbour view. Low-fat and low-cholesterol diets are accommodated. Check-in after 3:00 p.m.; check-out by 11:00 a.m. Visa. Not suitable for small children. Not suitable for pets. Smoking in front garden sitting area. **In the hosts' own words:** "We encourage guests to enter our home as visitors and to leave as friends. Enjoy the conveniences of downtown in a quiet, park, seaside location."

Kenya Court Oceanfront Guest House

Dr. and Mrs. H. R. Williams
2230 Cornwall Avenue
Vancouver, BC V6K 1B5
(604) 738-7085

• Five self-contained suites. Two people
$85–130. King-sized bed; queen-sized bed; twin
beds. Ensuite bathrooms.
• A three-storey building across the street from
Kitsilano Beach Park, which has an outdoor saltwater Olympic-sized heated swimming pool.
Seaside paths in Kitsilano Beach Park lead to Granville Island, a maritime museum, and a
planetarium. One-thousand-square-foot self-contained suites have private entrances and
views of water, city, and mountains. Five minutes' walk from tennis courts and ethnic restaurants. Ten minutes by bus from downtown. Near Jericho Beach, boutiques on Fourth Avenue,
and the University of British Columbia's Anthropology Museum. Full breakfast is served in
a rooftop solarium with panoramic view. Check-in times are flexible. No smoking. **In the
hosts' own words:** "A heritage building in one of the best locations in Vancouver."

Graeme's House

Ms. Graeme Elizabeth Webster
2735 Waterloo Street
Vancouver, BC V6R 3J1
(604) 732-1488

• Near West Tenth Avenue and Alma Street.
• Two rooms. One person $60; two people $70.
Queen-sized bed; twin beds. Shared guest bath-
room. Additional person $25. Child under 12
$15.
• A B&B with gardens, on a quiet street, one kilo-
metre from Jericho Beach and a few minutes by bus or car from the University of British
Columbia, the Aquatic Centre, Granville Island, and downtown. Close to shops on Broadway
and shops and services near Tenth and Sasamat. A variety of restaurants within two blocks.
Living room with fireplace, kitchen/family room with TV, and roof garden. Due to the hosts'
work schedules, guests sometimes help themselves to breakfast. No pets; cat in residence.
No smoking.

Penny Farthing Inn

Lyn Hainstock
2855 West Sixth Avenue
Vancouver, BC V6K 1X2
(604) 739-9002 Fax: (604) 739-9004

• Half a block west of MacDonald Street, on the north side of West Sixth Avenue.

• Two rooms. In summer, one person $75, two people $95. In winter, one person $65, two people $75. Double bed; twin beds. Shared bathroom. Two suites. In summer, one person $125–140, two people $150–165. In winter, one person $105–115, two people $125–140. Queen-sized bed and double sofa bed. Bathroom in suite.

• A 1912 house with stained glass windows, wood floors, and antiques brought by the host from England. Within walking distance of English Bay, shops, restaurants, and buses. Five minutes' drive from downtown and the University of British Columbia. Twenty minutes' from the airport. Honeymoon suite has a view of English Bay and mountains, skylights, a brass queen-sized bed, a private bathroom with shower, and a sitting room with a TV and a VCR. Another suite has a view of the mountains, a pine four-post queen-sized bed, a private bathroom, a sitting room with double sofa bed, a TV, a VCR, and a veranda overlooking the garden. Guest room with pine four-post double bed has a porch overlooking the front garden. Another guest room has brass twin beds or a king-sized bed. Guest living room with TV, VCR, collection of videos, and CD player. Breakfast is served on a brick patio in an English country garden. Cats in residence. Smoking on the porches. **In the hosts' own words:** "Warm hospitality and a delicious breakfast in a beautiful heritage setting. Designated as a heritage house by the City of Vancouver."

Bed and Breakfast by Locarno Beach

Elke Holm
4505 Langara Avenue
Vancouver, BC V6R 1C9
(604) 341-4975

• Ten minutes from downtown Vancouver.
• One person $60; two people from $75. Queen-sized bed and twin sofa bed.
Ensuite bathrooms. Additional person $20.
• A B&B in West Point Grey on a quiet side street, across the street from a city park and four houses from a two-kilometre sandy ocean beach and seaside trail. The beach and trail have a panoramic view of the North Shore and Howe Sound mountains, downtown, and Stanley Park. Within walking distance of tennis courts, boat rentals, and a beachside cafeteria. Five minutes' drive from the University of British Columbia and a public golf course. Close to bus route. Twenty minutes by bus or ten minutes by car from downtown. Each guest room has a TV. Guest fridge and telephone in hallway. Full breakfast is served in the dining room. Cash, traveller's cheques. German and some French spoken. Non-smokers. **In the hosts' own words:** "Enjoy our resort-like setting within minutes of downtown Vancouver."

Panorama B&B

Vlasta Vit
4326 West Point Place
Vancouver, BC V6R 4M9
(604) 224-7055 Fax: (604) 224-4973

• Room. Queen-sized bed. Ensuite bathroom. Call for rates.
• A contemporary house with a view, in West Point Grey, within walking distance of a beach, nature walks, the University of British Columbia Endowment Lands walking and biking trails, and tennis courts. Ten minutes' drive from downtown and Stanley Park. Guest room has a view, a sauna, and a TV. Bikes. Breakfast is served on the deck or in the sunroom, with city, ocean, and mountain views. **In the hosts' own words:** "Enjoy European-style hospitality."

Brown's UBC B&B

Douglas Brown
4128 West Twelfth Avenue
Vancouver, BC V6R 2P6
(604) 222-8073 Fax: (604) 222-9073

• Five blocks from the University of British Columbia, between Tenth Avenue and Sixteenth Avenue.

• Two rooms. One person $65–95; two people $75–105. Queen-sized bed. Ensuite and shared bathrooms.

• A contemporary West Coast–style cedar house in a quiet area, three blocks from the University of British Columbia Endowment Lands forest and walking trails in Pacific Spirit Provincial Park. Near a golf course, the Museum of Anthropology, the Botanical Gardens, the Nitobe Japanese Gardens, Spanish Banks and Jericho beaches and parks, and shops and restaurants on Tenth Avenue. Twelve minutes from Granville Island and downtown. Within twenty-five minutes' drive of the airport. Near a main street that intersects a direct route to the airport, the highway to the U.S., and the Tsawwassen ferry terminal. One of the guest rooms has an ensuite bathroom, a TV, and a private wooded deck. Another guest room has a shared bathroom, a TV, and a private deck with mountain and city views. Laundry facilities. Full breakfast with natural foods and tea and coffee. Diets are accommodated. Reservations required. MasterCard. **In the hosts' own words:** "We offer our restful, warm home to provide you with comfortable beds, a relaxed atmosphere, and nourishing food."

Dunbar Area B&B

Amy H. Cudney
3716 West Thirty-seventh Avenue
Vancouver, BC V6N 2V9
(604) 263-5428

• Half a block west of Dunbar Street, on the south side of Thirty-seventh Avenue.

• One person $55; two people $80. One twin bed; twin beds (or a king sized bed). Shared bathroom.

Two people $75–85. Double bed. Ensuite bathroom with shower.

Minimum stay two nights. Open May 15 to September 30.

• A B&B within walking distance of restaurants, theatre, shops, and the University of British Columbia Endowment Lands. Half a block from bus stop. Within twenty minutes' drive of airport, downtown, the University of British Columbia, Stanley Park, beaches, Queen Elizabeth Park, the VanDusen Gardens, and the Nitobe Japanese Gardens. Beds have cotton linen and down duvets (alternatives to down available). Hardwood floors throughout. Main floor guest living room with fireplace and TV. Deck off dining room with view of organic garden. Guests bring clean slippers. Hot breakfast is served in the dining room. Diets are accommodated. Children over eleven welcome. No pets. No smoking. **In the hosts' own words:** "Enjoy the comfort of our bright, beautifully renovated bungalow and good food."

Johnson Heritage House B&B

Sandy and Ron Johnson
2278 West Thirty-fourth Avenue
Vancouver, BC V6M 1G6
(604) 266-4175

• Near West Thirty-third Avenue and Arbutus Street.
• Three rooms. One person $60–120; two people $70–135. Twin beds; king-sized bed. Queen-sized bed. Ensuite and shared guest bathrooms.
• A renovated 1920s Craftsman-style house with antique furniture including iron and brass beds, Persian carpets, carousel horses, and gramophones. Living room with cottage windows, French doors, a TV, and a fireplace. Covered front porch. Rhododendron garden with benches. Some guest rooms have TVs. Within walking distance of buses, restaurants, shops, and banks. Five to fifteen minutes from airport, downtown, Stanley Park, the University of British Columbia, and the VanDusen Gardens. Breakfast, including fruit, yogurt, hot entrée, and homemade muffins, scones, or cinnamon buns, is served at a nine-foot oak table. Cash, cheques. Children over twelve welcome. No smoking.

A Tree House B&B

Barb and Bob Selvage
2490 West Forty-ninth Avenue
Vancouver, BC V6M 2V3
(604) 266-2962 Fax: (604) 266-2962

• One room and two suites. One person $80–115; two people $85–125. Queen-sized bed; queen-sized bed and hide-a-bed. Ensuite and private bathrooms. Additional person $25.

• A multi-level house with contemporary art and sculpture, close to hiking, horseback riding, golf, tennis, swimming pools, and a community centre. A few minutes' drive from the University of British Columbia, the airport, and ferries to the islands. One of the suites occupies the entire third floor and has private sun decks, a four-post queen-sized bed, a skylit bathroom with Jacuzzi, and a sitting room with small fridge and coffeemaker. A suite on the main floor has a queen-sized bed, a sitting area with TV and hide-a-bed, and a bathroom with Jacuzzi. A guest room has a queen-sized bed and a private bath, is decorated with Japanese crafts, and opens onto a Japanese courtyard garden. Guest living/dining room and covered deck. Kimonos, slippers, chocolates on pillows, telephones, and morning papers are provided. Children over ten welcome. Pets can be boarded nearby. Smoke-free environment. **In the hosts' own words:** "Our B&B provides a unique experience. Discover why our guests return year after year."

Arbutus House B&B

Gus and Lani Mitchell
4470 Maple Crescent
Vancouver, BC V6J 4B3
(604) 738-6432 Fax: (604) 738-6433

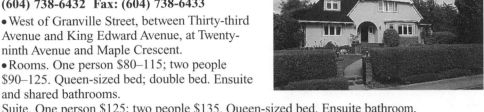

• West of Granville Street, between Thirty-third Avenue and King Edward Avenue, at Twenty-ninth Avenue and Maple Crescent.

• Rooms. One person $80–115; two people $90–125. Queen-sized bed; double bed. Ensuite and shared bathrooms.

Suite. One person $125; two people $135. Queen-sized bed. Ensuite bathroom. Additional person $20. Off-season rates. May to October, minimum stay two nights. Open January 15 to November 30.

• A 1920s character house in Shaughnessy, with antiques and contemporary furnishings. Within fifteen minutes' drive of downtown, Stanley Park, airport, beaches, Queen Elizabeth Park, the VanDusen Gardens, the University of British Columbia, and General Motors Place. Two blocks from public transit. Within walking distance of parks, shops, and restaurants. Guest rooms have sitting areas. One of the guest rooms has a private sun deck. Suite has a sitting area with a gas fireplace. Guest sitting room with fireplace and tourist information. Den with TV, VCR, and reading material. Sun decks and flower gardens. Tea, coffee, lemonade, and baked goods provided in the afternoon. Chocolates, sherry, dressing gowns, and slippers provided at bedtime. Hair dryers. Off-street parking. Full breakfast is served in the dining room. Children over twelve years welcome. No pets; cat in residence. Smoking outdoors. **In the hosts' own words:** "Our house is filled with warm hues, sunlight, and laughter; our breakfasts are tasty and creatively served; our gardens are lush, aromatic, and colourful; our approach is careful attention to detail and a sincere interest in the needs of our guests."

The Balfour Inn

Muni Nazerali
1064 Balfour Avenue
Vancouver, BC V6H 1X1
(604) 730-9927 Fax: (604) 737-2184
Toll-free from within Canada: 1-800-558-8878
Toll-free for reservations from within the U.S.: 1-800-643-4510

• Ten minutes from downtown Vancouver. North of King Edward Avenue and west of Oak Street.

• Ten rooms. Two people from $60. Queen-sized bed. Ensuite and shared guest bathrooms. Off-season and weekly rates.

• A 1913 mansion in Shaughnessy, surrounded by gardens, a few minutes' drive from Granville Island, Stanley Park, Gastown, Vancouver General Hospital, downtown shopping, and the Ford Centre for the Performing Arts. Near direct routes to the airport and to ferries to Vancouver Island and the Gulf Islands. Guest lounge with fireplace. Jacuzzi. Parking. Tea and coffee provided. Full breakfast with fresh fruit is served in the garden or in the dining room. Visa, MasterCard. Suitable for groups. No pets. Smoke-free environment. **In the hosts' own words:** "This is an oasis in the city. Come and enjoy it with us."

The French Quarter B&B

Ginette Bertrand
2051 West Nineteenth Avenue
Vancouver, BC V6J 2P5
(604) 737-0973 Fax: (604) 737-0973

• Between Burrard and Arbutus, near Sixteenth Avenue.
• One room. In summer (May 1 to October 1), at Christmas, and on holidays, one person or two people $125. In winter, one person or two people $105. Queen-sized bed. Ensuite bathroom.
Cottage. In summer (May 1 to October 1), at Christmas, and on holidays, one person or two people $195. In winter, one person or two people $165. Queen-sized bed. Ensuite bathroom.
Extended stay rates.
• A French country-style house on a half acre, in the Shaughnessy area, eight minutes from downtown. A five-hundred-square-foot cottage with an open floor plan has a bedroom with a four-post canopied queen-sized bed; a sitting room and a dining area with vaulted ceilings, French doors, dormer windows, and a fireplace; an ensuite bathroom with a Jacuzzi and a large shower; and an entertainment centre with TV, VCR, stereo, wet bar, and fridge. The cottage is adjacent to the house and has access to a pool, a pool-deck patio, and a garden. Guest room in the house has a queen-sized bed, a TV, and an ensuite bathroom. The house has an exercise room with stair climber, recumbent bicycle, aerobic rider, and free weights. Full breakfast is served at guests' convenience in the garden, weather permitting. Visa, MasterCard. **In the hosts' own words:** "An oasis of beauty and charm that offers you romance and tranquillity right in the midst of Vancouver. A honeymooners' paradise."

The Whitehead House B&B

Darlene Whitehead
901 West Twenty-third Avenue
Vancouver, BC V5Z 2B2
(604) 736-3050 Fax: (604) 736-3050

• One block east of Oak Street on the corner of Laurel Street and Twenty-third Avenue. Ten minutes from downtown.

• Room with sitting area. In summer, one person or two people $75. In winter, one person or two people $65. Queen-sized bed. Shared guest bathroom. Additional person $10. Cot available.

Room. In summer, one person or two people $65. In winter, one person or two people $60. Twin beds. Shared guest bathroom.

• A centrally located 1910 house within walking distance of Queen Elizabeth Park, the VanDusen Gardens, theatres, restaurants, and coffee bars. One block from bus route. Guest rooms have down quilts, feather pillows, and antiques. A shared guest bathroom has a shower big enough for two. Guest entrance. Guest sitting room with table, chairs, and antique sideboard. Coffee, tea, and biscuits provided. Full breakfast. Visa. Children welcome. No smoking. **In the hosts' own words:** "Enjoy a healthy West Coast breakfast in our heritage house."

Peloquin's Pacific Pad

Eugene and Janet Peloquin
426 West Twenty-second Avenue
Vancouver, BC V5Y 2G5
(604) 874-4529

• Near King Edward Avenue and Cambie Street.

• Two rooms. One person $50–55; two people $65–75. Shared guest bathroom. Additional person $25. Child $15–20.

• A B&B in a residential neighbourhood, within walking distance of restaurants, shops, parks, and bus routes. A few minutes by car or bus from downtown, the University of British Columbia, General Motors Place, the Ford Centre for the Performing Arts, B.C. Place Stadium, and Vancouver General Hospital. Easy access from the airport, ferries, and Highway 99 from the U.S. The hosts provide information about Vancouver. Guest rooms have private entrances and TVs. Guest common area has a fridge, a toaster, a microwave, and dishes and is stocked with coffee and tea. No cooking; the microwave is for warming food. Full breakfast, including homemade preserves, is served in a solarium-like kitchen. Check-in and check-out times are flexible. French and Ukrainian spoken. Children welcome. No pets. Non-smokers welcome. **In the hosts' own words:** "Have a happy holiday."

Beautiful B&B

The Sandersons
428 West Fortieth Avenue
Vancouver, BC V5Y 2R4
(604) 327-1102 Fax: (604) 327-2299

• First block east of Cambie Street on West Fortieth Avenue.
• $95–125; shared bathroom. $135–195; private bathroom.
Honeymoon suite.
• A colonial-style house with antiques and views of Vancouver Island, Mount Baker, and the North Shore mountains, centrally located on a quiet residential street. A few minutes' walk from Queen Elizabeth Park's sunken gardens and panoramic view of the city, the fifty-five-acre VanDusen Gardens, fine dining restaurants, a shopping centre, three cinemas, a fitness centre, hospitals, a public library, golf courses, tennis courts, and swimming pools. One block from buses to ferry terminal, airport, downtown (fifteen minutes by bus), the University of British Columbia, and Victoria. One block from shuttle bus to Bellingham, Seattle, and Tacoma and their airports. Ten minutes' drive from downtown. Twelve minutes' drive from the airport. Honeymoon suite is furnished with antiques and has a pink marble fireplace, French doors leading to a balcony, a private bathroom, and both northern and southern views. Large backyard with miniature Japanese pond, garden, and waterfall. The hosts help guests with travel plans. Breakfast is served in a formal dining room, with silver, on white tablecloths. Adult oriented. No pets. No smoking. **In the hosts' own words:** "Relax in elegance. For each guest, we try to find a little extra that will be uniquely pleasing. We also help our guests develop sightseeing plans to suit their tastes and resources. Public transportation is so accessible from our location that a car is not required."

Chickadee Tree B&B

Herb and Lois Walker
1395 Third Street
West Vancouver, BC V7S 1H8
(604) 925-1989 Fax: (604) 925-1989
E-mail: lowalker@direct.ca

- Two people $110–135. Additional person $20.
- Two self-contained suites. Bathrooms in suites.
Cottage. Private bathroom.
Group, family, and winter rates.
- A cedar and glass contemporary house with a solar-heated swimming pool, two pool decks, a sauna, and a guest indoor hot tub, surrounded by a high cedar fence and pine trees. Gazebo, greenhouse, and lily pond. Within fifteen minutes' drive of downtown Vancouver, Grouse Mountain and Cypress Bowl ski areas, and the Horseshoe Bay ferry terminal. Within a few minutes' drive of shops and restaurants in West Vancouver. Within walking distance, along a river trail, of the ocean, beaches, shops, the Capilano River fish hatchery, the Capilano Suspension Bridge, and the Grouse Mountain Skyride. Suites and cottage have TVs, VCRs, coffeemakers and private entrances. The cottage has a sitting room and a kitchen. One of the suites has a Jacuzzi and a balcony that overlooks the swimming pool. Another suite has a fireplace and is adjacent to the guest indoor hot tub. The hosts are former teachers and semi-retired Canadian children's television producers. Honeymoon guests receive wine and flowers. Breakfast, including fresh fruit, homemade bread, coffee or tea, and an egg entrée, is delivered to guests' suite or cottage. Or, if guests prefer, ingredients are supplied for them to make their own breakfast. Suitable for families and groups. No pets; cat and dog in residence. Smoking outside. **In the hosts' own words:** "This B&B is named for an ivy-draped mountain ash tree in the backyard—a meeting place for local chickadees. Our B&B is a sensible and convenient stopover point on the way to Whistler, Vancouver Island, and the Sunshine Coast. We love the variety, beauty, pace, convenience, and culture of North Shore life. Please come visit and we'll do our best to make your stay enjoyable."

Sunset Vista B&B

Helena Galas
815 Evelyn Drive
West Vancouver, BC V7T 1J1
(604) 925-3510 Fax: (604) 925-3510
Toll-free: 1-800-925-3510

• From Highway 1, turn south onto Taylor Way. After the light at Keith Road, turn right onto Evelyn Drive.
• Two rooms. One person $60–75; two people $75–85. Queen-sized bed. Ensuite and shared bathrooms.
One-bedroom suite. One person $100; two people $115. Queen-sized bed. Bathroom in suite. Extended stay rates, with or without breakfast.
• A B&B overlooking Stanley Park, the Lions Gate Bridge, the ocean, and Alaska cruise ships. Guest rooms and suite are a new addition to the house. One of the guest rooms has a private deck. The suite has a gas fireplace, a sink, a hotplate, a microwave, and a fridge. A few minutes from downtown Vancouver. Ten minutes from the Horseshoe Bay ferry terminal, a suspension bridge, and the ski slopes of Grouse Mountain and Cypress Bowl. An hour and a half from Whistler. A few minutes' walk from a shopping centre and an ocean beach. Smoking outdoors. **In the hosts' own words:** "Enjoy our European-Canadian atmosphere."

Cedardale

Joys Chow and Abdallah Jamal
694 Keith Road
West Vancouver, BC V7T 1L9
(604) 922-8888 Fax: (604) 925-9440
E-mail: relativeform@cyberstore.ca

• From Highway 1, take Taylor Way south to
Keith Road. The B&B is on the southeast corner
of Keith Road and Taylor Way.
• Room. One person $40; two people $50.
Double bed. Shared bathroom.
Self-contained one-bedroom suite (sleeps four). Two people $100. Queen-sized bed.
Bathroom in suite. Additional person $10. Weekly and monthly rates.
• A B&B with a guest room and a self-contained one-bedroom suite, ten minutes' drive from
downtown Vancouver and the Horseshoe Bay ferry terminal. Living room with fireplace,
piano, and views of the Lions Gate Bridge and Stanley Park. Guest room has a TV. Suite
sleeps up to four people, opens onto a terrace and a garden, and has a private entrance and
a kitchen. The suite's living room has a fireplace, a TV, a futon, and a view of the Lions Gate
Bridge. Across the street from buses to downtown Vancouver and Whistler. Five minutes'
walk from Park Royal shopping centre. Ten minutes' walk from the Capilano River. A riverside path leads to beaches and shops in Ambleside Village to the south and a fish hatchery,
the Cleveland Dam, and Grouse Mountain to the north. The suite is suitable for families.
Non-smokers.

Ambleside B&B

John and Jeannick Helm
1373 Haywood Avenue
West Vancouver, BC V7T 1V4
(604) 922-8485 Fax: 922-8485

• From Vancouver, cross the Lions Gate Bridge
and turn west onto Marine Drive. Turn north
onto Thirteenth Street and left onto Haywood
Avenue.
• Suite (rented as a one- or two-bedroom suite;
accommodates up to six people). Two people
$95–115. Twin beds (or a king-sized bed), queen-sized bed, and double bed. Private bath-
room. Additional person $35.
• A B&B with a ground-floor ocean-view suite and an English garden with a creek. Fifteen
minutes from downtown Vancouver and ferries to Vancouver Island and the Sunshine Coast.
Ten minutes from skiing at Grouse Mountain. Two minutes from Ambleside beach, parks,
shops, and restaurants. On bus route. The suite has a private entrance, a living/dining room,
a TV, a telephone, a sink, a fridge, and sliding glass doors leading to a covered patio overlooking the ocean. Continental breakfast is provided. French and Spanish spoken. Not suitable for young children or for pets. Smoke-free environment.

Ambleside-by-the-Sea B&B

Kenneth Walters
763 Seventeenth Street
West Vancouver, BC V7V 3T4
(604) 922-4873

• Near Seventeenth Street and Marine Drive.
• Two rooms. One person $40–45; two people
$55–65. Queen-sized bed; twin beds. Private and
shared guest bathrooms.
• A centrally located B&B close to shops, parks, a
seawall walkway, and restaurants with West Coast
menus. Ten minutes' drive from downtown Vancouver. Near bus stop. Off-street parking.
Full breakfast, with guests' preferences accommodated, is served in the dining room. Not
suitable for young children or for pets. **In the hosts' own words:** "You will enjoy our hospitality, friendship, and sincerity."

Creekside B&B

Donna Hawrelko and John Boden
1515 Palmerston Avenue
West Vancouver, BC V7V 4S9
(604) 926-2599 or (604) 328-9400
Fax: (604) 926-7545

• From Highway 1, turn south onto Fifteenth
Street. Continue to Palmerston Avenue and turn
right.
From Marine Drive in West Vancouver, turn
north onto Fifteenth Street. Continue to
Palmerston Avenue and turn left.
• Two rooms. From $100. King-sized bed, ensuite bathroom; queen-sized bed, private bathroom. Minimum stay two days.
• A B&B on a wooded lot with a small stream running through it. Close to transit, beaches,
wilderness and mountain areas, fine dining restaurants, antique shops, shopping malls,
ocean beaches, Stanley Park, and Grouse Mountain and Cypress Bowl ski areas. Each guest
room has a TV, a radio alarm clock, a coffeemaker, and a fridge with wines, beverages, and
snacks. Robes, toiletries, and half-price coupons for dining, sightseeing, and entertainment.
Honeymoon suite guest room is air-conditioned and has a king-sized bed, a gas fireplace,
and a two-person marble Jacuzzi bathtub with a glass roof through which trees can be seen
by day and stars by night. Another guest room has a brass queen-sized bed and a private bathroom with a six-foot Jacuzzi bathtub and skylights. Full breakfast including fresh fruit is
served. Visa, MasterCard. Not suitable for children under ten. Small pets permitted by
arrangement; small poodle in residence.

English Rose B&B

Mary Salvador
Dundarave, West Vancouver, BC
(604) 926-1902

• Suite. Double bed. Bathroom in suite. Call for further information. Open
May to October.
• A B&B with an English country garden, three blocks from Dundarave Village, an ocean
beach, and a seawall walkway. Twenty minutes' drive from downtown Vancouver. Ten minutes' drive from the Horseshoe Bay ferry terminal and Lighthouse Park's walking trails down
to the ocean. Suite occupies the main floor of the house and includes a guest living room and
dining room. Oils, watercolours, and etchings in each room. Chintz chairs, old pine furniture, and Persian rugs. Guest room with brass double bed. The dining room has a bay window with window seats and pillows and overlooks a treed back garden with old English roses
that climb thirty feet up evergreen trees. The host is originally from England. Full breakfast
is served at a pine table. Guests choose either to visit with the host at breakfast or to have
breakfast served for them in privacy. Spanish spoken. No pets. No smoking. **In the hosts'
own words:** "We especially invite garden lovers and those looking for a romantic getaway."

Beachside B&B

Gordon and Joan Gibbs
4208 Evergreen Avenue
West Vancouver, BC V7V 1H1
(604) 922-7773 Fax: (604) 926-8073
Toll-free from within Canada and the U.S.: 1-800-563-3311
E-mail: beach@uniserve.com

• From the Lions Gate Bridge, go 7 kilometres west on Marine Drive. Turn south onto Ferndale Avenue and continue for half a block. Turn left onto Evergreen Avenue. The B&B is at the end of the cul-de-sac.

• Five rooms. Two people from $110. Queen-sized bed. Ensuite and private bathrooms. Additional person $20. Off-season rates.

• A waterfront house at the end of a quiet cul-de-sac, with a sandy beach and a panoramic view from Vancouver to the Gulf Islands. Within twenty minutes of downtown Vancouver, Stanley Park, the Horseshoe Bay ferry terminal, and North Shore attractions. Half a block from the bus. Guests walk along the beach and watch sunrises, sunsets, Alaska cruise ships, seals, sea otters, birds, and eagles. Near fishing, sailing, wilderness hiking, skiing, golfing, parks, trails, tennis courts, antique stores, a convenience store, shopping, and fine dining restaurants. Guest lounge with fireplace, VCR, and collection of videos. Guest fridge. Board games, puzzles, and books. Guest outdoor beachside Jacuzzi and beach patios. Indoor Jacuzzi. Guest rooms have fireplaces, TVs, fresh flowers, fruit baskets, coffee pots, blow dryers, and curling irons. Two of the guest rooms have ocean views. The house has antique stained glass, old brick, and hanging baskets. One host is available as a tour guide. Off-street parking. Full breakfast with muffins, scones, fresh-ground coffee, and teas is served in a dining room with a view of the ocean. Deposit of 50 percent required. Cancellation notice fourteen days. Check-in from 5:00 to 6:00 p.m. or by arrangement. Cash, traveller's cheques, Visa, MasterCard. No pets; dog in residence. Smoking on covered patios. **In the hosts' own words:** "We are well-travelled former teachers, and we advise guests on local attractions. Relax, make new friends, and enjoy Vancouver's legendary scenery, cultural events, and attractions, in quiet seclusion just minutes from the city centre."

The Palms Guest House

Heidi Schmidt
3042 Marine Drive
West Vancouver, BC V7V 1M4
(604) 926-1159 Fax: (604) 926-1451
Toll-free from within Canada and the U.S.:
1-800-691-4455

• Three rooms. Two people $100–220. King-sized bed; queen-sized bed; twin beds. Ensuite bathrooms.

• A new semi-waterfront house with antiques, within walking distance of Dundarave Village, a seawall, and restaurants. On bus route to ferries at Horseshoe Bay and downtown Vancouver. Each guest room has a balcony that has a view of a garden and the ocean. One of the guest rooms has a canopied bed, a Jacuzzi, and a fireplace. TV, telephone, stereo, air conditioning, and down duvets. Tea is served in the guest living room or on the terrace. Breakfast is served in a formal dining room. Spanish, German, and Italian spoken. Adult oriented. No pets. Smoking on balconies. **In the hosts' own words:** "Experience unforgettable West Coast living."

The Vineyard at Bowen Island

Elena and Lary Waldman
Mail: Box 135
Bowen Island, BC V0N 1G0
(604) 947-0028 Fax: (604) 947-0693

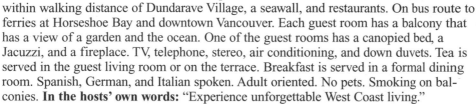

• One hour's drive and ferry ride from downtown Vancouver. From the Horseshoe Bay ferry terminal, take the ferry to Bowen Island.

• Rooms. Queen-sized bed and queen-sized futon sofa.

Suites. King-sized bed.

• A B&B on four landscaped, fenced acres with a two-acre vineyard on the property. Fifteen minutes' walk from shopping and restaurants. Near kayaking tours, fishing, mountain hiking, walking trails, and beaches. Each guest room or suite has a sun deck/patio, a private entrance, a fireplace, a TV, a VCR, videos, a microwave, a fridge, a coffeemaker, a radio, books, and magazines. Suites have living rooms and wet bars. One of the suites has a private garden courtyard and an ensuite bathroom with soaker tub and shower. Guest lounge with stone fireplace, books, puzzles, and games. Guest hot tub. Swimming pool and patio open until 9:00 p.m. The hosts offer tours of their other vineyards by arrangement. Picnic baskets, sit-down lunches, and dinner available by arrangement. Full breakfast, including farm-fresh eggs, local produce, homebaked muffins, and entrées such as apricot French toast, smoked salmon and brie omelettes, cheese blintzes, eggs Benedict, and potato latkes, is served 8:00 to 10:00 a.m. in the guest lounge or, by arrangement, in guests' rooms. Reservations recommended. Deposit of first night's rate required to hold reservation. Cancellation notice five days. Visa, MasterCard.

Union Steamship Company

Rondy and Dorothy Dike
Mail: Box 250
Bowen Island, BC V0N 1G0
(604) 947-0707 Fax: (604) 947-0708

• Fifteen minutes by ferry from the Horseshoe Bay ferry terminal. The B&B cottages are next to the ferry landing on Bowen Island.

• Two two-bedroom cottages and a one-bedroom float house. In summer (June 1 to October 15), two people $85. In winter, two people $65. Queen-sized bed and two sets of bunk beds. Breakfast not included. Additional person $10. Minimum stay two days on summer weekends. Discount of 15 percent on stays of five or more days.

• Two of the original cottages of the Union Steamship Company in a resort village in Snug Cove on Bowen Island, with views of mountains and Howe Sound. Bald eagles and deer can be seen. Each cottage has two bedrooms, a living room with wood stove, a TV, a kitchen, and a porch. A newly remodelled float house on a dock has a bedroom, a living room, a kitchen, a TV, and a futon sofa. Within one block of a bakery, a deli, and a restaurant. A few minutes from private coves, public beaches, parks, and hiking and biking trails. Bowen Island's port has boutiques, boardwalks, and turn-of-the-century buildings. Breakfast not included. Credit cards. Children and pets welcome. **In the hosts' own words:** "There's no place in the world like the B.C. coast, and there's no better way to see its scenery and natural sights than seated on the front porch of one of our rustic cottages."

Mountainside Manor B&B

Anne and Mike Murphy
5909 Nancy Greene Way
North Vancouver, BC V7R 4W6
(604) 985-8484 Fax: (604) 985-8484

• From Highway 1, take Capilano Road north. Follow signs for Grouse Mountain.
• Four rooms. $75–120. Queen-sized bed; king-sized bed; twin beds. Ensuite bathrooms and shared guest bathroom. Additional person $20. Extended stay rates.
• A contemporary West Coast–style house in a garden setting, with the forested slopes of Grouse Mountain as a backdrop. Within walking distance of Grouse Mountain's skyride, restaurants, skiing, hiking, logging shows, movies, and sleigh rides; the Cleveland Dam; Capilano Lake; a salmon hatchery; and a forest with large trees. Five minutes' drive from the Capilano suspension bridge. Fifteen minutes from Stanley Park and downtown Vancouver. Ninety minutes from Whistler Mountain. Guest rooms have TVs, flowers, and toiletries. Some guest rooms have views, balconies, and coffeemakers. One of the guest rooms has a queen-sized bed and an ensuite bathroom with Jacuzzi. Lounge with fireplace, contemporary and antique furniture, reading material, city and mountain views, and an adjoining deck with hot tub. Off-street parking. On bus route. Full, varied breakfast is served. Deposit of one night's rate required to hold reservation. Visa. No smoking. **In the hosts' own words:** "Our B&B in its colourful garden setting is spectacularly designed, hospitable, and yours to enjoy."

Cedar Hill B&B

Jean and Adolph Olson
1095 West Keith Road
North Vancouver, BC V7P 1Y6
(604) 988-9629
E-mail: cedarhil@citywidenet.com

• One and a half blocks from Marine Drive, near Capilano Road.
• Rooms and suite. One person $40–55; two people $75–95; four people (in suite) $135. The beds (queen-sized bed; double bed; twin beds; king-sized bed) and the layout of the rooms allow for many bedroom/bathroom/living room combinations. Bathroom in suite and shared guest bathrooms. Additional person $20.
• A B&B with rooms and a garden-level suite with a private entrance and a patio, ten minutes from downtown Vancouver. The suite's living room has a fireplace, a TV, a VCR, a bar, a piano, and an organ. One of the guest rooms in the suite has a king-sized bed. The other guest room in the suite has its own private entrance and a double bed. Guest rooms have TVs. Upstairs guest living room with TV. Large yard with gardens. Within walking distance of Capilano Mall, restaurants and shopping. Near hiking, beaches, and tourist attractions. Parking. Breakfast is served in the dining room, which has a bay window, or on the patio. Wheelchair accessible. Suitable for families and groups. Small pets welcome. Smoking outside. **In the hosts' own words:** "We offer comfort and a central location in quiet, secluded Pemberton Heights. A North Vancouver treat."

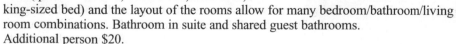

Summit View B&B

Sherri Kia
5501 Cliffridge Place
North Vancouver, BC   V7R 4S2
(604) 990-1089 Fax: (604) 987-7167
E-mail: summit@direct.ca

• From Highway 1, take the Capilano Road exit and go north on Capilano Road. Turn right onto Prospect Road, left onto Cliffridge Avenue, and left onto Cliffridge Place. The B&B is the first house on the left.
From Marine Drive, turn north onto Capilano Road.
• Rooms and honeymoon suite. In summer, from $75. In winter, from $55. Queen-sized bed; double bed; twin beds. Ensuite bathrooms, private bathrooms, shared guest bathrooms, and shared bathrooms. Extended stay rates.
• A B&B with mountain and forest views, close to hiking, skiing, swimming, and tennis courts. Bicycles and table tennis. Near public transportation. Close to Grouse Mountain, Cleveland Dam park, the Capilano suspension bridge, and the Capilano River fish hatchery. A few minutes from shopping and restaurants. Formal dining room and family room. Large balcony. Guest rooms have keyed entrances. Some guest rooms have TVs. Honeymoon suite has a queen-sized bed, a dormer window area with twin bed, an ensuite bathroom with skylight, and a walk-in closet. Pickup from plane or ferry for a fee. Full breakfast. Dinner on request. Diets are accommodated. Suitable for families or groups. Smoke-free environment.
In the hosts' own words: "We offer a gourmet breakfast. Come as a guest and leave as a friend."

Norgate Parkhouse B&B

Vicki Tyndall
1226 Silverwood Crescent
North Vancouver, BC V7P 1J3
(604) 986-5069 Fax: (604) 986-8810

• Fifteen minutes' drive from downtown Vancouver.
• Three rooms. One person $65; two people $85. Queen-sized bed; twin beds
(or a king-sized bed); one single bed. Shared guest bathroom. Minimum stay
two nights on holiday weekends.
• A cedar-sided ranch-style house with a patio and garden, fifteen minutes from downtown
Vancouver. Three blocks from public transit. Three to five blocks from restaurants and car
rentals. Within fifteen minutes of sailing, canoe rentals, hiking, nature viewing, horseback
riding, fishing, downhill and cross-country skiing, tennis courts, museums, galleries, Grouse
Mountain, and the Capilano suspension bridge. The guest area is a separate wing of the
house. Two of the guest rooms open into the back garden. The third guest room has a private
deck. Guest sitting room has a fireplace, books, tourist brochures, and a TV. Full breakfast
is served. Diets are accommodated with advance notice. Deposit of entire stay's rate required
to hold reservation; $20 non-refundable. Cancellation notice fourteen days. Cash, traveller's
cheques, credit cards. Not suitable for small children. Three resident cats and, at times, a
family of raccoons. Smoking outside.

The Nelson's B&B

Roy and Charlotte Nelson
470 West St. James Road
North Vancouver, BC V7N 2P5
(604) 985-1178

• From Highway 1, turn north onto Westview.
Turn right onto Windsor and continue for one
block. Turn left onto St. James.
• Rooms. One person $50, twin bed, ensuite
bathroom; two people $80, queen-sized bed and
single day bed, ensuite bathroom; two people
$65, double bed, private bathroom. Child under 6 $5. Child 6 to 12 $10. Child 13 to 15
$15. Open April 1 to November 15.
• A B&B on a quiet tree-lined street, three blocks from buses and ten minutes from restaurants, parks, sports facilities, beaches, and shopping. Ten minutes from Grouse Mountain, Cleveland Dam, the Capilano suspension bridge, a fish hatchery, par three golf, and Lonsdale Quay. Twenty minutes from Stanley Park, Gastown, Imax Theatre, downtown shopping, and ferries to Vancouver Island. Den with TV and VCR. Sun deck, garden, and heated swimming pool. Breakfast includes homemade jams and muffins. Check-in 2:00 to 6:00 p.m.; check-out by 11:00 a.m. No pets; cat in residence. No smoking. **In the hosts' own words:** "Your satisfaction is our pleasure."

Poole's B&B

Doreen and Arthur Poole
421 West St. James Road
North Vancouver, BC V7N 2P6
(604) 987-4594 Fax: (604) 987-4283

• Near Westview and Queens Avenue, a few
blocks north of Highway 1.
• Three rooms. One person $40; two people $55.
Queen-sized bed; double bed; twin beds. Shared
guest bathrooms. Additional person $10. Child 6
to 12 $5. Children under 6 free. Crib and cot
available. Off-season and weekly rates.
• A colonial-style house in a residential district, twenty minutes' drive from downtown Vancouver and two blocks from a bus stop. Within walking distance of restaurants, shopping, a golf course, and an indoor public swimming pool. Ten minutes by car or bus from the Capilano suspension bridge, the Grouse Mountain skyride, and the SeaBus to downtown Vancouver. Twenty minutes' drive from Stanley Park and the ferries to Nanaimo. Breakfast is served at a candlelit dining table with flowers from the hosts' garden. No pets. No smoking. **In the hosts' own words:** "We are retired and are happy to help with directions and information about our beautiful city and surrounding areas. We welcome guests to share our quiet, relaxed B&B."

Pacific View B&B

Sylvia and Gerhard Gruner
139 West St. James Road
North Vancouver, BC V7N 2P1
(604) 985-4942

• From Highway 1, take exit 18 to Lonsdale
Avenue. Go north on Lonsdale and turn left onto
St. James. The B&B is in the first block.
• One person $45; two people $60–80. Queen-
sized bed. Ensuite bathrooms.
• A B&B with city and ocean views in a residen-
tial neighbourhood, twenty minutes' drive from downtown Vancouver, Stanley Park, and the
Horseshoe Bay ferry terminal. A fifteen-minute drive from Grouse Mountain and a ten-
minute drive from the Royal Hudson steam train station, the Capilano River fish hatchery,
the Capilano suspension bridge, and the SeaBus, which takes passengers to downtown
Vancouver and a rapid transit station. Two minutes' walk from a bus stop. Guest rooms are
upstairs. Upstairs guest lounge with a TV and a balcony with panoramic views. Outdoor
heated swimming pool. Parking in the driveway. Full breakfast is served in a glass-enclosed
patio overlooking a garden. German and Polish spoken. Children welcome. No pets; small
bird in residence. Non-smokers welcome. **In the hosts' own words:** "Our home is your
home away from home."

Mavis's B&B

Mavis Walkley
1—269 East Keith Road
North Vancouver, BC V7L 1V4
(604) 986-9748

• From Highway 1, take exit 18 to Lonsdale
Avenue. Go south on Lonsdale and turn left onto
Keith Road. The B&B is between St. Georges
and St. Andrews avenues.
• Two rooms. One person $45–60; two people
$60–85. Twin beds; queen-sized bed. Private and
ensuite bathrooms. Child 2 to 6 $5. Child 7 to 12 $10.
• A B&B within walking distance of restaurants, Lonsdale Quay, and the SeaBus to
Vancouver. On bus route to Capilano Canyon and Grouse Mountain. Within ten minutes'
drive of Stanley Park, the Royal Hudson steam train, and Lynn Canyon. Twenty minutes'
drive from the Horseshoe Bay ferry terminal. Guest rooms have TVs. One of the guest rooms
has a queen-sized bed, an ensuite bathroom with Jacuzzi bathtub, and a private patio. Lounge
and family room. Full or Continental breakfast is served in the dining room. Children welcome. No pets; cats in residence. **In the hosts' own words:** "Enjoy your stay in an attractive, clean, comfortable house with friendly hosts."

Sue's Victorian Guest House

Sue Chalmers
152 East Third Street
North Vancouver, BC V7L 1E6
(604) 985-1523
Toll-free: 1-800-776-1811

• Half a block east of Lonsdale Avenue.
• Three rooms. One person $50–65; two people $60–75. Ensuite and shared guest bathrooms. No showers. Additional person $25. Breakfast not included. Seventh night free in the off season. Long-term rates.
• A 1904 house with original exterior finish, authentically framed double-glazed windows, original staircases, handcrafted décor, antiques, soaker tubs, and full-width front veranda. Each guest room has a TV, a VCR, a heater, a fan, a telephone (for short local calls), and an individually keyed door. Four blocks from the harbour and Lonsdale Quay. Close to a fitness centre, the Royal Hudson steam train, Grouse Mountain, two suspension bridges, and Stanley Park. A twelve-minute SeaBus ride across the harbour from Gastown, a conference centre, the Imax theatre, downtown Vancouver, and connections to rapid transit, buses, and Alaska cruise ship departures. Off-street parking behind the house and behind 158 East Third. Breakfast is not provided; there is a guest fridge, and nearby are restaurants and stores. Non-refundable deposit of first night's rate. Visa used for reservations only. Cancellation notice eight days. Cash, traveller's cheques. Adult oriented. Cats in residence. Non-smoking guests. **In the hosts' own words:** "Years of love and effort have restored this charming heritage house in North Vancouver. Why have so many guests stayed here? Because the price is right."

Helen's B&B

Helen Boire
302 East Fifth Street
North Vancouver, BC V7L 1L1
(604) 985-4869

• Follow Highway 1 over the Second Narrows Bridge to North Vancouver. Take exit 23A, which becomes Third Street. Turn right onto St. Andrews and continue for two blocks. The B&B is on the corner.
• Three rooms. One person from $65; two people from $75. Double bed. Ensuite and shared guest bathrooms.
• A restored 1906 Victorian-style house with antiques. Guest rooms have views of a harbour and the city of Vancouver. Seven blocks from the ocean. Two blocks from several bus routes. Within ten minutes' drive of Grouse Mountain, Stanley Park, the Royal Hudson steam train, Capilano and Lynn Canyon suspension bridges, and salmon fishing. Twenty minutes' drive from the Horseshoe Bay ferry terminal. Ninety minutes' drive from Whistler Mountain. Guest rooms have views, antique double beds, and TVs. Refreshments are served when guests arrive. Wake-up coffee service on request. Full three-course breakfast is served in the dining room. No pets. **In the hosts' own words:** "Your satisfaction is my mandate."

Jane's Gourmet B&B

Jane and Lorne Rae
4187 Fairway Place
North Vancouver, BC V7G 1Y8
(604) 929-6083

• Take Fairway Drive south to Fairway Place.
• Suite. Two people $95–110. Queen-sized bed and double pull-out sofa bed. Bathroom in suite. Additional person $20. Children free. Off-season and extended stay rates. Closed November and December.
• A B&B with a garden-level suite, in the quiet residential area of Deep Cove. The suite has a fireplace, English and Canadian antiques, a TV, a stereo, a living/dining room, a private bathroom, and a massage tub. Within five kilometres of theatre, restaurants, canoeing, golf, skin diving, swimming, hiking, and beach walks. Twenty minutes' drive from Lynn Canyon and hiking trails at Mount Seymour. Twenty-five minutes' drive from downtown Vancouver. One block from two bus stops. One host is a home economist. Coffee and tea supplies and homemade cookies are provided in the suite. Breakfast is different each day. Diets are accommodated. Children's menus are provided. Check-in times are flexible. Wheelchair accessible. No pets. Non-smokers welcome. **In the hosts' own words:** "A perfect honeymoon or anniversary hideaway."

The Kerr House B&B

Otto and Sheila Wetzlmayr
606 East Windsor Road
North Vancouver, BC V7N 1K7
(604) 987-3500 Fax: (604) 987-3500
Toll-free: 1-800-571-KERR (5337)

• From Highway 1, take Lonsdale exit north and turn right onto Twenty-ninth
Street. Turn left onto Regent and continue for three blocks.
• One room. One person $75; two people $85. Shared bathroom.
One suite. One person $100; two people $110. Bathroom in suite.
• A 1910 house restored by its current owners, with stained glass and antique sinks, showers, bathtubs, and furniture. Two blocks from city bus service. Close to churches, shopping, and recreation facilities. Heated swimming pool. One of the hosts gives guided tours of the North Shore mountains. Guest room is upstairs and has a fireplace and a recessed sleeping porch. Guest suite is on ground level and has a kitchen and a five-piece bathroom. Guests join the hosts for breakfast in the dining room or serve themselves in the suite. Cash, traveller's cheques, MasterCard. German spoken. No pets; dog in residence. Non-smoking. **In the hosts' own words:** "Relax and enjoy a step into the past."

Mousehole Waterfront B&B

Joan Elliot and John Surridge
2558 Panorama Drive
North Vancouver, BC V7G 1V5
(604) 929-0347 Fax: (604) 929-0347

• Twenty minutes' drive from downtown Vancouver; forty minutes by public transit.

• Self-contained suite. Two people $125. Double bed. Bathroom in suite.

• A modern house with a terraced garden on the Deep Cove waterfront, twenty minutes' drive from downtown Vancouver and five minutes' walk from restaurants, theatre, kayak and canoe rentals, and hiking. Suite has a TV, facilities for making coffee and tea, and a sitting room with French doors that lead to a waterfront patio and a private dock. Rowboat. Varied breakfast is served in the dining room, which has a view of the ocean and mountains. Not suitable for the disabled or children, as there are several stairs from the road down to the house. No pets; small dog in residence. No smoking indoors. **In the hosts' own words:** "Who could ask for anything more?"

Gloria's B&B

Gloria and Tim Enno
6191 Madrona Crescent
Richmond, BC V7C 2T3
(604) 277-7097

• Near Westminster Highway and Gilbert Road.
• Two suites. Two people $50–60. Queen-sized
bed and sofa bed. Ensuite bathrooms. Additional
person $15. Minimum stay two nights.
• A B&B in the suburb of Richmond, twenty minutes' drive from downtown Vancouver, ten min-
utes' drive from Vancouver International Airport, and thirty minutes' drive from the U.S. border. Each suite accommodates up to four people and has a separate entrance, an ensuite bathroom, a TV, and a fridge. Full breakfast, with homemade bread and fresh-ground coffee, is
served. Children over nine welcome. No pets. No smoking indoors.

The Corner House—Sue's B&B

Sue and Norm Richard
11220 Second Avenue
Richmond, BC V7E 3K5
(604) 275-0913
Cellular: (604) 220-3740

• From Highway 99, exit west onto Steveston
Highway. Cross Number One Road and take the
first left onto Second Avenue. The B&B is on
the southeast corner of Second Avenue and Hunt.
• Two rooms. One person $50; two people $55,
double bed, private bathroom. One person $55; two people $60, queen-sized bed and sofa
bed, ensuite bathroom. Additional person $15. Child 2 to 14 $1 per year of age. Children
under 2 free. Off-season rates.
• A new house in a historical fishing village, ten minutes' drive from Vancouver International
Airport and within twenty minutes' drive of ferries to Vancouver Island and the Gulf Islands.
On bus route to Richmond and downtown Vancouver. Close to restaurants, shopping, and
Garry Point Park. Guests rent bicycles, walk on dike trails, and walk on the quay to shop for
local fresh fish. Guest rooms have TVs and facilities for making coffee and tea. Guest sitting room. Reservations recommended. Children welcome. No pets. No smoking. **In the
hosts' own words:** "We really enjoy meeting such interesting people as our guests. We look
forward to meeting you and sharing with you the magic of Steveston."

Blueberry Farm Guest House

Nermin Jadavji
10731 Blundell Road
Richmond, BC V6Y 1L2
(604) 273-8293 Fax: (604) 278-6745

• On Blundell Road between No. 4 Road and No. 5 Road. Call for directions.
• Two rooms. One person $40–50; two people $55–65. Twin beds, shared guest bathroom; queen-sized bed, ensuite toilet and washbasin, shared guest bathroom. Additional person $10–15. Child 2 to 6 $5; child 7 to 12 $10–15. Two-bedroom suite. Two people $60–80. Queen-sized bed, double bed, and hide-a-bed. Private bathroom. Additional person $10–15. Child 2 to 6 $5; child 7 to 12 $10–15.
• A B&B on a blueberry farm, with a view of the North Shore mountains. Patio and guest living room with TV and VCR. Two-bedroom suite with living room and dining room. Ten minutes' drive from shopping, restaurants, theatres, parks, and recreation. Within thirty minutes' drive of Stanley Park, English Bay, downtown Vancouver, the Vancouver Trade and Convention Centre, the University of British Columbia, the Museum of Anthropology, Grouse Mountain, ferries to Vancouver Island, a heritage fishing village, and art galleries. Guests wake up to the sounds of birds. Breakfast is served in a dining room that has sliding doors to the garden; while eating breakfast, guests watch birds feed and bathe. French spoken. **In the hosts' own words:** "Warm and friendly hospitality in a bright, comfortable, and spacious house, in a tranquil country setting."

Brigadoon B&B

Tom Hamilton
4180 Lancelot Drive
Richmond, BC V7C 4S3
(604) 271-7096 Fax: (604) 271-7099

• From Highway 99, take Steveston Highway westbound exit. Turn right onto Gilbert Road. Turn left onto Francis Road and continue past Railway Avenue to the next road, Lancelot Gate. Turn right onto Lancelot Gate.

• Three rooms. In summer, one person $70, two people $75, queen-sized bed, ensuite bathroom with shower; one person $60, two people $65, double bed or twin beds, shared guest bathroom. In winter, one person $60, two people $65, queen-sized bed, ensuite bathroom with shower; one person $50, two people $55, double bed or twin beds, shared guest bathroom.

• A B&B ten minutes from Vancouver International Airport and close to ferries and the U.S. border. Within a block of direct buses to downtown Vancouver. Five minutes from cycling, an ocean dike to walk on, shops, boardwalk restaurants, and a historical fishing village at Steveston. Guest sitting room has a TV, a VCR, and books. Terrace garden. Reservations recommended. Visa, MasterCard, American Express. Adult oriented. Corgi dog in residence. Smoke-free environment. **In the hosts' own words:** "We invite you to enjoy a full and delicious breakfast."

Ocean View Lodging

Mary Lou Stewart
246 Centennial Parkway
Delta, BC V4L 1K5
(604) 948-1750 Fax: (604) 948-1751

• Four rooms. One person or two people (in winter) $79–119. One person or two people (in summer) $139–229. King-sized bed; queen-sized bed.
Suite. One person or two people $498.
Family rates.

• A Victorian-style B&B with antiques, on the beach at Boundary Bay. Migrating birds, bald eagles, and blue herons can be seen. Guest living room with books and tourist information. Guest rooms have TVs. Suite has bay windows, round rock fireplace, three decks, and two lofts. Hot tub on beach. Continental breakfast is served in the dining room with a view of the ocean and Mount Baker, in front of the fireplace in the living room, on the patio, or in guests' rooms. Check-in after 3:00 p.m. or by arrangement; check-out 12:00 p.m. or by arrangement. Cash, cheques, Visa, MasterCard, American Express. Smoking on porches. **In the hosts' own words:** "Experience our Victorian-style bed and breakfast at Boundary Bay. Boundary Bay and Tsawwassen are part of a sunny belt that has less annual rainfall than Vancouver. Boundary Bay is a part of the Pacific flyway of migrating birds. A birdwatcher's delight."

River Run Floating Cottages

Bill and Janice Harkley
4551 River Road West
Ladner, BC V4K 1R9
(604) 946-7778 Fax: (604) 940-1970

• On the Fraser River in Ladner.

• Three cottages. Two people $150, one night; two people $250, two nights; two people $345, three nights. After three nights, $115 per night. Discount of 15 percent, January to March.

• A floating cottage on the Fraser River and two cottages on the bank of the river, each with a private deck overlooking the river. The floating cottage rises and falls with the tides and gently rocks with the river traffic. It has a fireplace, a CD player, a telephone, and, on request, a TV. One of the cottages has a fireplace, a double Jacuzzi, a kitchen, and a bedroom with a river view. The other cottage has a loft bedroom, a fireplace, a wet bar, and a deck with a double soaking tub. Bicycles, rowboats, and a kayak available to explore the delta and the Reifel Migratory Bird Sanctuary. Ten minutes' drive from ferries to Victoria and the Gulf Islands. Twenty minutes' drive from Vancouver International Airport. Breakfast is delivered to the cottages at a time specified by guests. Breakfast choices include French toast and eggs Benedict with fresh salsa. Deposit of one night's rate required to hold reservation. Cancellation notice ten days; full refund also given if hosts are able to rebook room. Visa, MasterCard. **In the hosts' own words:** "Share with us the experience and the joys of living on a river."

An English Garden B&B

Norma McCurrach
4390 Frances Street
Burnaby, BC V5C 2R3
(604) 298-8815 Fax: (604) 298-5917
Toll-free: 1-800-488-1941

• From Highway 1A or 99A, turn north onto
Willingdon Avenue. Continue to Frances, which
is two blocks south of Hastings Street, and turn
left. The B&B is one block west of Willingdon.
• Two rooms. One person $45–55; two people
$60–75. King-sized bed and one twin bed, private bathroom; queen-sized sofa bed, shared
bathroom. Additional person $20. Child 2 to 6 $10. Off-season and extended stay rates.
• A white stucco bungalow ten minutes' drive from the top of Burnaby Mountain with its
view of Vancouver, Burrard Inlet, and Grouse and Seymour mountains. A fine dining restaurant on the top of Burnaby Mountain has a view and a varied menu. Five minutes from a
pasta restaurant. Fifteen minutes from most Vancouver tourist attractions. Guest rooms have
TVs. One of the guest rooms has a view of the mountains. Full breakfast. A quick phone call
in advance is appreciated. No pets; cat in residence. **In the hosts' own words:** "We pride
ourselves on the full breakfast we serve. We are an average family home."

Welcome B&B

Gerard and Alice Van Kessel
325 Pine Street
New Westminster, BC V3L 2T1
(604) 526-0978

• Off Fourth Avenue, between Fourth Street and
Third Street, near Queen's Park.
• Three rooms. In summer (April 1 to September
30), one person $40, two people $50. In winter,
one person $35, two people $45. Queen-sized
bed; twin beds. Shared guest bathroom and
shared bathroom.
• A renovated 1905 house in a residential area, near parks, shopping, and restaurants. A few
minutes' bus ride and a half-hour rapid transit ride from downtown Vancouver. Guest rooms
are upstairs and have TVs. Guest sitting room. Snacks provided. Full breakfast. Check-in
and check-out times flexible. Adult oriented. Dog in residence. Smoking in restricted areas.
In the hosts' own words: "See all the exciting sights of Greater Vancouver, and enjoy morning and evening quiet amidst heritage houses in New Westminster. We invite you to share
our home and enjoy Dutch hospitality."

Sheridan Hill B&B

Gerry and Wendy Gillan
20289 Menzies Road
Pitt Meadows, BC
Mail: 2139 Audrey Drive
Port Coquitlam, BC V3C 1G9
(604) 460-0009
Cellular: (604) 351-0060

• Room. One person $65; two people $80. Double bed. Private bathroom. Suite. One person $80; two people $100. Queen-sized bed and two pull-out couches. Ensuite bathroom. Optional choice of being served breakfast or of having breakfast ingredients supplied. Additional person $25.

• A Victorian-style B&B on five and a half acres in a mountain forest setting with views of farmland, the Coast Mountains, and Mount Baker. Outdoor hot tub overlooks a pond. Wildlife can been seen. Five minutes' walk from dike trail for cycling, hiking, and fishing. Within ten minutes' drive of canoeing, boating, and backpacking at Pitt Lake; golfing at Swan-E-Set Bay, Pitt Meadows Golf Club, Meadow Gardens, and Golden Eagle golf courses; horseback riding; a wildlife reserve; shopping; restaurants; and theatres. Forty-five minutes' drive from downtown Vancouver. Outdoor swimming pool, covered porches, sun decks, and fire pit. Guest room has a private bathroom with a claw-foot tub. Self-contained suite accommodates up to six guests and has a private entrance, an ensuite bathroom with Jacuzzi, a kitchen, a bedroom with a queen-sized bed, and a living room with two pull-out couches. Guest room and suite have antiques and down duvets. Breakfast is served in the dining room or in the atrium. Guests in the suite have the option of having breakfast ingredients supplied in the suite for them to make their own breakfast. Check-in between 3:00 and 5:00 p.m.; check-out by 11 a.m. Cancellation notice seven days. Visa. Not suitable for young children. No pets; cats and dogs in residence. Smoking on covered porch.

Bob's B&B

Bob and Margaret Timms
21089 Dewdney Trunk Road
Maple Ridge, BC V2X 3G1
(604) 463-5052 Fax: (604) 467-2795

• One hour from Vancouver. Five minutes west of downtown Maple Ridge.
• Room. Two people $65. Queen-sized bed. Ensuite bathroom. Additional person $10. Sofa bed and cot available. Weekly and monthly rates.
• A B&B near Golden Ears Park, riding and hiking trails, golfing, swimming, and boating. Guest room has a dining area, a fridge, a TV, and an ensuite bathroom with soaker tub. Fenced backyard with fruit trees; flower, vegetable, and herb gardens; patios; and wading pool. On bus route. Off-street parking. Breakfast, including fresh fruit and berries in season and homemade jams, jellies, and preserves, provides traditional, low-sugar, and low-fat choices. Wheelchair-accessible entry and bathroom. Cancellation notice three days. Visa. Children welcome. Pets welcome; several pets in residence. Smoking outdoors. **In the hosts' own words:** "This area is famous as the horse capital of the West. Home preserves, crisp, clean sheets, and our warm welcome await you."

Gunilda's Guest House B&B

Patricia Gunilda Drew
26683 Dewdney Trunk Road
Mail: RR 4
Maple Ridge, BC V2X 8X8
(604) 462-7509

• Eleven kilometres east of downtown Maple Ridge.
• Suite. Two people $75. King-sized bed, twin beds, and two day beds.
Half bathroom and ensuite bathroom in suite. Additional person $15.
• A B&B with a view of Blue Mountain, on nine and a half acres of farm and woodlands.
Suite has two storeys, high open ceilings, a cedar interior, and a separate entrance. The upper
floor of the suite has a bedroom with king-sized brass bed, a TV, a writing area, and an
ensuite bathroom with soaker tub and shower. French doors open into a sunroom with sitting areas and two twin beds and two day beds for up to four additional guests. The suite has
a dining area with a small fridge. On the ground floor of the suite are a living room with TV
and wood-burning stove, a laundry room, and a half bathroom. The hosts, who have lived on
the property for thirty-two years, share their knowledge of the area with guests. Five to fifteen minutes' drive from hiking, nature, and riding trails. Near several lakes, including
Whonnock, Alouette, and Rolley. Full, varied breakfast is served in the hosts' dining room
or, if guests prefer, in the dining area of the suite. Cancellation notice three days. Cash, traveller's cheques. Adult oriented. No pets; dog in residence. Non-smokers preferred. **In the
hosts' own words:** "Perfect for a romantic getaway or for relaxing after a day of sightseeing
and outdoor activities."

Fence Post Lane B&B

Fran and Martin Perdue
8575 Gaglardi Street
Mission, BC V4S 1B2
(604) 820-7009

• Eight kilometres west of Mission, in the Silverdale area. From Mission, take the Lougheed Highway. Turn right onto Chester Street, left onto Silverdale Avenue, and right onto Gaglardi Street.

• $45–50, double bed; $55–60, queen-sized bed. Private bathrooms.

• A ranch-style house on one acre in a quiet country setting, ten minutes from Whonnock Lake, hiking at Rolly Lake, golfing, and Westminster Abbey in Mission. Forty-five minutes from Harrison Hotsprings and Vancouver. Fifteen minutes from Abbotsford. **In the hosts' own words:** "Fraser Valley B&B has become Fence Post Lane B&B. Come and enjoy our hospitality in the quiet country—you'll love it."

Fenn Lodge

Diane Brady and Gary Bruce
15500 Morris Valley Road
Mail: Box 28
Harrison Mills, BC V0M 1L0
(604) 796-9798 Fax: (604) 796-9798
Web site:
http://www.tbc.gov.bc.ca/chamber/fenn.html

• Ninety minutes from Vancouver. Thirty minutes from Mission.

• Six rooms. $70–85. Ensuite and shared guest bathrooms.

• An eight-thousand-square-foot house built in 1903 on ninety acres, ninety minutes from Vancouver, with forest trails leading to one-half mile of riverfront and a two-hundred-foot waterfall. Porch and swimming pool with patio. Guest library and living room with fireplace. Twenty minutes from Harrison Hot Springs and skiing at Hemlock Valley. Near hiking, biking, downhill and cross-country skiing, canoeing, kayaking, birdwatching, and fishing for steelhead, trout, and salmon. Reservations recommended. Smoking outdoors. **In the hosts' own words:** "Built to welcome guests in 1903, this beautifully restored house still extends a warm invitation to relax and revitalise. The Chehalis River curls around the property from northwest to south, providing deep fishing pools and pleasant paths for strolling. Share a healthful and delicious breakfast with us, and then set out to explore the surrounding towns and farmlands."

Little House on the Lake

Arla and Wayne Swift
6305 Rockwell Drive
Mail: Box 492
Harrison Hot Springs, BC V0M 1K0
(604) 796-2186 Fax: (604) 796-2186
Toll-free from within Canada and the U.S.: 1-800-939-1116

• Three hours from Seattle. Ninety minutes from Vancouver. From Highway 1, turn north onto Highway 9. Turn right at the four-way stop in Harrison Hot Springs and continue for 3 kilometres to the B&B.

• Three rooms. One person $115–130; two people $140–165. Queen-sized bed; queen-sized bed and twin day bed; two double beds. Ensuite bathrooms. Additional person $25. Off-season, one person $100–130, two people $125–155. Extended stay rates.

Boston Whaler boat charters.

• A new hand-hewn log lodge with a private beach on the shore of Harrison Lake. Each guest room has a sitting area, a balcony, a skylight, a CD player, and fresh flowers. Lake, mountain, and forest views. Hand-carved mahogany four-post, iron, and brass beds with down comforters (alternatives to down available). Two of the guest rooms have fireplaces. Guest living room with billiards, ping-pong table, games table, upright grand piano, TV, VCR, conversation area, and washroom with utility sink for painters. Books, videos, hot tub, dock, and canoe. Bathrobes provided. Roof-top, middle, and lower decks. Work by B.C. artists throughout. Skiing, swimming, windsurfing, sailing, kayaking, hiking, mountain biking, golfing, reading, and writing. Hosts conduct tours of the lake in a Boston Whaler. In the area are art and music festivals and country fairs. Near fine dining restaurants. Afternoon tea and evening snack are provided. Morning coffee and muffins are delivered to rooms. Full breakfast is served in a lakeside library/dining room. Visa, MasterCard. Children over fifteen welcome. No pets; German shepherd, hamsters, and squirrels in residence. A non-smoking establishment. **In the hosts' own words:** "A warm welcome in a beautiful setting awaits you with an invitation to retreat, relax, and renew. Permission to do absolutely nothing is gladly given."

Sunshine Hills B&B

Putzi and Wim Honing
11200 Bond Boulevard
North Delta, BC V4E 1M7
(604) 596-6496 Fax: (604) 596-2560

• From Highway 1, take exit 66 onto Highway
10. Turn right onto 120th Street (Scott Road),
left onto Sixty-fourth, right onto McKenzie, and
left onto Bond Boulevard. The B&B is the second
house on the left.
From Highway 99, take exit 16 onto Highway
91. Turn right onto Sixty-fourth Avenue. Halfway up the hill, turn left onto McKenzie.
Turn left onto Bond Boulevard.
• Two rooms. Two people $55. Double bed; twin beds. Shared guest bathroom. Additional
person $15. Open March to November.
• A B&B in quiet surroundings across from a park with tennis courts. Near buses to downtown Vancouver (thirty minutes), the airport, the U.S. border, and ferries to Vancouver Island
and the Gulf Islands. Guest rooms have sitting areas and TVs. A guest room with twin beds
has an additional twin bed in a sitting area separated from the guest room by a sliding glass
door. Fridge, microwave, kettle, toaster, dishes, and cutlery in common area. Guest entrance.
Full breakfast is served in the dining room, which has a view of the park. Dutch, German,
some French, and some Spanish spoken. Cat in residence. Non-smokers preferred. **In the
hosts' own words:** "We welcome you to our friendly home and wish you a memorable stay
in beautiful British Columbia."

White Heather Guest House

Glad and Chuck Bury
12571 Ninety-eighth Avenue
Surrey, BC V3V 2K6
(604) 581-9797

• Ten minutes from Highway 1. Twenty-five
minutes from the U.S. border.
• Two rooms. One person $45–50; two people
$55–60. Queen-sized bed; double bed. Ensuite
half bathroom and shared guest bathroom.
Children's rates negotiable.
• A house with mountain views, in a quiet suburb close to rapid transit, with easy access to
the highway to downtown Vancouver and the tourist attractions of the Lower Mainland.
Guest rooms, breakfast room, TV, and living rooms are on the main floor. Patio, sun deck,
and guest TV room. The hosts share their knowledge of the area and Vancouver Island.
Pickup from plane, ferry, train, and rapid transit. Full English breakfast with homemade
bread is served in a sunroom that has a panoramic view of the mountains on the north shore.
Children welcome. No pets. No smoking. **In the hosts' own words:** "We are well travelled
and enjoy sharing our home with you."

Country Lane B&B

Brian and Julie
15493 Kildare Drive
Surrey, BC V3S 6L2
(604) 574-5246 Fax: (604) 574-4182
Toll-free: 1-800-228-7833

• From 152nd Street and Highway 10, go north on 152nd Street. Turn right onto Kildare Drive. The B&B is the last house on the left.
• Two rooms. One person $60–80; two to four people $70–130.Two double beds. Ensuite bathrooms.
Bicycle tours and rentals.
• A B&B in a quiet country setting, thirty minutes from the airport and fifteen minutes from the U.S. border. Guest lounge with TV and fireplace. Guest gardens, barbecue, and fire pit. Hot tub and pitch and putt. Guest rooms have TVs and a panoramic view of rolling hills and mountains. Two minutes' walk from a seventeen-acre park with tennis courts and walking and jogging trails. The hosts rent bikes and conduct guided cycle tours of Vancouver, Whistler, and Vancouver Island for all levels of cyclists. Three minutes' drive from the Northview Golf Club. Within fifteen minutes' drive of several golf courses. No pets. No smoking. **In the hosts' own words:** "Our B&B is much more than just a B&B, you'll see."

B&B on the Ridge

Dale and Mary Fennell
5741—146th Street
Surrey, BC V3S 2Z5
(604) 591-6065

• From Highway 1, take exit 66 or exit 53 onto Highway 10. Turn right onto 146th Street. The B&B is the eighth house on the left.
From Vancouver, take Highway 99 and then take exit 16 onto Highway 10. Turn left onto 146th Street.
From the Victoria ferry or the U.S. border, take exit 10 onto Highway 10. Turn left onto 146th Street.
• Four rooms. One person $45–65; two people $55–95. Queen-sized bed; queen-sized bed and day bed; twin beds. Ensuite, private, and shared guest bathrooms. Additional person $15. Two cots, pull-out couch, and crib available.
• A B&B on half an acre in a quiet country setting, with skylights, antiques, and a wraparound sun deck. Ten minutes' drive from White Rock and Crescent beaches, shopping malls, golf courses, rapid transit, and the U.S. border. Twenty-five minutes' drive from ferries, airport, and cruise ship terminal. Pickup from plane and cruise ship terminal. The house accommodates up to twelve guests. Three of the guest rooms are on the upper floor. One of the guest rooms is suitable for honeymoons and has an ensuite bathroom with Jacuzzi. Guest sitting area with TV, reading material, and music. Living room. Cookies and tea are served when guests arrive. Full breakfast is served on china with silver and fresh flowers. Diets are accommodated. Wheelchair accessible.

Crescent Green B&B

Louisa and Keith Surges
3467—141st Street
Surrey, BC V4P 1L7
(604) 538-2935

• Thirty minutes from Vancouver. Ten minutes from the U.S. border.
From Vancouver, take Highway 99 south. Take the Crescent Beach exit. On
Crescent Road, continue southwest past an Esso gas station. Turn left onto
142A Street (Elgin Hall), right onto Green Crescent, and left onto 141st Street.
From the U.S. border, take Highway 99 north for 9 kilometres. Take exit 10 to
Highway 99A south and continue for 10 kilometres. Turn right onto Crescent
Road.

• Three rooms. Two people $90, queen-sized bed, ensuite bathroom; two peo-
ple $75, double bed, shared bathroom. Additional person $20. Crib available.

• A single-level house on a quiet acre with a patio garden, a container garden, an English garden, a cut flower garden, and theme gardens including white, golden, and alpine. Evergreens,
ornamental trees, flowering shrubs, and perennials. Guest rooms have private entrances from
patios. Guest lounge has a stone fireplace, a piano, and a TV. Wood furniture, plants, art, and
antiques. Swimming pool and sauna. Near golf, tennis, nature walks, a bird sanctuary,
beaches, and fine dining restaurants. Coffee provided at any time. Breakfast, with ethnic
choices and, in season, fruit, herbs, and bouquets of flowers from the garden, is served in a
conservatory overlooking the garden. Visa, MasterCard. No smoking. **In the hosts' own
words:** "Tranquillity, beauty, comfort, and hospitality. Enjoy a memorable vacation stop, a
getaway retreat, or a special occasion celebration."

Dorrington B&B

Pat and Helen Gray
1385—19A Avenue
White Rock, BC V4A 9M2
(604) 535-4408 Fax:(604) 535-4409

• From Highway 99A south, turn right at exit 10. Follow Crescent Beach Road. Turn left onto 140th Street. Turn right onto 19A Avenue.

• Two rooms. One person $65–80; two people $75, queen-sized bed, private bathroom; two people $90, double bed, private bathroom. Off-season rates. Minimum stay two nights.

• A B&B on over half an acre of gardens, with an outdoor tennis court and hot tub, within five minutes of White Rock's beach promenade, cafés, specialty shops, art galleries, antiques, and restaurants. Ferries to Victoria and the Gulf Islands are thirty minutes away. Sitting room has twelve-foot ceilings, a river rock fireplace, and a view of the gardens. Guest rooms have Victorian or rustic décor. Towels, robes, slippers, scented soaps, and tennis rackets and balls are provided. The hosts provide menus and recommendations to local restaurants and picnic baskets for outings to Stanley Park. Full breakfast is served indoors or on the patio. Deposit of one night's rate required to hold reservation. Cancellation notice seven days. Check-in 2:00 to 9:00 p.m.; check-out 11:00 a.m. Visa, MasterCard. Adult oriented. No pets; miniature dachshund in residence. No smoking. **In the hosts' own words:** "Luxury and elegance in a peaceful setting."

Country Elegance B&B

16651 Nineteenth Avenue
Surrey, BC V4B 5A8
(604) 538-8289 Fax: (604) 538-8289

• From King George Highway, turn east onto
Sixteenth Avenue. Turn north onto 168th Street.
Turn west onto Twentieth Avenue and continue
to 167th Street.
From 176th Street (Pacific Highway), turn west
onto Twentieth Avenue and continue to 167th
Street.
• One person $50; two people $70. Private bathrooms.
• A West Coast–style house with slate floors, a marble fireplace, a deck, a curving staircase, and guest rooms with balconies. The house is set among large maple trees on one acre in the countryside. Five minutes' drive from the centre of White Rock, the U.S. border crossing, Dartshill private gardens, Redwood Park, and the beach. **In the hosts' own words:** "Guests feel pampered with breakfasts that cater to all tastes, crystal, fresh-cut flowers, co-ordinated colour schemes, and stimulating conversation."

St. Elmo's Inn B&B

Elmo and Margo Berlinghof
678—176th Street (Pacific Highway)
Surrey, BC V4P 1M7
(604) 538-7585 Fax: (604) 538-7585

• One kilometre north of the U.S. border. Forty-
five minutes from Vancouver. Two kilometres
west of White Rock.
• One person $35; two people $55. Child $10.
Honeymoon room $75.
• A B&B in a parklike setting on two and a half
acres. In the area are geese, ducks, and horses. Close to sandy ocean beaches, golf courses, tennis courts, airports, and shopping centres. Guest living/dining room. Picnic grounds. The hosts are originally from Hamburg and Heidelburg and were the hosts at the Edelweiss Inn in White Rock for twenty years. Breakfast is served brunch style. Dinner and garden parties by arrangement. **In the hosts' own words:** "We will make your stay a wonderful experience; we want you to come back as a friend and stay longer."

Hall's B&B

Iris and Bruce Hall
14778 Thrift Avenue
White Rock, BC V4B 2J5
(604) 535-1225 Fax: (604) 535-0088

• Five minutes from the U.S. border and from Interstate Highway 5, which goes to Seattle. Five minutes from Highway 99, which goes to Vancouver and towards the ferries to Vancouver Island and the Gulf Islands.

• Three rooms. One person $40–55; two people $50–65. Queen-sized bed. Ensuite and shared guest bathrooms. Additional person $15.

• A B&B in a quiet residential area, five minutes' walk from a seaside promenade, a pier, and sandy beaches. Two guest rooms on the lower floor have a guest entrance and share a lounge area with ocean view, double hide-a-bed, fireplace, TV, fridge, microwave, bar sink, table and chairs, bath and shower, and patio. One party of guests can occupy both rooms. A guest room on the main floor has a TV and an ensuite bathroom. Five minutes' drive from golf courses. Within ten minutes' walk from tennis courts, a curling rink, an ice arena, Softball City, a swimming pool, shopping malls, movies, theatres, a seniors' centre, and the Evergreen Baptist complex. Guests explore Vancouver, Seattle, and Victoria on day trips. On bus route. Off-street parking. No pets. No smoking. **In the hosts' own words:** "Let our home be your vacation retreat."

Sausalito by the Sea

Robert and Jacqueline Yearsley
1185 Oxford Street
White Rock, BC V4B 3P5
(604) 538-3237 Fax: (604) 538-6862

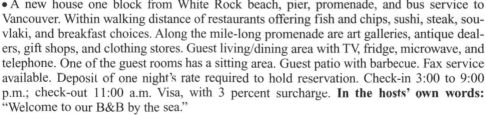

• In White Rock, forty-five minutes from downtown Vancouver and five minutes from the U.S. border.

• Two rooms. One person $44.95–$49.95; two people $49.95–$54.95. Queen-sized bed. Breakfast not included. Juice, coffee, and muffin $3; full breakfast $6. Both rooms $99.95.

• A new house one block from White Rock beach, pier, promenade, and bus service to Vancouver. Within walking distance of restaurants offering fish and chips, sushi, steak, souvlaki, and breakfast choices. Along the mile-long promenade are art galleries, antique dealers, gift shops, and clothing stores. Guest living/dining area with TV, fridge, microwave, and telephone. One of the guest rooms has a sitting area. Guest patio with barbecue. Fax service available. Deposit of one night's rate required to hold reservation. Check-in 3:00 to 9:00 p.m.; check-out 11:00 a.m. Visa, with 3 percent surcharge. **In the hosts' own words:** "Welcome to our B&B by the sea."

Fisher's B&B

Jill and Royce Fisher
5033—209th Street
Langley, BC V3A 5Y4
(604) 534-1104

• Two rooms. $50. Double bed; twin beds.
Shared guest bathroom.
• A B&B beside a golf course and within walking
distance of Langley. Near a swimming pool, a
park, and horseback riding. Sixteen kilometres
from the U.S. border. Easy access to the highway.
Family room, TV, VCR, fireplace, sunroom, sun deck, and enclosed backyard. One host is
from Ontario, the other from New Zealand. Off-street parking with space for RV. Breakfast
includes juice, fruit, cereal, toast, and homemade muffins and jams. Full hot breakfast for a
fee. No pets. No smoking. **In the hosts' own words:** "We have travelled widely. Enjoy the
friendly warmth of our hospitality. Feel free to put your feet up and relax."

The Goose Green B&B

Lynn Moore and Chris Mion
7047—210th Street
Langley, BC V2Y 2R8
(604) 533-3456 Fax: (604) 533-3453

• Five minutes' drive from Highway 1. Take
200th Street exit southbound. Turn left onto
Seventy-second Avenue. Turn right onto 210th
Street and look for the B&B's sign.
• Two rooms. One person $50–65; two people
$60, queen-sized bed, private bathroom; two
people $75, queen-sized bed, ensuite bathroom.
• A ranch-style house on an acreage, with a hot tub, a sauna, and an outdoor pool. Within a
few minutes' drive of golf courses, horseback riding, the original trading post at Fort
Langley, restaurants, shopping malls, and the U.S. border. Guest rooms have queen-sized
brass beds and TVs. One of the guest rooms has an ensuite bathroom, a queen-sized bed
chesterfield, a fireplace, a VCR, and a private patio. The other guest room has a private bathroom with a claw-foot tub. Full breakfast includes eggs from the hosts' free-range chickens.
Wheelchair accessible. Children over six welcome. No pets; cat and dogs in residence. No
smoking indoors. **In the hosts' own words:** "Our B&B's peacefulness and space provide a
perfect retreat from the hectic pace of city life."

Cedaridge Country Estate

Lucille Johnstone
9260—222nd Street
Langley, BC V1M 3T7
(604) 882-8570 Fax: (604) 888-7872

• From Highway 1, take exit 58 onto 200th Street. Go north over the freeway and continue to the end of 200th street. Turn right onto 96th Avenue and continue for 5 kilometres. Turn right onto 222nd Street and continue for 1 kilometre. The B&B's sign is on the left.

• Three rooms. $75, king-sized bed, ensuite bathroom; $60, queen-sized bed, private bathroom; $60, twin beds, private bathroom.
Group rate for the three rooms. Off-season rates. On-site equestrian centre.

• A B&B on fifty acres by the Salmon River, one hour's drive from Vancouver, with an eastern view that extends 120 kilometres, to the mountains in the Hope area, and a southern view that extends 120 kilometres, into the state of Washington. Guest indoor swimming pool, sauna, games room, library, sitting rooms, tennis court, lawns, and patios. Five kilometres of nature trails for walking, jogging, and cycling on the property and immediate area. On-site equestrian centre; riding and training lessons and accommodation for guests' horses available for additional fees. Riding on the property and on eight kilometres of off-site riding trails. Within five minutes' drive of three golf courses. Fifteen minutes from a shopping centre. Near historical Fort Langley, a winery, restaurants, ice rinks, and a bowling alley. Guest rooms are on the top floor. One of the guest rooms has a king-sized bed with duvet, a gas fireplace, a covered balcony, two vanity areas, and a sunken tub. Full breakfast and afternoon coffee or tea are provided. Deposit of one night's rate required to hold reservation. Check-in 1:00 to 6:00 pm.; check-out by 11:00 a.m. Cash, traveller's cheques, Visa. Adults only. No pets. Smoking outdoors. **In the hosts' own words:** "You will enjoy our scenic, spacious, spectacular, and secluded retreat."

Country Style B&B

Ingrid Wetzel
20324—49A Avenue
Langley, BC V3A 6R3
(604) 530-6647 after 6:00 p.m. and on weekends
(604) 530-9796 days

• Near Fraser Highway and 203rd Street.
• Three rooms. One person $40; two people $55.
Queen-sized bed. Ensuite, private, and shared bathrooms. Additional person $20. Child $15. Extended stay rates.
• A B&B within ten minutes' drive of Fort Langley, White Rock beaches, a game farm, a wave pool, golf courses, and restaurants. Easy access to Highway 1. Near direct routes to the ferry to Victoria, the U.S. border, and the Langley airport. Garden-level guest room has an adjacent sitting room with TV, a private entrance and patio, a private bathroom, a wood stove, a coffeemaker, and a queen-sized hide-a-bed for additional members of the same party. Guest rooms have TVs. Living room, patio, and treed yard. Cookies and tea served when guests arrive. Full breakfast is served in a dining area. German spoken. No pets. No smoking. **In the hosts' own words:** "We offer an average family home and serve a delicious breakfast."

Big Sky B&B

Cindy and Rob Kugel
21333 Allard Crescent RR 16
Langley, BC V1M 3H8
(604) 888-8102

• Ten minutes' drive from Fort Langley. Ten minutes' drive from Highway 1. Within an hour's drive of downtown Vancouver.
• Room. One person $50; two people $55.
Queen-sized bed. Private bathroom.
Hot tub heated for a $5 fee.
• A B&B in the country with a heated indoor swimming pool, a sauna, a hot tub, and a sun deck with views of meadows, mountains, and the Fraser River. Near Fort Langley's Hudson's Bay Fort historical site. On bicycle route. Guests walk to the Fraser River through meadows behind the house. Antique stores and gift shops in Fort Langley. One kilometre from fishing, picnicking, and camping at Derby Reach regional park. Five minutes' ride across the Fraser River on the Albion ferry from Fort Langley to hiking at Golden Ears provincial park. Within thirty minutes of three golf courses. Guest living room with fireplace. Jacuzzi. Use of kitchen by arrangement. Hot tub heated for a $5 fee. Reservations recommended. **In the hosts' own words:** "Surround yourself with the peace of our pastoral setting and all the comforts of a luxurious home. The sunsets are spectacular—remember to leave time to enjoy the big sky."

Salmon River Guest House

Casey and Gay Smith
8812 Glover Road
Mail: Box 725
Fort Langley, BC V1M 2S1
(604) 888-7937

• Forty minutes from downtown Vancouver.
• Two rooms. In summer (May 1 to September 30), one person $55, two people $65. In winter, one person $50, two people $60. Queen-sized bed. Shared guest bathroom.

• An older, character house on a large treed lot with gardens and a small barnyard with miniature goats and bantam chickens. A few minutes from the village of Fort Langley and three golf courses. Within walking and driving distance of restaurants, antique and gift shops, a riverfront park, and museums. On bus route. Across the river from Golden Ears Provincial Park. Near fishing at Derby Reach regional park. Near the U.S. border. Living room, dining room, sitting room, patio, and outdoor areas. One of the guest rooms has a sleigh bed and rustic décor. Another guest room has a sitting area and southern exposure. Guest bathroom has a claw-foot tub. Full breakfast is served in the dining room. Traveller's cheques, personal cheques with ID, Visa, MasterCard. No children. No pets; small dogs and a rabbit in residence. Smoking on the patio and in the garden. **In the hosts' own words:** "Wonderful breakfasts in a relaxed, friendly atmosphere. The quaintness of our house and community will make your visit a special one."

Aaron House B&B

Kim and Rob Chikites
34745 Arden Drive
Abbotsford, BC V2S 2X9
(604) 850-5085 Fax: (604) 850-5069

• From Highway 1, take exit 92 to Abbotsford town centre. Call for directions to be faxed or mailed.
• Room. Two people $65. Ensuite bathroom.
Suite. Two people $80. Bathroom in suite.
Queen-sized bed; twin beds (or a king-sized bed).
Additional person $15. Child 3 to 11 $10. Children under 3 free. Roll-away beds, crib, child's bed, and queen-sized sofa bed available. Extended stay rates.
• A B&B on a quiet cul-de-sac surrounded by tall trees, a few minutes from downtown Abbotsford, in the Ten Oaks area. Within walking distance of restaurants, shops, and parks. Guest TVs, VCRs, fax machines, and telephones. Living room with fireplace and French doors leading to a garden patio. Suite has a kitchen. Children welcome. **In the hosts' own words:** "Come stay today."

Everett House B&B

Cindy and David Sahlstrom
1990 Everett Road
Abbotsford, BC V2S 7S3
(604) 859-2944 Fax: (604) 859-9180

• From Highway 1, take exit 92 (Sumas Way) north for two blocks. Turn right onto Marshall and continue for about six blocks. Turn right onto Everett Road. The B&B is the first house on the left.

• Two suites and one room. Two people $65–105. Queen-sized bed; king-sized bed. Ensuite and private bathrooms. Additional person $15.

• A Victorian house on a third of an acre in the central Fraser Valley, with a view of the Sumas Prairie and Mount Baker. Guest room beds have Battenburg lace duvets. Each guest room has a claw-foot bathtub, a double-head shower, a private sun deck, or a sitting area. In the area are golf, horseback riding, hiking, and fishing. Forty minutes from skiing at Mount Baker. Thirty minutes from shopping in Bellingham. Guest hot tub in the garden. Living room has a home theatre and movies. Breakfast is served in guests' rooms, in the dining room, or outside. Cash, traveller's cheques, Visa. Smoking outside. **In the hosts' own words:** "An ideal retreat from the world or a romantic getaway. When you are our guest, we want you to feel special."

Glacier Valley Farm

Sue and Marty Vanderhoef
Mile 16.5 Upper Squamish
Mail: Box 30
Brackendale, BC V0N 1H0
(604) 898-2810 Fax: (604) 898-2776
Messages: (604) 892-7533

• Ninety minutes from Vancouver. Forty-five minutes from Whistler. Twenty minutes from Brackendale. Call for directions.

• Three rooms. One person $60. Two people $75.
Double bed and twin beds; queen-sized bed. Shared guest bathroom. Additional person $15. Cots available.
Raft or sea kayak float trip packages November to March.

• A farm house with an open-beamed living room with fieldstone fireplace, in the Upper Squamish Valley, surrounded by glacier views, hillsides, and waterfalls. Guest rooms have views of Tantalus Glacier. South-facing patio with a view of fields with horses and sheep. Hiking, cycling, fishing, photography, sketching, and birdwatching from the B&B. Horseback riding available. Farm animals on property. Full breakfast includes homemade breads and jams. Additional meals provided with advance notice. Deposit requested. Cash, cheques, Visa. **In the hosts' own words:** "Need to escape hectic city life? Experience our unique bed and breakfast. Our large rambling farm house is in a very private and scenic valley. The perfect place to unwind."

Hummingbird Pension

Abe and Yoko Kushida
Mile 18.5 Upper Squamish
Mail: Box 3653
Garibaldi Highlands, BC V0N 1T0
(604) 898-2809 Fax: (604) 898-2809

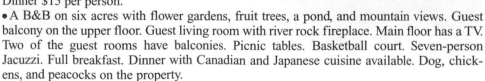

• Ninety minutes from Vancouver. Forty-five minutes from Whistler. Twenty minutes from Brackendale.

• Five rooms. One person $70 85. Double bed; single bed. Ensuite and shared bathrooms.
Dinner $15 per person.

• A B&B on six acres with flower gardens, fruit trees, a pond, and mountain views. Guest balcony on the upper floor. Guest living room with river rock fireplace. Main floor has a TV. Two of the guest rooms have balconies. Picnic tables. Basketball court. Seven-person Jacuzzi. Full breakfast. Dinner with Canadian and Japanese cuisine available. Dog, chickens, and peacocks on the property.

Brew Creek Lodge

Peter and Susan Vera
1 Brew Creek Road
Whistler, BC V0N 1B1
(604) 932-7210 Fax: (604) 932-7223

• Fifteen minutes south of Whistler Village. At the lodge's signpost on Highway 99, turn west onto Brew Creek Road and continue for 1 kilometre.

• Six lodge rooms. One person or two people $85. Ensuite bathrooms. Additional person $25.

Two-storey guest house (sleeps thirteen). One to six people $450. Two private bathrooms. Additional person $75.

Three-storey guest house (sleeps eight). One to six people $450. Two private bathrooms. Additional person $75.

Cabin. One to four people $200. Private bathroom.

Breakfast not included; Continental breakfast provided for a fee.

• A lodge, a two-storey guest house, a three-storey guest house, a meeting house, and a cabin on two landscaped acres in a wilderness setting fifteen minutes' drive south of Whistler. The lodge has a bar and a sitting area with a stone fireplace. The two-storey guest house, which accommodates up to thirteen people, has a kitchen, a dining room, a living room, a Jacuzzi, and a suite with king-sized bed, fireplace, bathroom, and private entrance. The three-storey guest house, which accommodates up to eight people, has a kitchen, a dining room, a living room with stone fireplace, a dry sauna, a Jacuzzi, and a living room that has a stone fireplace and opens onto a sun deck. The log meeting house, built over Brew Creek, has a stone fireplace and views of the surrounding forests and mountains and accommodates meetings of up to thirty people. On the grounds are a guest outdoor hot tub that accommodates up to six people, a volleyball court, and a natural swimming pond. Easy access to hiking and biking trails. Close to tennis, golf, horseback riding, and river rafting.

Brio Haus B&B

Diana and Les Habkirk
3005 Brio Entrance
Whistler, BC V0N 1B3
(604) 932-3313 Fax: (604) 932-4945
Toll-free: 1-800-331-BRIO (2746)
E-mail: briohaus@whistler.net

• One-half kilometre south of Whistler Village, in Brio.
• Two rooms. In winter, one person $80, two people $90. In summer, one person $65, two people $75. Queen-sized bed; twin beds.
Room for families. In winter, $105–145. In summer, $90–130. King-sized bed and bunk beds.
• A Swiss-style alpine house ten minutes' walk from ski lifts, Whistler Village, shopping, dining, and Whistler Golf Course. Guest rooms have down duvets. Each guest room has a view of Blackcomb Mountain or Rainbow Mountain. Guest living room with fireplace, TV, VCR, and stereo. Guest sauna and two-person Jacuzzi. Guests prepare dinner in guest kitchen. Afternoon tea. Two-course breakfast. Smoking on decks.

Haus Landsberg B&B

Heinz and Donna Wango
3413 Panorama Ridge
Whistler, BC V0N 1B3
(604) 932-5233 Fax: (604) 932-5233

• From Vancouver, go north on Highway 99 to Whistler. In Whistler, go 3.5 kilometres past the first traffic lights and turn at the second entrance to the Brio subdivision. Turn right onto Panorama Ridge.
• Two rooms. Two people $65–125. Queen-sized bed and one twin bed; double bed and twin bunk beds. Ensuite bathrooms. Additional person $25. Off-season rates.
• A quiet house with a view of Alta Lake, Blackcomb ski runs, and mountains. Within fifteen minutes' walk of Whistler Village via the Valley Trail, which is lit at night. Guest sauna and living room with fireplace. Guest rooms have TVs and down comforters. Ensuite bathrooms have Jacuzzis. Pickup from bus and train. Hosts provide transportation to ski lifts. Parking. Bicycle and ski storage. Full breakfast includes homemade bread and jam. Check-in between 4:30 and 10:00 p.m.; check-out by 10:00 a.m. Cancellation notice fifteen days. Visa. No smoking. **In the hosts' own words:** "We offer a European and truly Canadian high alpine experience."

Whistler B&B Inns

Whistler, BC
Toll-free: 1-800-665-1892 (for all three inns)
• In summer, one person $60–99; two people $69–119.
In winter, one person $80–129; two people $105–159.
Additional person $25. Child 7 to 12 $10.

Edelweiss Pension

Ursula and Jacques Morel
7162 Nancy Greene Drive
Mail: Box 850
Whistler, BC V0N 1B0
(604) 932-3641 Fax: (604) 938-1746

• Eight rooms. King-sized bed; queen-sized bed;
twin beds. Ensuite bathrooms.
• A B&B within walking distance of Whistler
Village, ski lifts, lakes, and cross-country skiing
and biking trails. Guest rooms have down com-
forters. Some of the guest rooms have balconies and mountain views. Honeymoon suite.
Guest dining/sitting room with fireplace. Whirlpool, sauna, garden, patio, and balcony. Full
breakfast includes the cuisine of a different country each day. Raclette and fondue dinner on
some evenings. Tea, coffee, and Glühwein are provided. Licensed. German and French spoken. Non-smoking environment. **In the hosts' own words:** "A charming B&B with an international atmosphere and traditional European hospitality."

Cedar Springs B&B Lodge

Joern and Jacqueline Rohde
8106 Cedar Springs Road
Whistler, BC V0N 1B8
(604) 938-8007 Fax: (604) 938-8023
Toll-free: 1-800-727-7547

• Eight rooms. King-sized bed; queen-sized bed;
twin beds; one twin bed. Ensuite and shared
guest bathrooms.
Ski, summer, and golf packages.
• A B&B near Meadow Park Recreation Complex
and the Valley Trail. Five minutes' drive from Whistler Village and ski lifts. Near lakes and
mountain bike trails. Hot tub, patio, sauna, and Jacuzzi. Dining room with fireplace. Guest
lounge with fireplace, TV, and VCR. Guest rooms have fireplaces and balconies. Parking
and ski storage. Full breakfast includes homemade baked goods. Dinner is available most
evenings for an additional fee. Traveller's cheques, Interac, Visa, MasterCard. German spoken. No pets. A non-smoking environment. **In the hosts' own words:** "Relax and unwind.
An unforgettable gourmet experience."

Chalet Luise

Luise and Eric Zinsli
7461 Ambassador Crescent
Mail: Box 352
Whistler, BC V0N 1B0
(604) 932-4187 Fax: (604) 938-1531

• Eight rooms. King-sized bed; queen-sized bed; twin beds. Ensuite bathrooms.
Ski and summer packages.
• A B&B in a quiet garden setting within walking distance of Whistler Village and ski lifts. Close to tennis courts, Lost Lake Park, and cross-country skiing, walking, and cycling trails. Whirlpool, sauna, and garden with patio. Guest lounge with fireplace. Guest rooms have down comforters. Some of the guest rooms have balconies. Honeymoon rooms have fireplaces. Full breakfast. Daily maid service. Parking. Bicycle and ski storage. No smoking. **In the hosts' own words:** "Swiss hospitality and charm in the Canadian alps."

Stancliff House B&B

Stan and Shirley Langtry
3333 Panorama Ridge
Mail: Box 995
Whistler, BC V0N 1B0
(604) 932-2393 Fax: (604) 932-7577

• From Vancouver or the Horseshoe Bay ferry terminal, take Highway 99 north. Drive through Whistler Creek to the Brio area. Turn right onto Panorama Ridge.
• Two rooms. In summer, two people $75–95. In winter, two people $85–120. Queen-sized bed; twin beds. Additional person $20.
• A house on the side of Whistler Mountain, with a view of a valley. Close to lakes, a golf course, tennis courts, and the seventeen-kilometre Valley Trail. Within walking distance of Whistler Village. Guest hot tub, TV lounge, microwave, sink, and fridge. Piano, small art collection, wood stove, patio, parking, ski/bike storage, and boat/bike rentals. Pickup from bus and train can be arranged. The hosts help guests plan activities. Tea and coffee supplies provided. Full breakfast. Smoking on decks. **In the hosts' own words:** "Welcome to our home. Enjoy warm hospitality and hearty Canadian breakfasts in our contemporary-style house."

Wedgewood Inn

Carolyn and David Hornsby
6460 St. Andrews Way
Whistler, BC V0N 1B6
(604) 905-0185 Fax: (604) 905-0186
E-mail: wedgwood@whistler.net
Web site: http://www.whistler.net/wedge-wood/

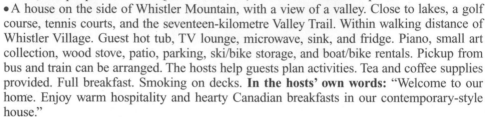

• From Highway 99, take the Lorimer Road exit and turn left onto St. Andrews Way, or take the Eagle Drive (Whistler Cay Heights) exit and turn left onto Wedge Lane and continue to the corner of St. Andrews Way. The B&B is on the corner of Wedge Lane and St. Andrews Way, in Whistler Cay Heights.
• Three rooms. In summer, two people from $85. In winter, two people from $95. Queen-sized bed; twin beds. Private bathrooms. One-person rates $10 less. Group rates. Ski, golf, and dinner packages.
• A timber-framed house constructed with wooden pegs rather than nails. Extensive wood-work throughout. Eight minutes' walk or two minutes' drive from Whistler Village and ski lifts. Mountain views from guest rooms. A few steps from the Valley Trail and Whistler Golf Course. Local bus service. Pickup from bus and train. Guest rooms have down duvets, TVs, VCRs, and small fridges. Guest lounge with thirty-five-foot floor-to-ceiling fireplace. Outdoor Jacuzzi hot tub and garden patio. Ski storage. Fax machine and e-mail address available for guests' use. Full breakfast includes homemade breads, fresh fruit, and juices. Check-in after 4:00 p.m.; check-out by 10:00 a.m. Visa, MasterCard. A non-smoking estab-lishment. **In the hosts' own words:** "Great location and gourmet breakfasts. Only an eight-minute walk from Whistler Village and the ski lifts and steps away from the Valley Trail. Quiet, secure, and peaceful surroundings with mountain views all around."

Renoir's Winter Garden

Paul and Helga Ruiterman
3137 Tyrol Crescent
Whistler, BC VON 1B3
(604) 938-0546 Fax: (604) 938-0547
E-mail: paulr@whistler.net

• From Vancouver, take Highway 99 north.
Continue past the Whistler Creek traffic lights
for 3 kilometres. Turn left at Blueberry Hill sign,
turn left after 30 metres, and turn left again after
250 metres.

• Three rooms. In winter, two people $95–135. In summer, two people, $75–105. Queen-sized bed; twin beds. Ensuite and shared guest bathrooms. Additional person $25.
One-person, extended stay, and off-season rates.

• A new, three-level house on treed grounds with hillside and lake views. Three minutes' drive or ten minutes' walk from Whistler Village and Whistler and Blackcomb ski lifts. Three kilometres from the Whistler Mountain ski lift at Whistler Creek. Guest rooms have TVs and VCRs. Guest entrance and terrace. One of the guest rooms has a balcony and an ensuite bathroom with a steambath. Guest Jacuzzi hot tub. Laundry facilities and parking. Hosts provide transportation to ski slopes. Pickup from bus and train. Full breakfast is served in a treetop-level dining room with a mountain view. Dutch and German spoken. Children over five welcome. No smoking. **In the hosts' own words:** "You will be impressed and happy to see that we deliver what we promise. We want to make sure that you will come again."

Lorimer Ridge Pension

Eva and Stan Plachy
6231 Piccolo Drive
Whistler, BC VON 1B6
(604) 938-9722 Fax: (604) 938-9155

• Eight rooms. In winter, one person $88–148,
two people $98–158. In summer, one person
$80–110, two people $90–120. Queen-sized bed;
extra-long twin beds. Ensuite bathrooms.
Five-day and seven-day skiing packages.
Summer packages.

• A West Coast–style mountain lodge within walking distance of Whistler Village and ski hills, with views of Blackcomb, Fissile, and Rainbow mountains. Near golf and hiking. Guest room beds have duvets. Two of the guest rooms have gas fireplaces. Guest living room with TV and VCR. Guest living room and billiards room have river rock fireplaces. Heated floors throughout. Guest outdoor whirlpool, deck, and sauna. Ski lockers and storage for sports equipment. Daily housekeeping. Parking. Full breakfast. Deposit of one night's rate required to hold reservation; full payment required thirty days before arrival date. Cancellation notice thirty days. Check-in 3:00 to 10:00 p.m.; check-out 10:00 a.m. Visa, MasterCard. No pets. No smoking. **In the hosts' own words:** "Our mountain lodge, set in spectacular surroundings, with Canadian hospitality, will make the perfect setting for your holiday."

Idylwood Inn

Lily Antunes
8725 Idylwood Place
Mail: Box 797
Whistler, BC V0N 1B0
(604) 932-4582 Fax: (604) 932-4556
E-mail: gbsa@whistler.net
Web site: http://www.whistler.net/accomadate/idylwood

• From Whistler Village, go 4 kilometres north on Highway 99. Turn left onto Alpine Meadows and go up Alpine Way. Take the fourth left turn onto Idylwood Place. The inn is the second house on the right.

• Three rooms and a loft in an inn separate from the hosts' house. In summer, two people $80–105. In winter, two people $100–125. King-sized bed, queen-sized bed, and twin beds. Ensuite and shared guest bathrooms.

The entire inn. In summer, $225–325. In winter, $300–400. Breakfast not included in rental of entire inn; breakfast available for additional fee.

• A B&B on a quiet cul-de-sac a few minutes from Whistler Village, with a view of Blackcomb and Whistler mountains. Within walking distance of a swimming pool, an ice rink, squash and tennis courts, a playground, the Valley Trail, and the Nicklaus North golf course. The inn is separate from the hosts' house. One of the guest rooms has an ensuite bathroom with a Jacuzzi. Guest outdoor hot tub, barbecue, fireplace, stereo, selection of music, TV, and VCR. Rental of the entire inn does not include breakfast; breakfast is available for an additional fee. Guest room rates include breakfast. Breakfast is served in the dining room. Suitable for families. Smoking outdoors. **In the hosts' own words:** "Soak up the spectacular view from our outdoor hot tub and stay in the lap of luxury by joining us at the inn."

Chalet Beau Séjour

Sue Stangel and Hal Mehlenbacher
7414 Ambassador Crescent
Mail: Box 427
Whistler, BC V0N 1B0
(604) 938-4966 Fax: (604) 938-4966

• From Whistler Village, go 1 kilometre north on Highway 99. At Nancy Green Drive, turn right into White Gold Estates. Turn right onto Ambassador Crescent.

• Three rooms. In winter, one person $75–85, two people $90–99. In summer, one person $60–70, two people $70–80. Queen-sized bed; twin beds. Ensuite bathrooms. Additional person $20. Off-season rates.

• A new alpine house with mountain views from the front deck, fifteen minutes' walk from ski lifts, cross-country ski trails, Whistler Village, golf courses, and Lost Lake Park. Hot tub. Living room with fireplace, TV, and VCR. Pickup from bus and train. Parking and ski storage. Full breakfast includes fresh fruit and homemade baked goods. Deposit of one night's rate required to hold reservation. Cancellation notice twenty-one days. German, French, and Spanish spoken. Children welcome by arrangement. No pets. No smoking. **In the hosts' own words:** "We invite you to enjoy a relaxed atmosphere and our warm Canadian hospitality during your stay at Whistler."

Alta Vista Chalet B&B Inn

Tim and Yvonne Manville
3229 Archibald Way
Whistler, BC V0N 1B3
(604) 932-4900 Fax: (604) 932-4933

• Two kilometres north of Whistler South (Creekside). Turn left onto Hillcrest Drive, immediately right onto Alpine Crescent, and left onto Archibald Way.

• Eight rooms. In summer, one person from $69, two people from $79. In winter, one person from $109, two people from $119. Queen-sized bed; twin beds. Ensuite bathrooms. Additional person $20–25. Child 3 to 10 $10.

• A B&B on the Valley Trail in a forest overlooking Alta Lake, two kilometres from the ski centres of Whistler Village and Whistler South. Fifteen minutes' walk via the Valley Trail from Whistler Village. Close to Lakeside Beach, which has swimming, picnic tables, barbecues, and canoe, kayak, and windsurfer rentals. Two of the guest rooms are larger than the other six and have TVs and sofa beds; one of these rooms has a fireplace. Antiques and collectibles. Guest lounge that leads onto a sun deck with Jacuzzi. Adjoining games room with TV, VCR, and guest fridge. Sauna. Off-street parking and ski storage. Pickup from bus and train. Afternoon tea is served. Breakfast is served in the dining room. No smoking.

Golden Dreams B&B

Ann and Terry Spence
6412 Easy Street
Whistler, BC V0N 1B6
(604) 932-ANNS (2667) Fax: (604) 932-7055
Toll-free: 1-800-668-7055

• From Vancouver, follow Highway 99 for 111 kilometres to Whistler. At Whistler's third traffic light, turn left onto Lorimer. Go down the hill past the school and turn right onto Balsam Way. Take the first left onto Easy Street. The B&B is the third house on the left; enter through the separate arched guest entrance.

• Rooms. In winter, one person $75–95, two people $85–105. In summer, one person $55–75, two people $65–85. Queen-sized bed; two double beds. Private bathroom or shared guest bathroom. Additional person $25. Child over 5 $10.

• A B&B with mountain views, one mile from ski lifts, restaurants, and village shops. Bike rentals at the B&B. Valley trail system leads from the B&B to several golf courses, Rainbow Beach, and Meadow Park Sports Centre. Guest rooms are decorated with Victorian, Asian, and Aztec themes and have down comforters and sherry decanters. Guest living room with fireplace and mountain view. Guest kitchen. Jacuzzi. Full breakfast includes whole grains, homemade preserves, local farm-fresh eggs, and cappuccino. Vegetarian diets are accommodated. Visa, MasterCard. Children welcome. No smoking indoors. **In the hosts' own words:** "Be surrounded by nature's beauty and pampered with a wholesome breakfast at our B&B. Experience Whistler's real value and get the inside edge on Whistler."

Haus Stephanie B&B

Willi and Doris Weh
7473 Ambassador Crescent
Mail: Box 1460
Whistler, BC V0N 1B0
(604) 932-5547 Fax: (604) 932-5547

• From Vancouver, drive past the centre of Whistler Village. Turn right onto Nancy Greene Drive and right again onto Ambassador Crescent.

• Three rooms. In summer, two people $70–80. In winter, two people $99–105. Queen-sized bed; twin beds. Ensuite bathrooms. Additional person $20.

• A B&B within ten minutes' walk of Whistler Village, Blackcomb Mountain, and cross-country ski trails. Guest entrance, guest lounge, down comforters, and outdoor Jacuzzi. Full breakfast is served in the guest lounge. Deposit of one night's rate required to hold reservation. A non-smoking establishment. **In the hosts' own words:** "Enjoy our European hospitality. Make our home your home away from home."

Rainbow Creek B&B

Heidi Lieberherr
8243 Alpine Way
Mail: Box 1142
Whistler, BC V0N 1B0
(604) 932-7001

• From Highway 99, four kilometres north of Whistler Village, turn left at
Alpine Meadows onto Alpine Way and continue for three blocks. The B&B is
on the right.

• Three rooms. In summer, two people $60–75. In winter, two people $85–95.
Ensuite and private bathrooms. Additional person $20.

• A log house surrounded by evergreens, five minutes' drive from Whistler and Blackcomb
ski lifts. A few minutes' walk from an ice rink, a swimming pool, a playground, tennis courts,
picnic areas, and riding and walking trails at Meadow Park. Living room with fireplace and
TV. Guest rooms have mountain views; one has a balcony. Full breakfast is served in the dining room. Afternoon tea. Visa, MasterCard. German spoken. No smoking. **In the hosts' own
words:** "Nothing is more spectacular than a Whistler winter—except perhaps a Whistler
summer. Enjoy Swiss hospitality at this great year-round escape."

The Log House B&B Inn

Margaret and Bill Scott
1357 Elmwood Drive
Mail: Box 699
Pemberton, BC V0N 2L0
(604) 894-6000 Fax: (604) 894-6000
Toll-free: 1-800-894-6002

• Thirty-two kilometres past Whistler, in the village of Pemberton. Cross the railroad tracks and turn left at the Bank of Nova Scotia. Go one block and turn right onto Aster. Go one block towards mall; before entering mall, turn right onto Dogwood. Go up slight hill to Fernwood; Elmwood is 100 metres farther. The B&B is on the corner.

• Seven rooms. One person $70; two people $80–90. Ensuite and private bathrooms. Additional person $25.

• A five-thousand-square-foot log house with a deck with mountain view, hot tub, lounge chairs, and barbecue. Lofts and living areas have exercise equipment, a TV, a VCR, books, and a fireplace. A guest lounge with woodstove overlooks Mount Currie. In the area are golfing, sailplane gliding flights, skiing, fishing, rafting, snowmobiling, biking, and trail riding. Robes are provided. Full breakfast is served in the dining room. Reservations recommended. Cancellation notice seven days for holidays; twenty-four hours at other times. Visa, MasterCard. Children welcome by arrangement. No pets. No smoking. **In the hosts' own words:** "Our goal is to make your stay as comfortable and relaxing as we can, so you will keep coming back to our house and tell all your friends."

Chris's Corner B&B

Chris and Fred Einarson
7406 Larch Street
Mail: Box 636
Pemberton, BC V0N 2L0
(604) 894-6787 Fax: (604) 894-2026

• Two and a half hours from Vancouver. Twenty-five minutes north of Whistler. From Vancouver, follow Highway 99 north to Pemberton. At the Petro Canada gas station, turn right. Turn at the next left onto Harrow Road and then take the third left onto Hemlock Street. The B&B is the second house on the left.
• Three rooms. One person $45–50; two people $65–75. Twin beds (or a king-sized bed). Ensuite and shared guest bathrooms. Additional person $20. Reflexology session $25.
• A new air-conditioned house with a fireplace and mountain views, in a rural area a few minutes' walk from the village of Pemberton and restaurants. Hiking, biking, and cross-country skiing from the B&B. Ten minutes' walk from swimming, fishing, and boating on a small lake. Twenty minutes' drive from larger lakes. Five minutes' drive from golf, horseback riding, jet boating, and gliding (at an airport). Twenty-five minutes from Whistler. An hour and a half from hot springs. Guest sitting room with TV, VCR, and piano. Reflexology sessions are available from one of the hosts, who is a certified practitioner. No pets. No smoking. **In the hosts' own words:** "Let us pamper you with our friendly B&B hospitality to make this an experience to remember."

The Farmhouse B&B

Carol and Peter Shore
6711 Meadows Road
Mail: Box 121
Pemberton, BC V0N 2L0
(604) 894-6205 Fax: (604) 894-6205

• In the Pemberton Valley. Off Highway 99, 20 minutes north of Whistler; $1^{1}/_{2}$ hours south of Lillooet. Turn right at the Scotiabank in Pemberton onto Pemberton Meadows Road. Continue for 3 kilometres. The B&B is on the left.
• One person $65; two people $75; three people $95. Private and shared bathrooms. Extended stay and seniors' rates.
• A sixty-five-year-old farmhouse on ten acres with horses and cattle, with mountain, meadow, and garden views. Art collection and books. Close to Whistler's attractions, skiing, and dining. Pickup from plane, train, and bus. Full breakfast is served in a country-style kitchen. No pets; cats in residence. Smoking on veranda. **In the hosts' own words:** "We offer you a unique and charming retreat in a character house removed from all urban influence. The narrow, green Pemberton Valley, Canada's seed potato home, is surrounded by steep Coast Mountains and, although it is close to Whistler, has different enough topography and climate from Whistler to warrant a visit. The Pemberton Valley offers many outdoor activities year-round, and its reputation for tranquil solitude is as yet little known. Its nearness to Whistler allows guests to enjoy the resort's events, skiing, and dining while staying with us in Pemberton. "

Patchwork Place Guest House

Trish White and Gerry Onischak
9 Marmot Crescent
Mail: Box 49
Bralorne, BC V0K 1P0
(250) 238-2592
(area code 604 before October 1996)

• Ninety-five kilometres from Pemberton, including 60 kilometres on gravel logging road.
One hundred fifteen kilometres from Lillooet, including 50 kilometres on gravel highway.
• Two rooms. One person $25. Queen-sized bed; twin beds. Shared bathroom and half bathroom. Children's rates.
• A B&B in a remote mountain valley, at 1,077-metre elevation, surrounded by 2,154-metre to 2,769-metre mountain peaks. The house was built in the early 1930s, when the Bralorne gold mine was being developed. In the area are fishing, hunting, hiking, gold panning, wildlife viewing, and hundreds of kilometres of old trails and roads. The hosts help plan activities. Living room, wood stove, balcony, stereo, and games. Beds have handmade patchwork quilts. Coffee, tea, and juice available at any time. Evening tea. Full breakfast including free-range eggs and homemade baked goods is served at guests' convenience. Diets are accommodated by arrangement. Reservations recommended. Cash, travellers cheques. Cat in residence. Smoking outdoors. **In the hosts' own words:** "Today, Bralorne's population hovers around one hundred, and the attraction is outdoor activities. This is a very informal establishment. We treat our guests as we do our friends."

Bonniebrook Lodge B&B

Karen and Philippe Lacoste
1532 Ocean Beach Esplanade
Mail: RR 4 Site 10 C–34
Gibsons, BC V0N 1V0
(604) 886-2887

• Take the ferry from Horseshoe Bay to Langdale. From the Langdale ferry terminal, follow Highway 101. Turn left onto Pratt Road, follow it to the bottom, and turn right onto Gower Point Road. The B&B is at the foot of Gower Point Road.

• Four rooms. Two people $75–95. Ensuite and three shared guest bathrooms. Additional person $10.

• A 1920s oceanside lodge with a restaurant. Guest rooms are on the upper floor. Guest sun deck. Sunsets over Georgia Strait can be seen from a patio. The lodge's restaurant has a stone fireplace and candlelit tables with flowers and linen. French cuisine with West Coast influence. Wine list. Breakfast includes homemade baked goods and is served in the dining room between 8:30 and 10:00 a.m. No pets; cat in residence. No smoking in the guest rooms.

The Maritimer B&B

Noreen and Gerry Tretick
521 South Fletcher Road
Mail: Box 256
Gibsons, BC V0N 1V0
(604) 886-0664

• From the Langdale ferry terminal, take the lower road along the water 5 kilometres to Lower Gibsons. Turn right at Molly's Reach and continue up School Road hill. Take the first left onto South Fletcher. The B&B is the fourth house on the right.

• Two suites. One person $65–70; two people $75–80, one bed; two people $80–85, two beds. Additional person $15.

• A fifty-year-old renovated house in Lower Gibsons with trees, flowers, and a view of harbour, mountains, and islands. One block from Molly's Reach, restaurants, shops, museums, wharf, tennis courts, and kayak rentals. Two-bedroom suite has a queen-sized sleigh bed, a single bed, and a harbour view. Another suite has twin beds or a king-sized bed, a double bed, and a private sun deck with mountain and water view. Both suites have sitting areas, private entrances, and books. Full breakfast is served in the dining room or on a canopied sun deck that overlooks the harbour. Deposit of one night's rate required to hold reservation. Cash, Visa, MasterCard. No pets. No smoking. **In the hosts' own words:** "Let my East Coast hospitality spoil you on the West Coast."

Casita B&B

Diana Unwin
744 Hillcrest Avenue
Mail: RR 1 Site 6 C–82
Gibsons, BC V0N 1V0
(604) 886-0686

• From the Langdale ferry terminal, take Highway 101. Turn right onto North Road and then right onto Hillcrest Avenue.

• Two rooms. One person $35; two people $45. Shared guest bathroom.
Cottage. Two people, variable rates. Breakfast optional.

• An English-style B&B with a cottage, in Gibsons, five minutes from the Langdale ferry terminal. Within walking distance of waterfront and shops. Picnic lunches on request. Full breakfast includes homemade preserves. Pets welcome. **In the hosts' own words:** "Welcome to our B&B in the heart of Gibsons. Our B&B is English style. Our cottage is hostel-like and suitable for cyclists, kayakers, and hikers. Excellent breakfasts await you."

Ocean-View Cottage B&B

Dianne and Bert Verzyl
1927 Grandview Road
Mail: RR 2 Site 46 C–10
Gibsons, BC V0N 1V0
(604) 886-7943 Fax: (604) 886-7943

• Three kilometres west of Sunnycrest Mall in Upper Gibsons. From the Langdale ferry terminal, take Highway 101. Turn left onto Lower Road, left onto Pine Road, and right onto Grandview Road.
• Two rooms. One person $50–55; two people $65. Queen-sized bed; twin beds. Ensuite bathrooms.
Self-contained cottage. Two people $95. Double bed, sofa bed, three-quarter-sized futon bed, and cot. Private bathroom. Additional person $25. Child under 12 $10.
• A B&B on three acres, overlooking Georgia Strait and Vancouver Island. Guest rooms have sliding glass doors that open to a guest sun deck. A self-contained cottage has a bedroom with double bed, a kitchen, a sofa bed, a three-quarter-sized futon bed, a cot, a TV, skylights, and a sun deck with tables and chairs. Near shopping and restaurants. Coffee and tea are served any time. Full breakfast is served in the dining room or in a sunroom. Cash, traveller's cheques, Visa, MasterCard. French and Dutch spoken. No pets. No smoking. **In the hosts' own words:** "Relax and enjoy the spectacular ocean and mountain views of the Sunshine Coast. Beautiful sunsets."

Sunshine Coast Country Hide-Away

Günter and Marcelina Beyser
1148 Reed Road
Mail: RR 4 Site 1B C–17
Gibsons, BC V0N 1V0
(604) 886-7261 Fax: (604) 886-7261

• Two kilometres from the upper town centre of Gibsons.
• Two suites. One person $45; two people $50. Twin beds; queen-sized bed and futon. Ensuite bathrooms. Additional person $15.
• A B&B on a quiet parklike acreage surrounded by fir trees and cedar trees. One of the suites has twin beds and a fridge. Another suite accommodates two to four people and has a queen-sized bed, a fold-out futon in an adjoining room, a TV, and a VCR. Both suites have private entrances. Guests walk in the garden and the wooded parts of the acreage. Tea and full breakfast are served in the dining room or on a terrace. German spoken. **In the hosts' own words:** "Enjoy an easy getaway from the city, relaxing in a country setting on the beautiful Sunshine Coast, or plan to make your stay part of the Vancouver Island circle tour."

Cattanach's B&B

Ian and Barbara Cattanach
1756 Hanbury Road
Roberts Creek, BC
Mail: RR 5 Site 18 C–7
Gibsons, BC V0N 1V0
(604) 885-5444

• Halfway between Gibsons and Sechelt. From the Langdale ferry terminal, take Highway 101. One kilometre past golf course, turn right onto Lockyer. Turn left onto Hanbury and continue for 1 kilometre.

• Two rooms. One person $40; two people $50. Queen-sized bed; twin beds. Shared guest bathroom. Child 7 to 12 $7.50. Child 2 to 6 $5. Crib available. Horse stalls and pasture available.
Open March to October.

• A log house on five acres in a rural area, halfway between Gibsons and Sechelt. Within one and a half kilometres of the Sunshine Coast Golf and Country Club, the Roberts Creek picnic site and beach, and Cliff Gilker Park's hiking trails. Accommodation available for horses in a barn on the property. Near riding trails. Guest sitting room with a TV and two couches is sometimes used as a third guest room. An upstairs alcove has a crib. Breakfast includes honey from the hosts' bees and homemade muffins and jams. Children welcome. No smoking. **In the hosts' own words:** "A charming log house in quiet surroundings."

Country Cottage B&B

Philip and Loragene Gaulin
1183 Roberts Creek Road
Mail: General Delivery
Roberts Creek, BC V0N 2W0
(604) 885-7448

• From the Horseshoe Bay ferry terminal (half an hour from Vancouver), take the Sunshine Coast ferry (40 minutes). Go 25 minutes along the Sunshine Coast Highway (101). Past the golf course, turn left onto Roberts Creek Road.

• Self-contained cottage. One person $85; two people $95. Extra-long double bed. Private bathroom.
Self-contained lodge. One person $99; two people $115. Three queen-sized beds. Private bathrooms. Additional person $50.

• A farmhouse, a cottage, and a lodge, five minutes' walk from Roberts Creek, a beach, swimming, golfing, parks, and fine dining at a French restaurant. The hosts help plan and book day trips for hiking, kayaking, scuba diving, fly fishing, and cross-country skiing. The self-contained cottage has a wrought iron extra-long double bed, a kitchen, antiques, and a wood stove. The lodge, which overlooks an acre of cedars and a grassy pasture, is decorated in Adirondack style, with a river rock fireplace, fly-fishing memorabilia, Navaho rugs, and Arts and Crafts antique furniture. The lodge has a kitchen, a wood-fired sauna, and a campfire circle. Two queen-sized beds are in the lodge's loft, and one queen-sized bed and a private bathroom are in a separate cottage connected to the lodge by a walkway. The lodge accommodates up to six people and is rented to one couple or group at a time. English country gardens, croquet equipment, and bicycles. Guests feed the hosts' chickens and sheep. One host is a spinner and weaver. The other host is a wood worker and antique car and motorcycle enthusiast. Tea and scones are served at 4:00 p.m. on the lawn or in the living room in front of a fire. Full breakfast is cooked on a 1927 Etonia wood-burning cookstove in an antique-furnished kitchen and served in the hosts' farmhouse. Adults only. No pets. Non-smokers. **In the hosts' own words:** "Quality service, hospitality, and attention to detail. A visit to our B&B is like staying with friends in their country home."

The Cottage on Driftwood Beach

Evan and Eleanor Abercrombie
3807 Beach Avenue
Mail: General Delivery
Roberts Creek, BC V0N 2W0
(604) 885-3489 Fax: (604) 885-3724

• Eighteen kilometres from the Langdale ferry
terminal, off Highway 101. Call for directions.
• Two-bedroom cottage. One person $75; two
people $90. Queen-sized beds. Private bathroom.
Additional person $30.
• A waterfront cottage surrounded by cedar trees, on a walk-on beach, twenty metres from
high tide. Low tide exposes a sandy beach. Seven acres of forest. Four kilometres from
Sunshine Coast Golf Club and Cliff Gilker Park. The cottage's sitting room has a fireplace,
a TV, and windows that provide a 180-degree ocean view. An eagle perched in an old growth
tree can be seen from the window. The cottage has a patio with a barbecue. Continental
breakfast includes fresh fruit frappé and homemade baked goods. No pets. No smoking. **In
the hosts' own words:** "This is a tranquil romantic retreat. Experience the magical atmosphere of a rustic cottage snuggled between the beach and the forest. The sunsets are incred-
ible."

A Room with a View

Bonnie Paetkau
5293 Selma Park Road
Mail: RR 1 Cedarview Site C–4
Sechelt, BC V0N 3A0
(604) 885-5636

• One and a half kilometres south of the town of
Sechelt. Twenty-five minutes from the Langdale
ferry terminal.
• Two rooms. One person $50; two people $60.
Queen-sized bed; twin beds and day bed. Shared
guest bathrooms. Additional person $15.
• A B&B on five wooded acres with gardens, walking paths, and a view of Georgia Strait.
Close to Sechelt's restaurants and shopping. Guest patio and guest sitting room with TV.
Living room, with fireplace, for quiet reading. Guest rooms, patio, and sitting, dining, and
living rooms have views. Birds in a backyard aviary. Hiking on trails in the neighbourhood.
Continental breakfast, including fresh-ground coffee, Swiss-style muesli, homemade
muffins, fresh fruit, eggs from the hosts' chickens, and, in season, the hosts' grapes and kiwi
fruit, is served in the dining room. Cash, cheques. Calico cat and golden lab in residence. **In
the hosts' own words:** "Enjoy our quiet oasis."

Pacific Shores B&B

Dorothy Dolphin
5853 Sunshine Coast Highway (Highway 101)
Mail: Box 614
Sechelt, BC V0N 3A0
(604) 885-8938

• From Langdale, take Highway 101 through Sechelt. One hundred metres
past the end of town and the T junction, turn into the second driveway on the
left.
From Earls Cove, take Highway 101 to Sechelt. Just before town and the T
junction and immediately in front of a highway sign for Highway 101
South, turn right into driveway.
• Two rooms. $90–120. Queen-sized bed. Ensuite bathroom. Extended stay rates.
• A B&B on the waterfront, five minutes' walk from Sechelt. Garden-level guest room has
a private entrance, a fireplace, and picture windows with views of the garden and the sea.
Birds, sea life, and wildlife including herons, eagles, seals, and deer are often seen. A peb-
ble swimming beach is across the lawn. Five minutes' drive from an eighteen-hole golf
course. Full breakfast is served in guest rooms or on a patio that overlooks Trail Bay and
Georgia Strait. Deposit of one night's rate required to hold reservation. Visa, MasterCard.
Adult oriented. No pets. No smoking. **In the hosts' own words:** "Independent serenity and
a romantic aspect with direct beach access."

Four Winds B&B

David Fedor and Brenda Wilkinson
5482 Hill Road
Mail: RR 1 Blacks Site C–33
Sechelt, BC V0N 3A0
(604) 885-3144 Fax: (604) 885-3182

• From Langdale, take the Sunshine Coast Highway (101) to Sechelt. On the highway after Sechelt, watch for the Wakefield Inn (3 kilometres); Hill Road is 2 kilometres farther. Turn left on Hill (no through road), keep left, and continue to the end of the cul-de-sac.

From Earls Cove, on Highway 101, watch for Hill Road on the right, 1 kilometre past the second entrance to Redrooffs Road, 5 kilometres before Sechelt.

• One person $80–90; two people $95–105. Queen-sized bed; twin beds. En-suite and private bathrooms.

• A B&B on a rocky point jutting out into the ocean. The water surrounds the living room on three sides and is ten feet away from the window seats of the guest rooms. Winter storms. Heavy quilts and wool mattress covers. While eating breakfast, guests often see seals and a resident heron. One of the hosts is a registered massage therapist and takes advance bookings. Pickup can be arranged for guests coming by bus from Vancouver and Powell River. Hot tub on a deck. Breakfast is served on the deck or in the dining room. Visa, MasterCard. No children. No pets. No smoking. **In the hosts' own words:** "Celebrate a special occasion or plan a healthy weekend retreat."

Diane Mazzei/93

Summer Hill House B&B

Christa Rost
6282 Norwest Bay Road
Mail: RR 1 Drapers Site C–32
Sechelt, BC V0N 3A0
(604) 885-6263 Fax: (604) 885-0196

• From the Langdale ferry terminal, follow Highway 101 to Sechelt. Two kilometres past Sechelt, turn right onto Norwest Bay Road and continue for another kilometre.

• Three rooms. Two people $60, queen-sized bed, ensuite bathroom; two people $45, double bed or twin beds, shared guest bathroom.

• A B&B on a wooded property overlooking Georgia Strait and Vancouver Island. A few minutes' drive or half an hour's walk from the village of Sechelt, a beach, shops, and restaurants. Ten minutes' drive from Porpoise Bay Park. Near boat charters into Sechelt Inlet, kayak tours, scuba diving, mountain trails for hiking or bicycling, a golf course, birdwatching, and freshwater and saltwater fishing. The host arranges charters and reservations. The property is kept in a natural state and attracts robins, woodpeckers, hummingbirds, and chickadees. One of the guest rooms has a private balcony and a view of the ocean. The living room is a gathering place for talking and watching TV. Parking on the property. Coffee and tea are served when guests arrive. Breakfast is served in the dining room, which has a view of treetops and Georgia Strait. Reservations recommended. German spoken. Children welcome. No smoking in the guest rooms. **In the hosts' own words:** "Welcome to our B&B on the Sunshine Coast. We offer a variety of delicious breakfasts."

SUMMER · HILL · HOUSE SECHELT

Mason Road B&B

Joyce Rigaux and John Rayment
5873 Mason Road
Mail: RR 1 TLC Site C–73
Sechelt, BC V0N 3A0
(604) 885-3506 Fax: (604) 885-3506

• Five kilometres north of Sechelt. From Highway 101, turn right onto Norwest Bay Road. Turn right onto Mason Road and continue for 1 kilometre.

• Two rooms. One person $50; two people $75. Queen-sized bed; twin beds. Ensuite bathrooms. Additional person $25.

Adventure travel tours.

• A new timber-frame house on a forty-acre farm, a few minutes' drive from Sechelt Inlet and Georgia Strait. Horses, chickens, and border collies on the property. Guests pick their own berries in season from pesticide-free berry fields. A few minutes' drive from Porpoise Bay Provincial Park on Sechelt Inlet, where there are a beach, a children's play area, and barbecue pits. Sechelt Inlet has reefs and a sunken destroyer for scuba divers to explore. A few minutes' drive from hiking, cycling, golf, tennis, horseback riding, and backcountry skiing. Hosts arrange adventure travel tours for scuba diving, salmon fishing, kayaking, canoeing, sailing, hiking, and cycling. Guest rooms have separate entrances, private decks, and wool duvets. Eight-person guest hot tub on a cedar deck. Breakfast, including farm-fresh eggs, berries (in season), bread baked in a wood stove, and homemade muffins, is served on the cedar deck or in a guest sitting/dining room. Cancellation notice seven days. Children welcome. No pets. No smoking.

Davis Brock Retreat

John and April MacKenzie-Moore
7079 Sechelt Inlet Road
Mail: RR 1 Sandy Hook Road C–17
Sechelt, BC V0N 3A0
(604) 885-9866

• Eight kilometres northwest of the village of
Sechelt.
• Two suites. One person $70; two people
$80–100. Queen-sized bed; queen-sized bed and
sofa bed. Bathroom in suites. Additional person
$10. Weekly rates.
• A B&B on four wooded acres, with a swimming pool, a hot tub, and a fish pond on parklike grounds. Each suite has a fireplace, a private deck, and a private entrance. The larger
suite has a kitchen and a private yard area. Two minutes' drive from kayak and canoe rentals
and lessons on Sechelt Inlet. Five minutes' drive from Porpoise Bay Provincial Park. Twenty
minutes' drive from Tetrahedron recreation plateau. Continental breakfast with fruit is
served at guests' leisure. No pets. No smoking. **In the hosts' own words:** "Relax and refresh
yourself in our beautiful surroundings."

Inlet View Guest House

Gloria and David Pye
6937 Porpoise Drive
Sandy Hook, BC
Mail: Box 1873
Sechelt, BC V0N 3A0
(604) 885-4490

• Self-contained two-bedroom chalet (sleeps eight).
One person $75; two people $90. Queen-sized bed,
double bed, and two foam futons. Breakfast not
included. Additional person $10. Children under 5
free.
• A waterfront chalet near Sechelt, accessed by a ten-minute hike along a wooded trail.
Open-plan kitchen, dining room, and living room. Views from all rooms. Fireplace. Guest
hot tub, patio, private waterfront, and boat dock with deep water moorage. Fifteen minutes
from shopping, hiking, bicycling, diving, golfing, horseback riding, windsurfing, fishing,
and boating. **In the hosts' own words:** "After a day of adventuring or just relaxing, enjoy a
spectacular sunset across the water. The best of both worlds—solitude and adventure."

Burchill's B&B by the Sea

Jack and Millie Burchill
5402 Donley Drive
Mail: RR 2 Donley Site C–17
Halfmoon Bay, BC V0N 1Y0
(604) 883-2400

• Off Highway 101, twenty-four kilometres north of Sechelt.
• Self-contained cottage. One person or two people $80. Queen-sized bed and two bunk beds. Private bathroom. Breakfast ingredients supplied. Additional person $35. Child $20.
• A self-contained cottage a few steps from the ocean, with a panoramic view of Malaspina Strait and Texada Island. The cottage accommodates eight people and has a master bedroom with queen-sized bed, two bedrooms with bunk beds, a living room with fireplace, a kitchen, and a deck. Guests swim and row boats; boats available. Saltwater swimming pool at front deck level. Breakfast supplies, including homemade bread, muffins, and jams, are provided in the cottage kitchen. No pets. Non-smokers. **In the hosts' own words:** "There is always a lot to see and do on the Sunshine Coast, or you can just relax at the beach or on the deck by the pool."

Seawind B&B

Pat and George Larsen
9207 Regal Road
Mail: RR 2 Curran Site C–17
Halfmoon Bay, BC V0N 1Y0
(604) 885-4282

• From the Langdale ferry terminal, follow
Highway 101 for 42 kilometres through Sechelt
to Curran Road. Turn left onto Curran and at the
second intersection turn left onto Regal Road.
From Earl's Cove, follow Highway 101 for 40
kilometres to Curran Road.

• Two rooms. One person $65; two people $75. Queen-sized bed. Ensuite bathrooms.
Additional person $20.

• A contemporary West Coast–style house among Douglas fir and cedar trees, overlooking
Halfmoon Bay and the Strait of Georgia. Each guest room has an ocean view, a covered
deck, and a private entrance. Guest sitting room with games, books, TV, VCR, sink, fridge,
and microwave. In the area are fishing, sea kayaking, cycling, swimming, golfing, birdwatching, and summer and winter scuba diving. Multi-course breakfast is served in the dining room, which overlooks the ocean, or in the guest lounge. Deposit of one night's rate
required to hold reservation. Cancellation notice seven days. Check-in after 4:00 p.m.;
check-out by 11:00 a.m. Cash, Visa. No pets. Smoking on the deck. **In the hosts' own
words:** "Let us pamper you with elegant comfort, fine linen, and gourmet breakfasts."

Beaver Island B&B Inn

Diane and Chris Kluftinger
4726 Webb Road
Mail: RR 1 Site 4 C–6
Madeira Park, BC V0N 2H0
(604) 883-2990

• From Langdale, take Highway 101 north, turn
onto Francis Peninsula Road and continue for 2
kilometres. The B&B is on the left, at the corner
of Francis Peninsula and Webb.

• Two rooms in a guest house. Two people $65,
double bed; one person $50, two people $55, twin beds. Ensuite bathrooms. Cot available
in room with double bed. Additional person $15.
Tugboat charters.

• A B&B on one of Pender Harbour's original homesteads, with a private beach and a view
of Bargain Harbour and Thormanby Island. Orchard and gardens with flowers and shrubs.
Farmyard with dogs, pygmy goats, cats, potbellied pigs, and chickens. Canoe. Vintage 1920
tugboat available for charters. Five to forty minutes from hiking, swimming, fishing, and
water sports. Breakfast, including farm-fresh ingredients, is served on the patio or in the sun
room. Visa, MasterCard. German spoken. No pets. **In the hosts' own words:** "Enjoy our
oceanfront hobby farm in beautiful Pender Harbour."

Herondell B&B

Nancy and Alex Hollmann
11332 Highway 101
Mail: RR 1 Black Point 29
Powell River, BC V8A 4Z2
(604) 487-9528 Fax: (604) 487-9528

• On Highway 101, 12.5 kilometres north of Saltery Bay ferry terminal. Eighteen kilometres south of the Westview ferry terminal. Look for the B&B's white sign at 11332 Highway 101.

• Three rooms. One person $40; two people $50. King-sized bed, ensuite bathroom; double bed, private bathroom; double bed and one twin bed, private bathroom. Additional person $15. Cot available. Extended stay rates on stays of three or more days.

• A B&B on a forty-acre private wildlife sanctuary. A one-acre pond in front of the house is visited by wild ducks, great blue herons, bald eagles, and kingfishers and has resident beavers during most of the year. Well-marked trails through the woods. Swimming and fishing in a river on the property. Twenty minutes' walk from ocean swimming. Twenty minutes' drive from the Powell Forest canoe route. The hosts arrange canoe rentals and help plan day trips to nearby lakes. Children help gather eggs and feed chickens. Breakfast includes sourdough pancakes, homemade jam, and fresh eggs from the hosts' chickens. MasterCard, Diners Club. German spoken. No pets. Smoking on porches.

Beacon B&B

Roger and Shirley Randall
3750 Marine Avenue
Powell River, BC V8A 2H8
(604) 485-5563 Fax: (604) 485-9450

• On Marine Avenue, 2.2 kilometres south of the Comox ferry; 30 kilometres north of the Saltery Bay ferry terminal on Highway 101. Watch for the B&B's sign.

• Two rooms and one two-room suite. One person $65–95; two people $75–95. Queen-sized bed; queen-sized bed and one twin bed; queen-sized bed, one twin bed, and pull-out couch. Ensuite and private bathrooms. Additional person $20.

• A modern waterfront house with a panoramic view of Georgia Strait and Vancouver Island's snow-capped mountains. Half a block from beach access. Thirty minutes' drive from hiking trails, lakes, canoe rentals, a canoe route, an eighteen-hole golf course, diving grounds, and heli-mountaineering. Five minutes' drive from fishing. The hosts arrange advance bookings for various charters, for diving, and for sightseeing at Desolation Sound. Indoor hot tub with ocean view. One host offers body work (massage). Full breakfast is served between 7:00 and 9:00 a.m. Cash, traveller's cheques, Visa, MasterCard. Adult oriented; children over twelve by arrangement. Cat in residence. Smoking outside. **In the hosts' own words:** "If you are trying to get away from all the hustle and bustle of city life, you will truly enjoy our modern house and waterfront setting."

Texada Shores B&B

Robert and Kathleen Hagman
2790 Sanderson Road
Mail: Box 222
Gillies Bay, BC V0N 1W0
(604) 486-7388

• On the western side of Texada Island.

• Two self-contained suites. One person $40–50; two people $50–60. Queen-sized beds. Private and ensuite bathrooms. Breakfast ingredients supplied. Additional person $10.

• Two self-contained suites in a new house with an oceanside sun deck, on the western side of Texada Island, facing south and west to Vancouver Island and the Strait of Georgia islands—Denman, Hornby, and Lasqueti. Suites have private entrances, kitchens, laundry facilities, telephones, TVs, and picture windows. One of the suites has a fireplace. Patio with barbecue. Within walking distance of a general store. Five kilometres from a regional park with nature trail and a paved airstrip with scheduled flights. Air charters available. Pickup from the airstrip. There are ferries to Texada from Courtenay and Powell River. Hiking on logging roads and trails. There are no predators on Texada and there are said to be more deer than people on the island. Fishing charters available. Government wharf in Van Anda and Blubber Bay. Swimming and scuba diving at Shelter Point Park. Boat ramp at Shelter Point. Boat moorage at Marble Bay. Small golf course in Crescent Bay. Breakfast ingredients are supplied. Reservations recommended. Adult oriented. Smoking outdoors.

Cedar Lodge B&B Resort

Renate and Erwin Schulz
C–8 Malaspina Road RR 2
Powell River, BC V8A 4Z3
(604) 483-4414 Fax: (604) 483-4414

• Twenty-six kilometres north of Powell River, near the coastal village of Lund.

• Three rooms. One person $40–45; two people $45–50, queen-sized bed, ensuite half bathroom, shared guest bathroom with shower; two people $45–50, double bed, ensuite half bathroom, private bathroom; two people $50–55, twin beds, ensuite half bathroom, shared guest bathroom with shower.

Self-contained suite. Two people $75. Queen-sized bed, double sofa bed, and hide-a-bed. Additional person $15. Weekly and off-season rates.

Sailboat charters. Sea kayak and boat rentals.

Overnight adventure tours to a wilderness camp, by arrangement.

• A rural B&B on acreage on Okeover Arm, near Powell River, at the entrance to Desolation Sound Marine Park. Ten minutes' walk from Okeover Arm Provincial Park. Sailboat charters and sea kayak and boat rentals at the B&B. Overnight adventure tours to a wilderness camp by arrangement. In the area are sightseeing, hiking, scuba-diving, fjords, and fishing. Near pub and restaurants. Suite and two of the guest rooms have guest entrances. Barbecue and fire pit. Continental breakfast. Reservations recommended. Visa, MasterCard. No pets.

In the hosts' own words: "Many people consider their stay at our B&B to be the highlight of their vacation."

Savary Island Summer House

Janice and Doug Dalzell
Vancouver Boulevard
Savary Island
Mail: 5305 Sprucefield Road
West Vancouver, BC V7W 3B1
Savary Island number: (604) 483-4727
Vancouver number for messages and fax:
(604) 925-3536

• On Savary Island, at the mouth of Desolation Sound, 140 kilometres north of Vancouver.

Accessible by water taxi from Lund, boat, or float plane. The B&B is 1 kilometre from the wharf, by land taxi.

• Two rooms. One person $125; two people $175. Queen-sized bed. Ensuite half bathrooms and shared guest bathroom. Additional person $50. Child $25. Rates include all meals. Group rates for groups of eight to ten people. Open June to October.

• A log house centrally located on Savary Island, with fireplaces in the living room and dining room. Guests explore sandy beaches, hike along wooded trails, and photograph wildlife. The hosts provide phone numbers and information on flights and water taxis. Picnic lunches available. Meals with local seafood, organically grown vegetables, and desserts are served by candlelight in the dining room. Full breakfast, including fresh-squeezed orange juice, fruit salad, and homemade bread, buns, and jams, is served in the dining room or on the patio. Deposit of one night's rate required to hold reservation. Visa. Not suitable for small children. No pets; dog in residence. Smoking outside.

Merritt's Finest B&B

Luke and Gale Grant
Grant Ranches, Aberdeen Road
Mail: Box 4040
Lower Nicola, BC V0K 1Y0
(250) 378-9865 Fax: (250) 378-4004
(area code 604 before October 1996)

• Fifteen minutes west of Merritt. Turn off Highway 8 at Lower Nicola, at the
Courtesy Corner Store, and go up Aberdeen Road two kilometres. Call
for exact directions.

• Two rooms. One person $45; two people $50. Queen-sized bed; two double
beds, queen-sized pull-out couch, and twin bed. Shared guest bathroom,
shower room, and half bathroom. Twin beds available for a fee.
Log cabin. Call for rates.

• A 1987 house on a working cow and calf ranch with seven hundred square feet of covered
decking and a bonfire area. Hosts arrange adult horseback rides and pack trips. Guests take
part in or watch ranch activities. Hiking and biking. Rooms are on ground level and are cool
in summer. One of the guest rooms accommodates up to seven people. Parking. Full breakfast. Fifty percent deposit required. Cash, cheques. No pets indoors; kennels available nearby. A non-smoking house. **In the hosts' own words:** "Our house specialty is our Belgian
waffles with all the fixings. The coffee pot is always on."

Daly House

Richard and Carrie Nitsch
Mail: Box 7
Hedley, BC V0X 1K0
(250) 292-8481 Fax: (250) 292-8600
(area code 604 before October 1996)

• Half a kilometre east of Hedley. From Highway 3, take exit onto Heritage Drive and continue for two blocks.

• Three rooms. One person $30–50; two people $60. Queen-sized bed; one twin bed. Ensuite and private bathrooms.

Guided hiking tours on request.

• A 1904 house in a historical gold mining town, with a view of Nickel Plate Mountain. Upper and lower wrap-around verandas accessible from guest rooms. Close to Twenty Mile Creek, hiking trails, the historical Mascat Mine buildings, fishing, gold panning, swimming, and sightseeing. Cash, traveller's cheques. Two cats and a small dog in residence. Smoking in common areas. **In the hosts' own words:** "Our house overlooks the quaint gold mining town of Hedley. Discover the unique history of our town and its people. Relax on the verandas and experience the luxury and antiquity of days gone by. Our home is your home."

Fossen's Bar 7 Ranch

Louise and Ed Fossen
Highway 3 West RR 1
Rock Creek, BC V0H 1Y0
(250) 446-2210
(area code 604 before October 1996)

• Off Highway 3, 40 kilometres east of Osoyoos.
• One room. One person $45; two people $55. Double bed. Private bathroom.
Guest log house (sleeps six). One person $50; two people $75. Double beds. Additional person $20. Child $10. Weekly rates.
• A five-hundred-acre working cattle ranch with trails for horseback riding, hiking, and cross-country skiing. Twenty minutes' drive from downhill skiing at Mount Baldy. Guest room on the lower floor of the hosts' house has an adjoining solarium with hot tub. Guest log house built in 1898 has been restored. It accommodates six people and has two bedrooms, a living room, a bathroom, and a kitchen. Breakfast includes farm-fresh eggs and homemade baked goods. Guests staying in the guest house are provided with breakfast supplies or have breakfast in the main house. Additional meals on request. Children's play area on the grounds. No smoking indoors. **In the hosts' own words:** "Enjoy fresh air and the friendly atmosphere of our working cattle ranch."

Wagon Wheel Guest Ranch

Annina and Jörg Hoffmeister
Highway 3
Mail: RR I
Bridesville, BC V0H 1B0
(250) 446-2466 Fax: (250) 446-2466
(area code 604 before October 1996)

• On Highway 3, 25 kilometres east of Osoyoos
and 25 kilometres west of Rock Creek.
• Three rooms. Two people $60. Shared guest
bathrooms.
Two cabins. Two people $60. Private bathrooms. Additional person $5.
Accommodation for horses.
• A three-hundred-twenty-acre farm with trails for horseback riding and cross-country
skiing. Fallow deer, wild boar, sheep, horses, and cows on the property. Stocked lake for
fishing. Thirty minutes' drive from skiing at Mount Baldy. Full breakfast includes farm-
fresh eggs and homemade baked goods. Children welcome. **In the hosts' own words:**
"Enjoy our Swiss hospitality."

Old Rickter Pass Road B&B

Lois and Bud Sharpe
333 Old Rickter Pass Road
Mail: RR 2 Site 78 C–9
Osoyoos, BC V0H 1V0
(250) 495-3357
(area code 604 before October 1996)

• Five kilometres west of Osoyoos on Highway
3. Watch for signs.
• Self-contained suite. One person $60. Queen-
sized bed, double sofa bed, and roll-away single
bed. Ensuite bathroom. Additional person $15.
Seniors' discount of 10 percent.
• A country house five minutes from beaches, cafés, and shopping. Ten kilometres from golfing and the U.S. border. Guests take nature walks. Near weekly rodeos. Self-contained suite
has a kitchen, a washer, a dryer, a radio, a TV, and a bathroom with old-fashioned tub and
hand-held shower. Separate guest entrance and parking. Air conditioning. Full breakfast. No
pets; dogs in residence. No smoking in the house. **In the hosts' own words:** "We offer a full
country cowboy breakfast."

Lake Osoyoos Guest House

Italia Sofia Grasso
5809 Oleander Drive (new name of Eighty-fifth Street)
Mail: Box 1323
Osoyoos, BC V0H 1V0
(250) 495-3297 Fax: (250) 495-5310
(area code 604 before October 1996)
Toll-free, for reservations: 1-800-671-8711

- Near downtown Osoyoos.
- Rooms. One person $50; two people $75–95. King-sized bed; queen-sized bed; twin beds. Ensuite bathrooms.
Self-contained suite. Two people $125–150. Queen-sized bed and queen-sized sofa bed. Bathroom in suite.
Off-season rates November to March. Discount of 10 percent on stays of six or more nights.
- A lakefront guest house with a garden, on a quiet street, ten minutes' walk from downtown Osoyoos. Self-contained ground-floor suite has a kitchen and sliding glass doors leading to a rose garden. Guest rooms and suite have private entrances. Guests swim in the lake and use a paddle boat, gas or briquet barbecue, and fire pits. Hot tub. Off-street parking. Breakfast, including juice, coffee or tea, fruit, cereals, eggs, and homemade muffins or scones made with organic ingredients, is served in a glassed dining room, or guests may serve themselves in the suite. Cash, traveller's cheques; no credit cards. No pets. Smoking in the garden. **In the hosts' own words:** "A B&B with a luxurious European atmosphere. An ideal location for a special vacation. If you are celebrating an anniversary, are on a second honeymoon, or are simply having a quiet, relaxing holiday, look no further. I take pleasure in pampering my guests."

Haynes Point Lakeside Guest House

John and June Wallace
3619 Jasmine Drive
Mail: RR 1   Site 93   C–2
Osoyoos, BC   V0H 1V0
(250) 495-7443   Fax: (250) 495-7443
(area code 604 before October 1996)

• Take Highway 97 south and watch for sign for Haynes Point Provincial Park. Turn left onto Thirty-second Avenue, go down a short hill, and turn left onto Eighty-seventh Street.

• Three rooms. One person $60–70; two people $85, queen-sized bed, ensuite bathroom; two people $75, queen-sized bed, shared guest bathroom; two people $70, double bed, shared guest bathroom.
Golf packages.

• A modern rancher with gardens and trees on a hillside overlooking Osoyoos Lake, five minutes' walk from Haynes Point Provincial Park. Near six golf courses, swimming, water sports, tennis, horseback riding, fishing, hunting, birdwatching, art gallery, museum, and winery tours. Guest rooms have honeymoon, Asian, or antique décor. Shared guest bathroom has a Jacuzzi. Living room with TV and view of the lake, deck with patio furniture and hammock, and campfire. The house is air-conditioned in the summer and heated by a Grandpa Fisher stove in the winter. Coffee or tea is served on the deck before breakfast. Full or light breakfast with homemade baked goods is served in the air-conditioned dining room. Adult oriented. No pets. Smoking restricted. **In the hosts' own words:** "We welcome you to experience an unforgettable holiday in one of Canada's most beautiful small towns."

Wildflower B&B

Ruth and John Haak
38950 White Lake Road (149th Street)
Mail: RR 2 Site 53A C–6
Oliver, BC V0H 1T0
(250) 498-4326
(area code 604 before October 1996)
E-mail: jhaak@cln.etc.bc.ca

• Ten minutes from Oliver. Follow Highway 97
four kilometres north. Turn left onto Secrest
Road and then right onto White Lake Road
(149th Street). Watch for the B&B's sign.
Thirty minutes from Penticton. Follow Highway 97 south. Turn right onto White Lake
Road. Pass the observatory and then turn left, towards Oliver. Watch for the B&B's sign.
• Two rooms. One person $45; two people $55–65. Double bed; queen-sized bed. Private
bathrooms.
• A new house with views of mountains and a nature reserve from a patio and a dining area.
Two mountain bikes for rent for bike riding on White Lake Road and more strenuous back
roads. Within walking distance of hiking. Within five minutes' drive of a horseback riding
stable. Within fifteen minutes' drive of four golf courses. Within one hour's drive of two ski
hills. Guest outdoor hot tub. Wood stove, ping-pong table, games, piano, and deck. Tea and
coffee provided. Full or Continental breakfast includes homemade baked goods and preserves. Packed lunches for a fee. Cash, cheques. Some German spoken. No pets. No smoking. **In the hosts' own words:** "Come home to relax in our outdoor hot tub, read on the patio
or in front of the wood stove, play ping-pong or table games, watch videos, play the piano,
or just sit on the deck and enjoy the natural scenery."

Anne Marie's B&B

Anne Marie Thibodeau
34427 Ninety-seventh Street
Mail: Box 1623
Oliver, BC V0H 1T0
(250) 498-0131 Fax: (250) 498-0131
(area code 604 before October 1996)

• Take Highway 97 to the south end of Oliver.
Watch for the B&B's sign, which shows a
woman holding a Canadian flag.
• Two rooms. One person $50; two people
$65–95. Queen-sized bed; twin beds. Ensuite bathrooms. Additional person $20.
• A B&B one block from a mall and restaurants, two blocks from the airport, and within five
to twenty minutes' drive of golfing, swimming, boating, horseback riding, a walking and
cycling path along the Okanagan River, winery and orchard tours, antique shops, flea mar-
kets, bighorn sheep, and the Vaseaux Lake Bird Sanctuary. Thirty-seven kilometres from
skiing at Mount Baldy. Guest rooms have TVs. One of the guest rooms is decorated with red
satin and white lace. The hosts are well travelled. Tea and coffee are available at any time.
Laundry facilities. Off-street parking. Breakfast is served in the dining room or on a sun
deck with a mountain view. No pets. Smoking outside. **In the hosts' own words:** "We are
well travelled. Our spacious luxury bedrooms are great for special occasions, and our breakfasts are scrumptious."

Mirror Lake Guest House

Gwen and Joseph Rundle
9551—306th Avenue (Road 20)
Mail: Box 425
Oliver, BC V0H 1T0
(250) 495-7959 Fax: (250) 495-7959
(area code 604 before October 1996)

• Between Oliver and Osoyoos, on the southeast
corner of Highway 97 and Road 20 (306th
Avenue).
• Rooms. One person $55–60; two people
$75–85. Queen-sized bed.
Honeymoon suite $95–120. Queen-sized bed. Ensuite bathroom.
Minimum stay two nights on weekends.
• A 1920s seven-gabled farmhouse with gingerbread trim. Guest rooms have antiques, sitting areas, air conditioning, and lake views. Honeymoon suite has a cherry wood canopied
bed, a TV, leaded French doors, and a bow window. Parlour, music alcove with fireplace,
lounge with TV and VCR, and veranda. In the area are six wineries, three golf courses, a
bike trail, water sports, fishing, and horses. Boat and bikes. Reservations required. Visa,
MasterCard. Not suitable for children or pets. No smoking indoors. **In the hosts' own
words:** "Follow your heart to Oliver's desert sky. Mirror Lake, mountains, twelve certified
organic acres, and a corral are a setting for leisurely holidays."

Fritzville B&B

Fred and Inga Fritz
34032 Highway 97 South
Mail: RR 1
Oliver, BC V0H 1T0
(250) 498-3645
(area code 604 before October 1996)

• Two long blocks south of Oliver on Highway 97.
• Self-contained one-bedroom suite. One person
$45; two people $55. Queen-sized bed. Bathroom
in suite. Additional person $10. Weekly and off-
season rates.
• A B&B in an orchard setting at the south end of the Okanagan Valley, with a guest suite
with mountain view. Ten minutes' walk from restaurants, a cinema, and downtown Oliver.
Within five to twenty minutes' drive of five golf courses, several cottage wineries, the White
Lake Astrophysical Observatory, the Okanagan Game Farm, water slides, horseback riding,
snowmobile trails, hiking, bike trails, and a community recreation complex with outdoor
pool, baseball camp, and curling and skating arenas. Within one hour's drive of skiing at
Mount Baldy and Apex. Self-contained suite is air-conditioned and has a bedroom, a
kitchen, a living room with TV, and a private entrance. Patio and swimming pool. Full or
light breakfast includes fresh fruit in season.

Olde Osprey Inn

Joy Whitley
Lot 2, Sheep Creek Road
Highway 3A at Yellow Lake
Mail: RR 1 Site 25A C–0
Kaleden, BC V0H 1K0
(250) 497-7134 Fax: (250) 497-7134
(area code 604 before October 1996)

• On Highway 3A at Yellow Lake. Twenty-two kilometres southwest of Penticton. Twenty-two kilometres northeast of Keremeos.

• Three rooms. One person $45–50; two people $50–75. King-sized bed; double bed; twin beds. Two shared guest bathrooms. Additional person $15. Child $10. Group rates.

• A log house at 860-metre elevation on ten acres of evergreen trees and meadow, overlooking Yellow Lake, twenty minutes southwest of Penticton and twenty minutes northeast of Keremeos. Five minutes from golfing at Twin Lakes Resort. Thirty minutes from skiing at Apex. In the area are hiking, fishing, cycling, horseback riding, beaches, and tours of wineries and orchards. Alpine hiking can be arranged at Cathedral Lakes Lodge. Guest living room with wood-stove fireplace; three balconies on the main floor; loft sitting room adjacent to the guest rooms; and library and music area. Each guest room has an in-room sink. Two of the guest rooms have private balconies. Private nature trails and creek, barbecue and bonfire area, and rowboat. The house was built by the owners and has antiques, art, and collectibles. Artist and artisan in residence. Full breakfast is served in the dining room or on the porch. Visa, MasterCard. Pets in residence. Smoking on porches. **In the hosts' own words:** "At this tiny inn, comfort is our main concern."

Riordan House B&B

John and Donna Ortiz
689 Winnipeg Street
Penticton, BC V2A 5N1
(250) 493-5997 Fax: (250) 493-5997
Cellular: (250) 490-7017
(area code 604 before October 1996)

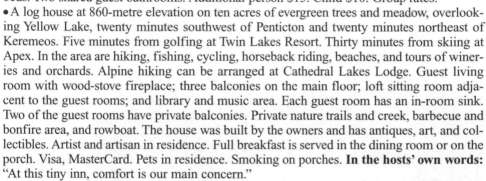

• At the corner of Winnipeg and Eckhardt, six blocks from the beach and two blocks from downtown.

• Two people $55–75. Additional person $15.

• A 1920 Arts and Crafts house known locally as "the house that rum built," within walking distance of a beach, galleries, and restaurants. Near estate wineries. Guest rooms have sitting areas, antique furnishings, TVs, VCRs, robes, slippers, glasses of lemon water when guests arrive, and treats on the pillows at night. One of the guest rooms has a fireplace and two bay windows. Antique shop on the property. Breakfast includes fruit dishes, juice, tea or coffee, and homemade croissants, scones, and muffins. Visa, MasterCard. Children over twelve welcome. No pets; small dog in residence. No smoking. **In the hosts' own words:** "We are in the heart of wine country."

God's Mountain Crest Chalet

Ghitta and Ulric Lejeune
RR 2 Site 15 C–41 Lakeside Road
Penticton, BC V2A 6J7
(250) 490-4800 Fax: (250) 490-4800
(area code 604 before October 1996)

• Two people $50–75. Additional person $15.
Holiday packages.

• A B&B at a vineyard, with lake and cliff views, on one hundred acres in the Okanagan Valley. Ten minutes' drive from downtown, airport, shopping, restaurants, wineries, golf courses, and beaches. Fireplace, sitting room, conference room, ponds, and patios. Educational adult and youth programs available. Full breakfast. Reservations recommended. French and German spoken. **In the hosts' own words:** "Come for holidays. Our chalet's warmth and atmosphere will inspire you. The corporate traveller will love the extraordinary peace and privacy of our one-of-a-kind setting. Use the uniqueness and comfort of our entire home to facilitate a corporate meeting, plan a private getaway, or celebrate a special occasion, no matter what the season."

The Brough House B&B

Heather Brough
185 Middle Bench Road South
Mail: Box 21068
Penticton, BC V2A 8K8
(250) 490-9958 Fax: (250) 490-9557
(area code 604 before October 1996)
Toll-free from within Canada: 1-800-774-4866

• Three rooms. Two people $70–90. Queen-sized bed; double bed; twin beds. Shared guest bathroom and shared bathroom. Additional person $10. Seniors' discount. Weekly rates.
• A 1916 house a few minutes from beaches, shops, restaurants, golf courses, and riding stables. Half an hour's drive from estate wineries, orchards, the Okanagan Game Farm, and skiing at Apex. Antiques. Gardens. Full breakfast is served in the dining room, on a covered veranda, or beside an indoor swimming pool. Visa. Children welcome by arrangement. No pets; cat in residence. Smoking on veranda. **In the hosts' own words:** "Relax and let us take care of your needs."

Eagles Point B&B

Barry Wilson
3145 Juniper Drive
Penticton, BC V2A 7T3
(250) 493-6555
(area code 604 before October 1996)

• Four rooms. $55–65. Queen-sized bed. Ensuite and private bathrooms.
• A ten-thousand-square-foot house in the Okanagan Valley, on a cliff overlooking Penticton, with a view of mountains and lakes.
Guest rooms have panoramic views and TVs. Robes are provided. Three of the guest rooms have private entrances and private decks. Great room, library, kitchen, and deck. Full breakfast. **In the hosts' own words:** "A picture is worth a thousand words. Come make a memory."

Paradise Cove B&B

Ruth Buchanan
3129 Hayman Road
Naramata, BC
Mail: Box 699
Penticton, BC V2A 6P1
(250) 496-5896 Fax: (250) 496-5896
(area code 604 before October 1996)

• From Westminster and Main in Penticton, follow Naramata Road for 13 kilometres. Turn left
onto DeBeck Road at the fire hall. Continue for
1 kilometre and turn right onto Hayman Road.
• Two rooms. Two people from $70. Queen-sized bed. Ensuite bathroom.
Self-contained suite. Two people from $95. Queen-sized bed and sofa bed. Bathroom in
suite.
Additional person $15.
• A modern two-storey house above Manitou Beach, among orchards and vineyards, with a
panoramic view of Okanagan Lake. Twenty minutes from downtown Penticton. Near swimming, hiking along the historical Kettle Valley Railway, three wineries, a wharf, two fine dining restaurants, and a pub. Forty-five minutes' drive from skiing at Apex. Self-contained suite
has a queen-sized bed, a sofa bed, a five-person hot tub, a fireplace, laundry facilities, and a
kitchen. The suite and guest rooms have lake views, private decks, telephones, TVs, fridges,
and beverage service. The suite and one of the guest rooms have private entrances. Full breakfast is served in the dining room or on the deck. One guest room is wheelchair accessible.
Cash, cheques, Visa, MasterCard. Adult oriented. No pets. No smoking indoors. **In the hosts'
own words:** "Idyllic surroundings with a panoramic lake view, friendliness, and comfort."

Lakeside Inn B&B

Mary and Ernie Ursuliak
7219 Nixon Road
Trout Creek, BC
Mail: RR 4 Site 104 C–1
Summerland, BC V0H 1Z0
(250) 494-1825
(area code 604 before October 1996)

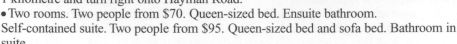

• East of Highway 97 at Johnston Street. Nine
kilometres north of Penticton and 4 kilometres
south of Summerland, in the suburb of Trout
Creek.
• Three rooms. One person $45; two people $60. Double bed; twin beds. Ensuite and private bathrooms.
• A beachfront house on the shore of Lake Okanagan. Guests swim from the beach, which
has a wharf. Guest living room with piano, fireplace, and TV. Two sun decks, garden, and outdoor hot tub. Two blocks from a park and public tennis courts. Four kilometres from
Summerland and nine kilometres from Penticton, where there are museums, libraries, winer-
ies, swimming pools, pubs, restaurants, shopping, art galleries, golf, squash, and badminton.
Near cross-country and downhill ski areas. One host is a potter and has a studio and gallery
on the premises. Breakfast is served in the dining room or on the upper sun deck. Visa,
MasterCard. No pets. No smoking in guest rooms. **In the hosts' own words:** "A touch of
Eden."

Lakeshore Memories B&B

Betty Raymond
12216 Lakeshore Drive
Mail: RR 1 Site 14 C–9
Summerland, BC V0H 1Z0
(250) 494-5134 Fax: (250) 494-5134
(area code 604 before October 1996)

• From Highway 97, turn onto Lakeshore Drive at the bottom of the hill at the south end of Summerland. Continue for two blocks. The B&B is on the left, on a corner.

• Three rooms. One person $50–65; two people $60–75. Queen-sized bed; double bed; twin beds. Ensuite and shared guest bathrooms.

• A restored turn-of-the-century house, a few steps from Lake Okanagan, on the original Summerland townsite. A few minutes' walk from beaches, sailing, and a fish hatchery. Near golf courses, wineries, a restaurant, art galleries, museums, orchards, and the gardens of an agricultural research station. Guests hike the Kettle Valley Railway line and ski at nearby downhill and cross-country ski areas. The host shares her knowledge about the local arts scene. Information on local fishing is available. Living room, a sunroom, and gardens. Air-conditioned. Full breakfast includes homemade baked goods and local products. Adults only. No smoking indoors. **In the hosts' own words:** "We invite you to relax in a lovingly restored heritage house. Each room has been furnished to provide an atmosphere of comfort and romance."

Heidi's B&B

Heidi Weisskopff
5811 Giants Head Road
Mail: RR 2 Site 69 C–9
Summerland, BC V0H 1Z0
(250) 494-0833 Fax: (250) 494-4428
(area code 604 before October 1996)

• In the Okanagan Valley, 400 kilometres from
Vancouver, 3 kilometres off Highway 97-S. Fif-
teen minutes north of Penticton. Half an hour
south of the Coquihalla Connector at Peachland.
• Three rooms. One person $39; two people $55. Double bed; queen-sized bed.
Llama cart tours and rides.
• A B&B on a four-acre hobby farm with dogs, cats, horses, and llamas. Near golf courses,
swimming beaches, boat and sailboat rentals, parasailing, bicycle rentals, go-carts, the his-
torical Kettle Valley Railway, a game farm, trail rides, a wilderness park, Apex Alpine and
Crystal Mountain ski areas, hiking, winery tours, night clubs, a cinema, and restaurants.
Barbecue, patio, garden area, and living room with TV and VCR. Full breakfast includes
German sausage. German spoken. Adults only. Pets welcome by arrangement. Smoking on
patio. **In the hosts' own words:** "Our specialty is German sausage. We invite you to enjoy
our relaxing country hospitality with a Bavarian touch."

Okanagan Lakeview B&B

Dorothy and Ron Deane
11591 Front Bench Road
Mail: RR 4 Site 82
Summerland, BC V0H 1Z0
(250) 494-9856 Fax: (250) 494-9856
(area code 604 before October 1996)

• Fourteen kilometres north of Penticton. Thirty
kilometres south of Kelowna. From Highway 97,
turn onto Walters Road. Turn right onto Front
Bench Road.
• Self-contained suite (sleeps four). One person $45; two people $55. Queen-sized bed and
double bed. Bathroom in suite. Additional person $15.
• A B&B on half an acre on a hillside, with fishponds, waterfalls, and a panoramic view of
Lake Okanagan. Suite with a private entrance accommodates up to four people and has a
kitchen, air conditioning, and a TV. Barbecue. Within a few minutes' drive of Summerland,
golfing, fishing, wineries, and rides on the Kettle Valley Railway. Within an hour's drive of
skiing at Penticton's Apex, Westbank's Crystal Mountain, and Kelowna's Big White.
Breakfast is served in the dining room, or, if guests prefer, guests prepare their own breakfast in the suite's kitchen, with coffee and tea supplied. Deposit of 50 percent required to
hold reservation. Cancellation notice seven days. Check-in 3:00 p.m.; check-out 11:00 a.m.
Visa, MasterCard. Adult oriented. No pets. Smoking outdoors. **In the hosts' own words:**
"Relax and enjoy our spectacular lakeview setting."

Peaches and Cream B&B

Sharin Lomax
6151 Davies Crescent
Mail: RR 1 Site 9 C–A6
Peachland, BC V0H 1X0
(250) 767-6206 Fax: (250) 767-6206
(area code 604 before October 1996)
Toll-free: 1-800-281-0177
Web site: http://www.achilles.net/~bb/302.html

• Halfway between Kelowna and Penticton, 5 minutes from the Coquihalla Connector.

• Rooms. Two people $65–100.
Honeymoon suite $125. Bathroom in suite.
Additional person $20. Weekly rates.
Ski, honeymoon, and anniversary packages.

• A modern house with a view of Okanagan Lake from each room, five minutes from golf, wineries, tennis courts, hiking, and beach. In the area are fishing, sailing, water sports, fine dining restaurants, hiking along the Kettle Valley Railway, and downhill and cross-country ski areas. Pickup from bus and plane at Penticton and Kelowna for a fee. The house has Persian carpets and a wrap-around deck with hanging flower baskets and white wicker furniture. Honeymoon suite has a canopied bed. One of the guest rooms has a four-post queen-sized bed. Afternoon tea is served on the deck. Full breakfast is served on Royal Albert or Royal Doulton china and crystal, on the deck or in the dining area, which has a panoramic view of the lake. **In the hosts' own words:** "Treat yourself to warm hospitality and an unforgettable experience in the Okanagan."

Caledon House B&B

Susan Obermeier
4666 Princeton Avenue
Mail: RR 1 Site X C–B1
Peachland, BC V0H 1X0
(250) 767-6656
(area code 604 before October 1996)

• Midway between Kelowna and Penticton. From Highway 97, turn uphill onto Princeton Avenue and continue 1.2 kilometres. The B&B's driveway is on the upper side of the road.

• One person $40–60; two people $50–70. Double bed; twin beds. Shared guest bathroom. Additional person $15.

• A house built circa 1905, with views of Okanagan Lake. Gardens, a veranda, and two sitting rooms furnished with period pieces. Ten minutes' drive from the Coquihalla Connector. Near restaurants, wineries, and facilities for water sports and other outdoor activities. One kilometre from Okanagan Lake. Five minutes' drive from Hardy Falls. Tea and coffee provided. Full breakfast is served in the dining room. Small pets welcome. No smoking indoors. **In the hosts' own words:** "Enjoy a traditional B&B with a wonderful heritage setting."

Cedar House Family B&B

Jenny and Adrian McGilvray
3760 Salloum Road
Westbank, BC V4T 1E4
(250) 768-1339
(area code 604 before October 1996)

• At Highway 97 and Glenrosa Road, the inter-section just south of Westbank and two kilome-tres north of Highway 97C, turn west (uphill). Take the first right onto Glenway and then the first left onto Salloum.

• Suite. Two people from $60. Queen-sized bed, double bed, and two cots. Child $5–20. Playpen available.

• A cedar and stone house on half an acre, with a panoramic view of Okanagan Lake, down-town Westbank, South Kelowna, a winery, and the surrounding Okanagan mountains. Twenty minutes south of Kelowna. Close to water slides, a children's amusement park, a go-cart track, and a shopping mall. Five minutes from a beach. Fifteen minutes from skiing at Crystal Mountain. Ninety minutes from skiing at Big White, Apex, and Silver Star. Guest suite with TV, VCR, fireplace, fridge, and microwave. Fenced backyard and playground. Babysitting available. The hosts have young children. Continental breakfast. Cash. No pets. No smoking. **In the hosts' own words:** "A perfect bed and breakfast for the young family."

Wicklow B&B

Johanne and Lloyd O'Toole
1454 Green Bay Road
Westbank, BC V4T 2B8
(250) 768-1330 Fax: (250) 768-1335
(area code 604 before October 1996)

• From Kelowna, take Highway 97 across the bridge. At the Esso gas station, turn left onto Boucherie Road and continue to Okanagan Lake. Make a sharp left turn onto Green Bay Road.

From Peachland, take Highway 97. At the McDonalds restaurant, turn right onto Gellatly Road and continue to Okanagan Lake. Turn left onto Boucherie Road and continue for 3 kilometres to Green Bay Road.

• One person $55–75; two people $85, queen-sized bed, ensuite bathroom; two people $75, queen-sized bed, shared guest bathroom; two people $65, double bed, shared guest bath-room.

Coach house: one person $75; two people $85, queen-sized bed and queen-sized sofa bed, ensuite bathroom. Additional person $15.

• A new waterfront house on half an acre on Okanagan Lake, with landscaped gardens, vine-yards, and a bird sanctuary. Ten minutes' drive from Kelowna. Private sandy beach and boat dock; boat tours available. Near horseback riding, golf courses, wineries, water slide, and Butterfly World. English-style guest rooms have TVs and air conditioning. The coach house and one of the guest rooms have private entrances. Full breakfast is served on a covered porch or in the dining room, both of which have a view of the lake and mountains. Visa, MasterCard. French spoken. No pets. Smoke-free environment. **In the hosts' own words:** "Enjoy the ambience of our waterfront home and friendly hospitality. On parle français."

Trenton's Hospitality Home

Daniel and Edith Trenton
855 Quigley Road
Kelowna, BC V1X 1A9
(250) 763-2892 Fax: (250) 763-9300
(area code 604 before October 1996)
Web site: htttp://www.achilles.net/~bb/154.html

• From Highway 33, turn south onto Hollywood
Road. Turn right onto Quigley Road and continue
for two blocks.

• Two-room suite. Two people $75. Queen-sized
bed and double hide-a-bed. Private bathroom with shower. Additional person $10.
Two rooms in suite rented individually. One person $40–50; two people $50–65. Queen-sized bed; double hide-a-bed. Shared guest bathroom with shower.

• A B&B in a residential area in the Okanagan. Five minutes drive from shopping, movie theatres, and restaurants. Near golf courses, beaches, art galleries, wineries, craft shops, hiking and fishing. One hour's drive from Big White ski area. City transit across the street. Suite has private entrance, tape deck, VCR, TVs, chesterfield and chairs, natural gas stove, air conditioning, fridge, and microwave. Parking. Full breakfast, including fruit from hosts' orchard, cereal, Canadian bacon and eggs, homemade muffins and preserves, and coffee and juice, is served on the covered deck or in the dining room. Visa, MasterCard. No smoking.
In the hosts' own words: "Your comfort is our first priority."

Point of View B&B

Cathy and Herb Comben
378 Sandpiper Street
Mail: RR 4 Site 10 C–2
Kelowna, BC V1Y 7R3
(250) 764-7378
(area code 604 before October 1996)

• Two rooms. One person $60; two people $70.
Queen-sized bed; twin beds. Private bathrooms.
Weekly and off-season rates.

• A B&B with a twenty-by-forty-foot heated
swimming pool and a view of Okanagan Lake, near beaches, three wineries, and Okanagan Lake Mountain Park. The hosts arrange hiking, cycling, and van tours of the valley. Guest indoor hot tub. Books, TV, VCR, and movies. Collection of telephones on display. Guest rooms have views of the lake. Coffee or tea is delivered to guest rooms before breakfast. Breakfast is served in the dining room. MasterCard. Adults only. No pets. Smoking outside.
In the hosts' own words: "Experience the Okanagan lifestyle in an atmoshpere of comfort and charm. Enjoy an invigorating swim in our pool or just lounge in the sun and admire the view of the lake. We look forward to offering you a memorable Okanagan experience."

Magpie B&B

Shirley Allnutt
1903 Rutland Road North
Kelowna, BC V1X 4Z9
(250) 765-2779 Fax: (250) 765-2779
(area code 604 before October 1996)

• Just off Highway 97 and Old Vernon Road.
• Rooms. $45–55. Child $10.
• A B&B with panoramic views of nearby hills and orchards, twenty minutes from Kelowna city centre and forty minutes from skiing at Big White. Within five minutes of restaurants, the airport, Bedrock City, and water slides. Ten minutes from shopping. Within walking distance of several golf courses. Guest hot tub, patio, TV, VCR, and reading material. Host is a retired professional cook. Full breakfast includes homemade breads. MasterCard. **In the hosts' own words:** "Come and visit our warmly decorated rooms in a quiet setting and relax on the patio."

The Grapevine B&B

Marilyn Rae and Andy Szita
2621 Longhill Road
Kelowna, BC V1Y 2G5
(250) 860-5580 Fax: (250) 860-5586
(area code 604 before October 1996)

• In Kelowna, turn north off Highway 97 onto Dilworth Drive. Turn right onto Longhill Road. Turn right onto Monford for parking.
• Four rooms. One person $55–65; two people $75, twin beds (or a king-sized bed) and double sofa bed, ensuite bathroom; two people $70, queen-sized bed, private bathroom; two people $65, queen-sized bed, ensuite bathroom; twin beds (or a king-sized bed), private bathroom. Additional person $15.
Golf and ski packages.
• A Cape Cod–style house in an orchard, six kilometres from Kelowna's city centre. Guest rooms are upstairs and have TVs. Guest entrance. Guest living room with fireplace and books. Covered patio and garden for guest use only. Hosts advise guests about touring the local wineries. Within thirty minutes' drive of a dozen golf courses. Within thirty minutes of beaches and water sports on three lakes. Within forty minutes of downhill and cross-country skiing at Big White, Silver Star, and Crystal Mountain. Full breakfast is served in the dining room; birds can be seen feeding outside. Cancellation notice seven days. Visa, MasterCard. Children over ten welcome. No pets. Smoking outdoors. **In the hosts' own words:** "Come and join us in the tranquil atmosphere and charm of our country home."

Sonora View B&B

Kurt and Edith Grube
998 Augusta Court
Kelowna, BC V1Y 7T9
(250) 763-0969
(area code 604 before October 1996)
Toll-free from within Canada and northwest
  U.S.: 1-800-801-2992

• Three rooms. One person $50–60; two people
$65, queen-sized bed or queen-sized bed and
one twin bed, ensuite bathroom; two people $75,
queen-sized bed, one twin bed, and double hide-a-bed, ensuite bathroom. Additional person $20. Child under 12 $10. Extended stay and off-season rates.

• A quiet, centrally located B&B with parklike gardens and fruit trees, overlooking Kelowna Golf and Country Club. Five minutes' drive from shopping, restaurants, golfing, and wineries. Within an hour of Vernon, Penticton, and ski hills. Air-conditioned rooms have panoramic views of city, lake, mountains, and golf course. Guest sitting room with antiques, collectibles, TV, VCR, telephone, books, fridge, and wood stove. One of the guest rooms has a private entrance. Two of the guest rooms share a guest entrance through the guest sitting room. A guest patio leads to the gardens. Full breakfast is served on a garden deck, weather permitting. Artists' work for sale on the premises. German spoken. No pets. No smoking. **In the hosts' own words:** "Experience a peaceful retreat nestled against the hills in our spacious house, decorated with antiques, collectibles, and an artist's touch. You'll feel our warm hospitality."

The Mad Cadder Guest House

Wayne Ross
409 Cadder Avenue
Kelowna, BC V1Y 5N2
(250) 763-3558
(area code 604 before October 1996)

• From Highway 97 north, turn south on Abbott Street and left onto Cadder Avenue.
• Three rooms. One person $40; two people
$55–75. Double bed. Ensuite bathrooms.
Cottage. Two people $75. Private bathroom.
Weekly and monthly rates.

• A two-storey English-style house built in 1933, with gardens and a detached cottage. Ten minutes' walk from downtown through a park. One block from hospital and beach at Okanagan Lake. Exhibits of fine art, antiques, and collectibles at the B&B. Sitting room with fireplace. Cottage has a kitchen. Continental breakfast is served on the stone patio or in the formal dining room. Credit cards. Children welcome. Kennel for pets available by arrangement. Smoke-free environment. **In the hosts' own words:** "The name need not worry you. Individuals seeking an enchanting destination should look no further. Our B&B boasts an eclectic atmosphere rich in the ambience of a house that has truly been lived in. A home away from home."

The Manor House B&B

Cheryl and Ted Turton
2796 K.L.O. Road
Mail: Box 202
East Kelowna, BC V0H 1G0
(250) 861-3932 Fax: (250) 861-4446
(area code 604 before October 1996)

• Detailed directions given at the time of booking.
• Two rooms. One person $60; two people $75. Queen-sized bed, ensuite bathroom; twin beds, private bathroom.
• A B&B with antiques and gardens, on a working orchard and vineyard, with a view of the Okanagan Valley. Two minutes' walk down a country lane from golf courses, a pub, and fine dining restaurants. Ten minutes' drive from shopping in Kelowna. The hosts share their knowledge about the history of the valley. Gardens and orchards to walk in. Full breakfast is served in the dining room or on a screened porch surrounded by a garden. Diets are accommodated. Check-in 4:00 p.m.; check-out 11:00 a.m. Cash, Visa. Adult oriented. No pets. Smoking outside only. **In the hosts' own words:** "Our elegant, antique-filled heritage house has been home to our family for three generations. We invite you to escape and enjoy an orchard experience."

The Schroth Farm B&B

Fred and Helen Schroth
3282 East Vernon Road
Vernon, BC V1B 3H5
(250) 545-0010
(area code 604 before October 1996)

• One kilometre east of Vernon.
• Room and suite. One person $30; two people $45–55. Double bed; twin beds. Ensuite and private bathrooms. Additional person $15. Child $10.
• A farmhouse with a patio and a view of cattle grazing on nearby pastures with mountains in the distance. Guests' children enjoy the miniature goats. Near sandy beaches for swimming, golf courses, trail riding, a water slide, and skiing at Silver Star. Guest room is on the upper floor and has a TV and a fridge. Suite is on the lower floor and has a private entrance and a living room with TV, VCR, and fridge. Breakfast is served in a sunroom. German spoken. Children welcome. Smoking outdoors. **In the hosts' own words:** "We have travelled to many parts of the world, and we enjoy having people visit from all parts of the world."

The Tuck Inn

Bill and Irene Tullett
3101 Pleasant Valley Road
Vernon, BC V1T 4L2
(250) 545-3252 Fax: (250) 549-3254
(area code 604 before October 1996)

• In Vernon, turn east from Highway 97 onto Thirtieth Avenue and continue for 1 kilometre to Pleasant Valley Road.

• Four rooms. One person $40–45; two people $65–75. Double bed; queen-sized bed; queen-sized bed and one twin bed. Additional person $15–20. Crib available.

Ski, golf, honeymoon, and anniversary packages.

• A house built in 1906 that has its original interior doors, casings, and mouldings and is furnished with antiques. Lounge with books and TV. Twenty-two kilometres from downhill and cross-country skiing at Silver Star. Ten minutes' drive from beaches at Kalamalka Lake and Okanagan Lake. Five minutes' walk from downtown Vernon's art galleries, museum, theatres, and playhouse. Fifteen minutes' drive from the historical O'Keefe Ranch. Ten minutes' drive from golf courses. Breakfast is served from 7:30 to 9:00 a.m. in a Victorian-style tea room with nine-foot ceilings and a circular fireplace. Deposit of 50 percent of total payment required to hold reservation. Cancellation notice seven days. Check-in between 3:00 and 7:00 p.m.; check-out by noon. Visa, MasterCard. Children welcome. No pets; cat in residence. No smoking indoors. **In the hosts' own words:** "Our large heritage house lets you step back in time to the Victorian era. Our specialty breakfast is a sumptuous delight."

Harbourlight

Helga and Peter Neckel
135 Joharon Road
RR 4   Site 11   C–50
Vernon, BC   V1T 6L7
(250) 549-5117   Fax: (250) 549-5162
(area code 604 before October 1996)

• Ten minutes' drive from downtown Vernon. Take Thirtieth Avenue west and continue on Bella Vista Road to Fleming Road (winding road). Turn right onto Fleming and right again onto Joharon. Watch for the B&B's sign.

• Three rooms. One person $45; two people $55–65. Ensuite bathrooms. Additional person $20.

• A custom-built house on two acres of quiet hillside. Guest rooms have picture windows and views of the lake and mountains. A base for exploring the Okanagan Valley and the Shuswap area. Hiking from the B&B. Five minutes' drive from Okanagan Lake. Ten to fifteen minutes' drive from golfing, fishing, boating, swimming, and trail rides. Forty-five minutes' drive from downhill and cross-country skiing at Silver Star. Living room, dining room, TV room, and garden. Central air conditioning. Full breakfast includes seasonal fresh fruit and homemade preserves and bread. German spoken. Adult oriented. No pets. No smoking. **In the hosts' own words:** "Each of our guest rooms is decorated with European flair."

Castle on the Mountain B&B

Eskil and Sharon Larson
8227 Silver Star Road
RR 8 Site 10 C–12
Vernon, BC V1T 8L6
(250) 542-4593
(area code 604 before October 1996)

• Ten kilometres east of Highway 97, on Forty-eight Avenue or Silver Star Road.
• Five rooms. One person $60–75; two people $65–145. Queen-sized bed;
king-sized bed; twin beds. Ensuite and private bathrooms. Additional person
$35. Child $15–30.
Special occasion packages.
• A Tudor-style house on the way to Silver Star Mountain, with views of the city of Vernon
and Okanagan and Kalamalka lakes. In the area are swimming, horseback riding, beaches,
winery tours, downhill and cross-country skiing, and snowmobiling. Hiking from the B&B.
Guest sitting room with fireplace and TV, kitchen for light snacks, and outdoor hot tub.
Playground and picnic area with fire pit. A new six-hundred-square-foot guest room has a
covered balcony with view, an open balcony, a gas fireplace, a stereo, a TV, and a Jacuzzi.
The hosts are artists and designed and built the house. Guests visit their gallery and studio.
Full breakfast with fresh fruit is served between 7:30 and 9:00 a.m. Credit cards. Suitable
for families. No pets. Smoking outdoors. **In the hosts' own words:** "Our home is your castle, with the view, the privacy, the space, the outdoors, and the artwork creating a special feeling that you must experience."

Melford Creek Country Inn and Spa

Steve and Karin Shantz
7810 Melford Road
Mail: RR 3 Site 11 C–102
Vernon, BC V1T 6L6
(250) 558-7910
(area code 604 before October 1996)

• From Highway 97, at the north end of Vernon, turn east onto Forty-eighth Avenue. Follow Silver Star Resort signs. Continue for 12 kilometres. Just past the Silver Star Nursery, turn left onto Keddleston Road. Continue for 1 kilometre to the B&B.
• Three rooms. One person $65–85; two people $75–95. King-sized bed; two queen-sized beds; pull-out sofa and one twin bed. Ensuite and private bathrooms. Additional person $25. Weekly rates.
Golf/ski, spa, and special occasion packages.
• A rock and wood chateau on five acres. Guest rooms have rock fireplaces, cathedral ceilings, and gothic windows. One of the guest rooms has a king-sized sleigh bed. Another guest room has a lodge-pole pine canopied queen-sized bed and a brass queen-sized bed. Guest loft has a rock fireplace and overlooks the living room. Indoor pool, whirlpool, and sauna. Therapeutic massage sessions available. Fifteen minutes from downtown Vernon and skiing at Silver Star. Twenty minutes from horseback riding, boating, and wineries. Breakfast includes light cuisine. Visa, MasterCard. German spoken. Adult oriented. Smoking outdoors. **In the hosts' own words:** "Experience the tranquillity and warm ambience of our country chateau, geared to replenishing the body, mind, and spirit—the perfect getaway for romance or rejuvenation."

Cherry Ridge B&B

Dave and Jill DeVries
648 North Fork Road RR 1
Cherryville, BC V0E 2G0
(250) 547-2257 or (250) 547-8919
(area code 604 before October 1996)

• Six kilometres off Highway 6, 45 minutes' drive east of Vernon on the way to Nakusp.
• Two rooms. One person $40; two people $50. Queen-sized bed; queen-sized bed and twin bed. Ensuite and private bathrooms. Additional person $15.
• A rancher built in 1992 with mountain views, on ten acres of forest with deer and birds. Within twenty minutes' drive of gold panning, golfing, fishing, horseback riding, lakes, and craft shops. The hosts have a craft and fabric shop attached to their house. One host makes quilts, dolls, and teddy bears. Quilting classes can be arranged. The other host makes rustic furniture. One of the guest rooms has a mountain view, the other a forest view. Each guest room has facilities for making tea and coffee. Breakfast is served beside a 1907 wood-burning cookstove. Other meals by request. No pets. No smoking. **In the hosts' own words:** "Welcome to our comfortable, quiet home in the Monashees."

Park Place B&B

Lynn and Trevor Bentz
720 Yates Road
Kamloops, BC V2B 6C9
(250) 554-2179 Fax: (250) 554-2179
(area code 604 before October 1996)

• From Highway 5, follow signs for north shore
and airport. After crossing the bridge, turn right
onto Westsyde Road and then take the fifth right
onto Yates Road.
• Three rooms. One person $40–50; two people
$55–65. Queen-sized bed; double bed. Ensuite and shared guest bathrooms.
Guided fishing trips.
• A riverfront B&B on landscaped grounds with a pool and a patio. Guest rooms are on
ground level. Two of the guest rooms have antique brass double beds. One of the guest rooms
has a view of river and mountains. Resident wild birds and beavers. Near golf, tennis, fishing, hiking, boating, shopping, and restaurants. Thirty minutes from skiing at Sun Peaks.
Guided fishing trips available. Full or light breakfast with homemade preserves is served in
a solarium with a view of Mount Paul and the North Thompson River. Not suitable for small
children. Pets on leashes welcome. Smoking outdoors. **In the hosts' own words:** "Enjoy our
delightful riverfront country home. Stroll around the landscaped grounds, swim in the large
pool, or lounge on the patio and watch the river flow by."

Reimer's B&B

Ray and Cookie Reimer
1630 Slater Avenue
Kamloops, BC V2B 4K4
(250) 376-0111
(area code 604 before October 1996)

• Take the Overlander Bridge to the north shore
and follow Fortune Drive, which becomes
Tranquille Road. Continue along Tranquille to
the light at Singh Road and turn left. Go one
block and turn right. The B&B is the fourth
house on the right.
• Three rooms. One person $30–35; two people $50, queen-sized bed or double bed,
shared bathroom; two people $60, queen-sized water bed, private bathroom with shower.
Open May 15 to December 15. Tent space available.
• A B&B with an outdoor pool on a landscaped, fenced lot, in a quiet area. One of the guest
rooms is downstairs and has a private entrance. Two of the guest rooms are upstairs. Outdoor
pool, patio, and sun deck. Ten minutes from golf, tennis courts, and a bike path at McArthur
Park. Ten minutes from the airport and downtown. Near shopping mall, theatre, and restaurants. Within an hour of Sun Peaks ski area at Todd Mountain and Harper Mountain. Varied
breakfast menu includes homemade jams and preserved fruits. Tea or coffee served any
time. Check-in any time; check-out 11:00 a.m. Cash, traveller's cheques. Adult oriented.
Alternative lifestyles welcome. Well-behaved pets welcome; dog in residence. Smoking outdoors. **In the hosts' own words:** "You'll feel at home in our friendly abode. Cookie likes to
cook, and it shows—breakfast is great here."

Ashram on the Lake

Doug and Tuni Bushey
224 Holbrook Road
Mail: General Delivery
Pinantan Lake, BC V0E 3E0
(250) 573-4087
(area code 604 before October 1996)

• Thirty minutes east of Kamloops. From Kam-
loops, turn off Highway 5 at the Husky gas sta-
tion. Go 29 kilometres east on Paul Lake Road.
Follow Jandana Ranch signs to Pinantan Lake.
Turn left at the first road past the store. Follow Holbrook Road to first house on the lake
past the school.
• Room. One person $40; two people $50. Queen-sized bed. Private bathroom.
Four-room suite. $70. Queen-sized bed and fold-out futon. Ensuite bathroom.
• A waterfront B&B on Pinantan Lake, with a private dock, a rowboat, and a deck. The lake
has rainbow trout that weigh up to three pounds. One host is available as a fishing guide.
Five minutes from horseback riding. Cross-country skiing from the B&B. Twenty-five minutes from downhill skiing at Harper Mountain. Eighty minutes from downhill skiing at Sun
Peaks. Ice skating on the lake in winter; swimming in summer. Thirty minutes from golf
courses in Kamloops. Guest room is on the second floor and has a TV. Suite has a private
entrance, a kitchen, and a living room with TV. Full breakfast is served in the dining room
or on the deck. **In the hosts' own words:** "The crystal-clear water invites swimmers from
our large deck."

Alpine Meadows B&B

Lorne and Lynn Isaac
RR 1 McKim Road
Pritchard, BC V0E 2P0   (250) 577-3726
(area code 604 before October 1996)

• From Kamloops, take Highway 1 east. Turn
right onto Highway 97 (Vernon/Falkland), left
onto Duck Range Road, and right onto McKim
Road. The B&B is an old log house on the left
side, at the end of the road. Ten minutes from
Highway 97.
• Two rooms. Two people $50. Double bed. Shared guest bathroom.
• A log house on a twenty-acre hobby farm, with covered and open sun decks and two rock
fireplaces. Walking, hiking, biking, cross-country ski trails, and tobogganning on the property. Guests watch hummingbirds and pick wild strawberries, salmonberries, and meadow
flowers. Farm animals during summer months. Thirty minutes from waterslides, a wildlife
park, golfing, and trout and salmon fishing in the South Thompson River. Eighty minutes
from downhill skiing at Sun Peaks. Ground-level entrance. Guest rooms are on the ground
floor. Sitting room, TV, drying room for snow gear, and sunken living room. Full breakfast,
including the hosts' wildflower honey, is served on the sun deck or in the dining room. Cash,
traveller's cheques. Some German spoken. No children. Cat and dog in residence; large sheltered dog kennel available. Smoking in designated area. **In the hosts' own words:** "Sit and
relax in tranquillity, and enjoy our one-of-a-kind two-storey log house nestled among pines
and meadows, with a panoramic view of the South Thompson River, Lake Kamloops, mountain ranges, and sunsets."

Freshwoods Country B&B

Margaret Abbott
Mail: Box 343
Pritchard, BC V0E 2P0
(250) 577-3269
(area code 604 before October 1996)

• From Kamloops, go 40 kilometres east on Highway 1. Turn right at the Pritchard Station store sign, right onto Duck Range Road, left onto Harrison Road, and right onto Schamp Road. The B&B is a grey house on the left. Seven minutes' drive from the Pritchard Station store.

• Four rooms. One person $35; two people $50–60. Queen-sized bed, ensuite bathroom; double bed, private bathroom; one twin bed, shared bathroom. Stalls and pasture for horses.

• A three-hundred-forty-acre farm high up in a quiet valley, with a panoramic view of the valley, mountains, and, at night, the lights of Kamloops forty kilometres away. Walking, hiking, and riding trails on the property. Mountain biking from the B&B. Within thirty minutes' drive of Kamloops, the Shuswap Lakes, four golf courses, a water slide, a wildlife park, trout fishing, and, in the fall, salmon fishing on the South Thompson River. Living room with eighteen-foot ceiling has a piano and a stone fireplace. Five-by-twenty-five-metre sun deck. Outdoor kitchen in a garden gazebo. Full or Continental breakfast, including farm-fresh eggs and garden produce in season, is served between 8:00 and 10:00 a.m. Picnic baskets available. Diets are accommodated with advance notice. Reservations recommended; best time to call is between 4:30 and 6:00 p.m. Cancellation notice forty-eight hours. Check-out 11:00 a.m. Traveller's cheques, cash. No small children. Well-behaved pets outdoors only; cat in residence. Smoking outdoors. **In the hosts' own words:** "Get away from it all at our country home with country hospitality. Sit high on a hill with only the sounds of nature. The sunsets can be breathtaking."

Country Corner B&B

Doreen and Tim McQuirter
20 Martin Creek Road
Mail: Box 295
Pritchard, BC V0E 2P0
(250) 577-3480
(area code 604 before October 1996)

• Thirty minutes east of Kamloops. Twelve minutes west of Chase. Two kilometres from Highway 1. From Highway 1, turn south at the Pritchard Station store. Take the first left, at Stoney Flats, and continue straight east to Martin Creek Road. Turn right and look for the B&B's large wooden sign.

• Two rooms. One person $35; two people $50. Queen-sized bed. Shared guest bathroom and shared bathroom.

• A cedar house on an acreage in a rural setting, with large cedar trees and country flower gardens. Twelve minutes from the Little Shuswap Lake. Fifteen to thirty minutes' drive from golfing, fishing, hiking, biking, trail riding, and cross-country skiing. House is decorated in country style with antiques. Full or light breakfast includes homemade jams, scones, and buns. Traveller's cheques, cash. Wheelchair accessible. Pets on leashes welcome. Smoking on porches. **In the hosts' own words:** "Come and enjoy our comfortable, casual, quiet country retreat."

The Sunset B&B

Kaj and Barbara Jensen
3434 McBride Road
Mail: Box 168
Blind Bay, BC V0E 1H0
(250) 675-4803
(area code 604 before October 1996)

• Twenty-four kilometres west of Salmon Arm. Ten kilometres east of Sorrento. From Highway 1, turn north onto Balmoral Road and continue for 6 kilometres. Turn right onto Reedman Point Road. Turn left onto McBride Road and continue up the hill.

• Two rooms. In summer, one person $40–45; two people $55–60. In winter, one person $35–40; two people $50–55. Queen-sized bed; twin beds. Shared guest bathroom. Day trip packages.

• A country house with a view of Shuswap Lake. Guest rooms have ceiling fans and private covered decks. Guest great room has TV, games, books, and sliding glass doors that lead to a patio and garden. Five minutes from marinas, a golf course, and fly fishing. Biking and hiking trails from the B&B. Ninety minutes from skiing at Sun Peaks, near Kamloops, and White Star, near Vernon. Near the Adams River fall salmon run. The hosts provide picnic lunches and backpacks and take guests on wilderness day trips for additional fees. Breakfast, including fruit from the hosts' garden and homemade breads and jams, is served on a covered veranda or in the dining room. Cash. German and Danish spoken. Not suitable for small children or for pets. Smoking outside. **In the hosts' own words:** "Let us make you feel special and pampered in spectacular surroundings. Get away from the highway and experience the serenity of the Shuswap."

Juniper Tree B&B

Dennis and Jeanne Hill
3662 Jackson Road
Salmon Arm, BC
Mail: Site 1 C–40
Tappen, BC V0E 2X0
(250) 835-4332
(area code 604 before October 1996)

• Twenty minutes west of Salmon Arm, 4.5 kilometres off Highway 1.
Turn off the Highway at Sunnybrae Road. Follow signs on Sunnybrae.
Call for detailed directions.

• Three rooms. One person $60–90; two people $80–100. Queen-sized bed;
twin beds (or a king-sized bed); double bed and one twin bed. Private and
shared guest bathrooms.
One suite (sleeps two to four) $100–140. Weekly rates.

• A log house at the foot of Bastian Mountain with a waterfront view of Shuswap Lake, overlooking a wild bird sanctuary. Refreshments served on arrival. Hosts help guests plan activities. Within walking distance or fifteen minutes' drive of Herald Park, Sunnybrae Beach,
Margaret Falls, hiking, cross-country skiing, and a golf course. Salmon run in the fall. Deck
with lakefront view. Dining room with fireplace. Rooms are decorated in Victorian, country,
and rose themes. Two of the guest rooms have private balconies with views. Suite has a private entrance and a private patio overlooking garden and lake. Full breakfast includes homemade muffins and rolls, fruit or juice, and a hot entrée. No pets. Smoke-free environment.
In the hosts' own words: "Enjoy warm hospitality and the uniqueness of a fine lakefront
log home. Breakfast is served on our rustic deck, with a panoramic view, or in our gracious
dining room, with a warm glowing fire in winter."

The Silvercreek Guesthouse

Gisela Bodnar
6820 Thirtieth Avenue SW
Salmon Arm, BC V1E 4M1
(250) 832-8870
(area code 604 before October 1996)

• From Highway 1 west of Salmon Arm, turn at flashing light onto Salmon River Road. Go 2.5 kilometres, turn right onto Thirtieth Avenue SW, and continue for 1.5 kilometres. Look for the B&B's sign on the left.

• One person $25–30; two people $40–45. Additional person $15. Child $5–10. Weekly rates.

• A log house with a deck and a garden, on forty acres, with a view of mountains and a valley. Five minutes' drive from shops, restaurants, a water slide, golf courses, and a community centre with pool and whirlpool. Near beaches and picnic grounds at Shuswap Lake. In the area are trail riding, hiking, biking, and fishing. Twenty-five minutes' drive from cross-country ski trails in the Larch Hills and Skimiken areas. Full breakfast includes eggs from the host's chickens and homemade jams and buns. Light breakfast available. Lunch and dinner available with advance notice. **In the hosts' own words:** "Enjoy your stay at this charming, comfortable, and spacious log house."

Shuswap View B&B

Gerald and Christa Jordan
5121 Fiftieth Street NW
Salmon Arm, BC V1E 4M2
(250) 833-0011
(area code 604 before October 1996)

• Halfway between Vancouver and Calgary. From Salmon Arm, go west on Highway 1. Turn left onto Fiftieth Avenue (Pierre's Point Road) and drive up the hill. Turn right onto Fiftieth Street.

• Two rooms. One person $45; two people $55. Queen-sized bed. Shared and private bathrooms.
One suite. Two people $65. Queen-sized bed and Murphy bed. Private bathroom.
Roll-away beds available. Additional person $15. Child under 15 $10. Open April 1 to October 15.

• A B&B overlooking the Salmon Arm of Shuswap Lake, with a view that extends to Sicamous, surrounded by acres of forest for hiking. Two minutes' drive from beaches. One guest room has a view of the lake. Another guest room has a view of the forest. Suite has a view of the lake and no stairs. Full breakfast is served in a breakfast room overlooking Shuswap Lake. Cash, cheques. No pets. No smoking indoors. **In the hosts' own words:** "We have a million-dollar view of Shuswap Lake and the surrounding area."

The Inn at the Ninth Hole

Henrietta and Henk Van Huigenbos
5091 Twentieth Avenue SE
Salmon Arm, BC V1E 4M3
(250) 832-5757 Fax: (250) 833-0113
(area code 604 before October 1996)
Toll-free from within Canada and the U.S.: 1-800-221-5955

• From Highway 1, go south on Highway 97B for 3 kilometres. Turn right on-to Twentieth Avenue SE. The B&B is the last house on the right.
• Three rooms. Two people $100–175. King-sized bed; queen-sized bed. En-suite bathrooms. Additional person $25.
• A colonial-style house overlooking the greens of the Salmon Arm Golf and Country Club. Ten minutes' drive from Salmon Arm. Each guest room has a sitting area, a fireplace, a TV, and an ensuite bathroom with jetted tub. Air conditioning. In the area are hiking, riding sta-bles, cross-country skiing, boating, shopping, and eighteen-hole and nine-hole golf courses. Full breakfast includes a choice of entrée. Reservations recommended. Cancellation notice five days. Visa, MasterCard. No pets. No smoking. **In the hosts' own words:** "A place for all seasons. Come and enjoy a relaxing time in peaceful surroundings."

Apple Blossom B&B

Paul and Lillian Scherba
3531 Tenth Avenue SE
Salmon Arm, BC V1E 4M3
(250) 832-0100
(area code 604 before October 1996)

• A few minutes from Highway 97B and High-
way 1. Call for directions.
• Room. $55–75. Queen-sized bed. Private bath-
room.
Extended stay rates.
• A B&B on a small acreage close to golf, tennis, horseback riding stables, hiking and cross-
country skiing trails, and historical sites. Within five minutes of downtown shopping malls
and fine dining restaurants. Private ground-level entrance, TV, patio, and flower garden.
Kitchen area with stove, fridge, sink, table and chairs, cooking utensils, dishes, and cutlery.
Guest family room with chesterfield, TV, and VCR. Parking. Light snack on arrival with
reservations. Continental breakfast, including homemade baked goods, preserves, and fresh
fruit, is served between 8:30 and 9:30 a.m. or earlier by request. Not suitable for children.
No pets. No smoking. **In the hosts' own words:** "Our B&B is designed with our guests'
comfort and privacy in mind. Our priority is that our guests are comfortable and enjoy a
relaxed stay."

Shawn's Inns B&B

Lyle Peterson and Kathy Watson
Mail: RR 1 Highway 1 East
Malakwa, BC V0E 2J0
(250) 836-3969
(area code 604 before October 1996)

• Twenty kilometres east of Sicamous, on Highway 1.
• Three rooms. One person $35–40. Two people
$40–45. Double bed and day bed; double bed
and single bed; two double beds and day bed.
Shared guest bathroom. Additional person $5.
Camping $5. RV hookup $15.
• A European-style house on forty acres on the Eagle River. One of the guest rooms has a
balcony; two other guest rooms have air conditioning. Close to golfing, swimming, and
houseboat rentals. Outdoor games, including horseshoes. Barbecues, fridge, and dance floor
for barn dances. Camping and RV hookups. Full breakfast. Visa. Children welcome. **In the
hosts' own words:** "Having a family reunion or another occasion? How about a barn dance
in our country setting."

Stone Castle B&B

Sherrin and Lawrence Davis
3325 Allen Frontage Road
Mail: Box 2113
Revelstoke, BC V0E 2S0
(250) 837-5266
(area code 604 before October 1996)

• Five kilometres west of Revelstoke, off Highway 1.
Six to seven hours from either Vancouver or Calgary.
• One room. One person $45, twin beds, private bathroom.
One suite. One person $65, two queen-sized beds and one twin bed, ensuite bathroom.
Additional person $15. Open December to March and June to September.
• A stone house with a hot tub and a view of Boulder Mountain. A stopover point between Vancouver and Calgary. Within walking distance of two fine dining restaurants. Within ten minutes' drive of Revelstoke, a tour of Revelstoke Dam, golfing, hiking, the Grizzly Plaza, and a train museum. In the area are downhill skiing, cross-country ski trails, and snowmobiling. Drying room for snow gear. Guest living room with TV. Suite has a sunroom. Full breakfast includes fresh fruit, homemade baked goods, muffins, and jams. Reservations recommended. Cancellation notice three days. Check-in 3:00 p.m.; check-out 11:00 a.m. Cat in residence. Smoking outdoors. **In the hosts' own words:** "We offer a warm welcome and a relaxed atmosphere."

Nehalliston Canyon Retreat B&B

Agnes and Paul Andrews
McNab Road, Nehalliston Canyon
Mail: Box 140
Little Fort, BC V0E 2C0
(250) 677-4272 Fax: (250) 677-4272
(area code 604 before October 1996)

• Six kilometres west of Little Fort, off Highway 24. Turn north onto McNab Road and continue for 3 kilometres.

• Two rooms. One person $44; two people $53–62. Queen-sized bed and one twin bed; double bed. Shared bathroom. Child 6 to 12 $10.
Two-bedroom cottage (sleeps six). Two people $71. Queen-sized bed, twin beds, and hide-a-bed. Private bathroom with shower. Additional person $20. Child 6 to 12 $10. Breakfast not included.
Canoe rentals.

• A hand-hewn log house in Nehalliston Canyon, overlooking Mount Loveway. Near hiking, walking, and a six-kilometre toboggan run. Wildlife in the area. Near lakes with rainbow trout. Canoes available for rent. One host conducts scheduled herb walks and gives Reiki sessions (an ancient healing art that relieves stress). Living room. Outdoor hot tub. Gardens with herbs and wildflowers. Two-bedroom cottage sleeps six and has cooking facilities and a wood stove. Full breakfast includes farm-fresh eggs, homemade baked goods, local wild-picked fruit in season, herbal teas, and coffees including espresso and Turkish. Breakfast for guests of the cottage is available on request. Macrobiotic breakfast available. Dinner available. Not suitable for small children. **In the hosts' own words:** "Enjoy the seclusion and peacefulness of our home."

Wooly Acres B&B

Chris Pirart and Jim Hetzler
1030 Bo Hill Place
Mail: RR 1 Box 1739
Clearwater, BC V0E 1N0
(250) 674-3508
(area code 604 before October 1996)

• Five kilometres from Highway 5. Turn onto Clearwater Valley Road (information centre on corner) and continue for 3.5 kilometres. Turn right onto Greer Road and continue for 1 kilometre. Turn right onto Bo Hill Place and continue for 500 metres to the gate. The B&B has signs on Greer Road and Bo Hill Place.

• Three rooms. One person $40; two people $58, queen-sized bed and twin beds, ensuite bathroom; two people $48, queen-sized bed and one twin bed, shared guest bathroom; two people $48, double bed and one twin bed, shared guest bathroom. Additional person $15. Child 2 to 6 $5. Child 7 to 12 $10.

• A house in the country, on ten acres with grazing sheep. Within ten minutes' drive of restaurants, shopping, and Clearwater's nine-hole golf course. Forty minutes' drive from hiking and sightseeing at Wells Gray Park. Den, yard, and gardens. Pickup from train and bus. Full breakfast, including muesli, fresh eggs, fresh berries in season, and homemade baked goods, jams and jellies, is served in the dining room. No pets; sheep, dog, and cats in residence. No smoking indoors. **In the hosts' own words:** "When visiting Clearwater, enjoy country comfort and sleep like a lamb."

Trophy Mountain Buffalo Ranch B&B

Joe and Monika Fischer
Clearwater Valley Road
Mail: Box 1768
Clearwater, BC V0E 1N0
(250) 674-3095 Fax: (250) 674-3131
(area code 604 before October 1996)

• Between Jasper and Kamloops, on Highway 5. In Clearwater, turn at the travel infocentre onto Wells Gray Park Road. Continue for 20 kilometres.

• Six rooms. One person $25–55; two people $50–60. Queen-sized bed and single bed; queen-sized bed; double bed; bunk beds. Ensuite and private bathrooms. Additional person $15–25. Children under 6 free.

• A restored 1926 log house in a quiet, rural setting. Horseback riding, hiking, biking, and cross-country skiing trails on property. Within an hour's drive of Wells Gray Provincial Park, Trophy Mountain hiking area, Helmcken Falls, canoeing, river rafting, hiking, cross-country and downhill skiing, and a shopping centre. Hosts keep bison and horses as a hobby. Hosts are outdoor adventure guides and provide information about the area and its outdoor activities. Horse, canoe, and bike rentals. Off-street parking. Visa, MasterCard. Pets welcome outside. Smoking outside.

Summit River B&B

Bill and Connie Achterberg
19345 Highway 5
Albreda, BC
Mail: Box 517
Valemount, BC V0E 2Z0
(250) 565-0396 Fax: (250) 566-4528
(area code 604 before October 1996)

• Twenty-three kilometres south of Valemount on
Yellowhead Highway 5, in Albreda.
• Five rooms. One person $50–60; two people
$60–75. Double bed and twin beds; two double beds; twin beds; two double beds and twin
beds; two double beds and one twin bed. Ensuite and private bathrooms. Additional person
$12–15. Rollaway cot available.
Twenty-three campsites. $10–15 pcr night.
Seniors' rates.
• A log house with a glacier-fed river running through the property. Fishing and gold panning in the river. Hiking, snowmobiling, and cross-country skiing on the property. Fifteen
minutes' drive from Valemount, a nature reserve, a golf course, helicopter tours, and a
salmon run in August. Forty-five minutes' drive from Robson Park. One hundred fifty kilometres west of Jasper. Hosts arrange adventure packages, including nature tours, guided
canoe trips, rafting, guided horseback riding, helicopter sightseeing tours, and golfing at an
eighteen-hole golf course. One host teaches guests tole painting on request. Twenty-three
wilderness campsites (without hook-ups) for tents and campers in a wooded area and a grass
field. Pickup from train and bus. Three of the guest rooms are wheelchair accessible. Deposit
of one night's rate to hold reservation. Visa, MasterCard. **In the hosts' own words:** "Our
area is a paradise for artists and camera enthusiasts."

Dream Catcher Inn

Noëlla and Harry Barber
310 Highway 5 North
Mail: Box 1012
Valemount, BC V0E 2Z0
(250) 566-4226 Fax: (250) 566-9128
(area code 604 before October 1996)
Toll-free from within B.C. and Alberta only:
1-800-566-9128

• Less than one-quarter kilometre north of
Valemount. Look for B&B's sign on the east side of the highway.
• Five rooms. Call for rates.
Three log cabins. In summer, one or two people $95; three to four people $110. In winter,
one or two people $75; three to four people $85. Breakfast not included.
• A B&B on ten acres in a parklike setting between three ranges of mountains—the
Cariboos, the Rockies, and the Monashees. Eighty minutes from Jasper, Alberta. Thirty minutes from Mount Robson Provincial Park's day hikes, rafting, and miniature golf. Within
walking distance of a salmon run in August, two golf courses, heli-hiking, a museum, birdwatching, snowmobile trails, and seasonal stock car races. Hosts rent bikes. Guest outdoor
hot tub. Badminton net, fire pit, covered sun deck, and heated garage for motorcycles, tents,
and snowmobiles. Children's playground. Parking. Visa, MasterCard. French spoken. **In the
hosts' own words:** "Our guest house is your home away from home. We want to share our
unique location with you. Welcome."

The Living Oasis B&B

Willis and Irene Blackman
6780 Blackman Road
Mail: Box 71
Valemount, BC V0E 2Z0
(250) 566-4274
(area code 604 before October 1996)

• From Valemount, go north on Highway 5 for 7 kilometres. Turn left onto Blackman Road and continue for 1 kilometre. Turn right at the log sign.

• Two rooms. One person $40; two people $50. Double bed, ensuite bathroom; queen-sized bed and one twin bed, private bathroom. Second room has an adjoining room with twin beds available. Additional person $10.

• A log house in a forested area with a mountain stream running through the yard. Children play in the stream and sandbox and play horseshoes. Twenty minutes from Mount Robson. Outdoor activities for people of all ages and abilities in the Robson Valley. McBride and Jasper are an hour away. Breakfast, including homemade jams, jellies, and syrups, is served in the dining area. Visa, traveller's cheques. Children welcome. Dog in residence. **In the hosts' own words:** "Our home is peaceful and comfortable. Our valley with its mountain peaks and rivers is truly an oasis for the traveller."

Brady's B&B

Alan and Mavis Brady
Mail: Box 519
Valemount, BC V0E 2Z0
(250) 566-9906
(area code 604 before October 1996)

• From Valemount, go north on Highway 5 for 7 kilometres. Turn left onto Blackman Road and continue for 5 kilometres. Turn left onto Buffalo Road. Turn right at the B&B sign.

• Two rooms and one semi-private loft. Two people $60. Queen-sized bed; two double beds. Shared guest bathroom and shared guest half bathroom.

• A log house built by the owners, on wooded acreage overlooking the McLennan River, with views of Mica Mountain and the Premier Range. Wildlife on the property. Two guest rooms have down comforters. Upstairs on a mezzanine, a semi-private loft with no door or wall on one side has two double beds. Living room with fireplace. Sun deck and backyard swimming pool. In the area are hiking, climbing, fishing, boating, river rafting, trail riding, cross-country skiing, heli-skiing, and snowmobiling. Full breakfast is served in a kitchen with a view of a field and mountains. No smoking indoors. **In the hosts' own words:** "Our home is quiet and comfortable, with spectacular views. Bring your camera; wildlife is just outside the door."

Rainbow Retreat B&B

Keith and Helen Burchnall
Mail: Box 138
Valemount, BC V0E 2Z0
(250) 566-9747 Fax: (250) 566-4528
(area code 604 before October 1996)

• Twenty kilometres north of Valemount. Half a kilometre west of the junction of the Yellowhead Highways (5 and 16). The B&B has signs on the highway and a large sign at the driveway.

• Two rooms. One person $55–60; two people $60–65. Double bed; queen-sized bed. Shared guest bathroom. Crib and highchair available. Infants free.

• A post and beam log house in old-growth forest on the western slope of the Rockies, overlooking the Cariboo Mountains. Ten minutes' walk from the Fraser River. Thirty minutes' walk from Lost Lake. Fifteen minutes' drive from Mount Robson, a world heritage site. One hour's drive from Jasper. A stopover point between Vancouver and Edmonton. Stained glass, original art, sitting/dining room, and stone fireplace. From a sun deck and a covered porch, hawks, hummingbirds, woodpeckers, swallows, and other birds can be seen among the forest trees and wildflowers. Deer, elks, bears, and other mammals often visit. One host is an experienced outdoorsperson and shares his knowledge about the history of the area. He is also a pianist and composer and plays for guests on a concert grand piano. Breakfast and dinner are served on fine china and with silver cutlery, in a licensed dining room. Diets are accommodated. Traveller's cheques, cash. Smoking outdoors. **In the hosts' own words:** "Your visit will be memorable. Be prepared to stay a while to enjoy scenic wonders, exciting activities, artists, and artisans in this easily accessible and undiscovered destination."

Blueberry Hill B&B

Marie and Mike Andrews
145 Fairview Drive
Castlegar, BC V1N 3S8
(250) 365-5583
(area code 604 before October 1996)

• Off Highway 22, 8 kilometres south of Castlegar, 18 kilometres north of Trail. Call for further directions.

• Two rooms. One person $50; two people $60. Double bed. Shared guest bathroom. Open May 1 to September 30.

• A quiet B&B on five acres with over thirty varieties of trees and a panoramic view. Sun deck. Living room with fireplace. A stopover point between Vancouver and Calgary. Hosts share their knowledge of the West Kootenays and help guests plan day trips. Breakfast includes tea or coffee, juice, home-grown fruit and preserves, cheese, and homemade blueberry muffins or waffles with blueberry topping. Adult oriented. Dog and cat in residence. No smoking indoors. **In the hosts' own words:** "Our B&B is relaxing and peaceful. Come and see for yourself."

Robson Homestead B&B

Linda and Rick Miller
3671 Broadwater Road
Robson, BC
Mail: RR 3 Site 4 C–23
Castlegar, BC V1N 4H9
(250) 365-2374 Fax: (250) 365-2374
(area code 604 before October 1996)

• Eight kilometres off Highway 3A, which joins Nelson and Castlegar. From Nelson, take the Robson turnoff and follow the signs for Syringa Creek Provincial Park. Or, from Castlegar, take Robson Bridge, and take the first left turn (towards Syringa Creek Provincial Park), which becomes Broadwater Road.

• Two rooms. One person $45; two people $55. Queen-sized bed. Shared guest bathroom. Child 6 to 12 $10. Off-season, seniors', and weekly rates.

• A restored 1909 house with antique-furnished guest rooms, on three acres across from the Columbia River. Ten minutes' drive from the Hugh Keenleyside Dam, Castlegar, the Doukhobor Museum, Pass Creek and Syringa Creek provincial parks, Selkirk College, golf course, airport, Arrow Lake, and marinas. On bus route. In the area are mountain biking, hiking, cycling, fishing, and wildlife viewing. Trail rides at a nearby stable. Forty-five minutes from cross-country skiing and three downhill ski areas. Pickup from plane. Babysitting by arrangement. Full breakfast includes fruit in season and homemade baked goods. Vegetarian, low-fat, and low-salt diets accommodated. Reservations and deposits recommended. Cash, cheques, traveller's cheques. Children welcome. No pets; goats, horse, and dog on property. Smoke-free environment. **In the hosts' own words:** "A warm Kootenay welcome awaits you."

Inn the Garden B&B

Lynda Stevens and Jerry Van Veen
408 Victoria Street
Nelson, BC V1L 4K5
(250) 352-3226 Fax: (250) 352-3284
(area code 604 before October 1996)

- Downtown, one block south of Baker Street, between Stanley and Ward streets.
- Five rooms. One person $65–80; two people $70–90. Queen-sized bed; double bed. Ensuite, private, and shared guest bathrooms. Additional person $15.
Suite. One person $100; two people $110. Additional person $20–25.
Ski and golf packages.
- A restored Victorian house with plants, wicker, and antiques. Two minutes' walk from shopping, restaurants, and theatre. Lake and mountain views, terraced front garden, and guest lounge. A seven-hundred-square-foot suite has a private entrance and is suitable for groups. In the area are historical walking tours, hiking, golfing, fishing, canoeing, and downhill and cross-country skiing. Off-street parking and ski/golf/bike storage facilities. Full, varied breakfast is served in an old-fashioned dining room. Check-in 4:00 to 8:00 p.m. Visa, MasterCard, American Express. Adult oriented. No pets. No smoking. **In the hosts' own words:** "We offer bright, comfortable rooms, modern amenities, and a friendly atmosphere, in our elegant turn-of-the-century heritage house."

Three B's Balfour B&B

Austen and Dianne Megyesi
7722 Highway 3A
Mail: Box 73
Balfour, BC V0G 1C0
(250) 229-5223 Fax: (250) 229-5223
(area code 604 before October 1996)

- Half an hour east of Nelson.
- Three rooms. One person $35; two people $60, queen-sized bed, ensuite bathroom; two people $55, double bed, shared guest bathroom; two people $55, twin beds, shared guest bathroom. Off-season rates.
- A country-style B&B overlooking Kootenay Lake, with lake access. Five minutes from golfing, fishing, and boating. Twenty minutes from hot springs. A few blocks from Kootenay Lake ferry. Near hiking. Hot tub. Guest rooms open onto a guest sitting area, which has books and a view of the lake. Full breakfast is served in the dining room. Cancellation notice two days. Cash. No pets. No smoking. **In the hosts' own words:** "Come and explore the beautiful Kootenay country. Our visits over breakfast are fantastic."

Trafalgar Mountain B&B

Barbara Neelands
Mail: Box 1079
Kaslo, BC V0G 1M0
(250) 353-7151
(area code 604 before October 1996)

• Ten kilometres north of Ainsworth Hot Springs; 10 kilometres south of Kaslo.
• Two rooms. One person $35–45; two people $45–55. Queen-sized bed, ensuite bathroom; double bed, shared bathroom. Child 6 to 12 $10.
• A log house in a rural setting, near Fletcher Falls and a beach on Kootenay Lake. Main-floor guest room has a queen-sized bed and an ensuite bathroom. Upstairs guest room has a shared bathroom with an old-fashioned bathtub and an antique dresser sink. Nine kilometres by four-wheel-drive vehicle from the trailheads of Woodbury Creek and Cody Caves. Fifteen minutes' drive from restaurants, Kaslo's historical Moyie Sternwheeler, and Ainsworth Hot Springs and hot mineral water caves. Full breakfast includes fruit from the garden in season. **In the hosts' own words:** "Huckleberry pancakes are a specialty."

The Beach House

Robert Wilson
5834 Morgan Road
Mirror Lake
Mail: Box 1375
Kaslo, BC V0G 1M0
(250) 353-7676 Fax: (250) 353-7676
(area code 604 before October 1996)

• Three kilometres south of Kaslo at Mirror Lake. The B&B is a yellow house.
• Three rooms. One person $55; two people $65–75. Queen-sized bed; double bed; twin beds. Private and shared guest bathrooms. Additional person $15.
• A newly renovated 1920s house with covered porch and sun decks, on Kootenay Lake. Close to hiking, bicycling, and boating. Three minutes' drive from Kaslo. Ten minutes' drive from Ainsworth hot springs. Full breakfast. Adult oriented. Smoke-free environment. **In the hosts' own words:** "Come and enjoy this spectacular setting on Kootenay Lake. Water, mountains, sky, and sunglasses all served daily with a delicious breakfast."

Three Maples B&B

Ann Barkley
710 Arthur Street
Mail: Box 270
Slocan, BC V0G 2C0
(250) 355-2586
(area code 604 before October 1996)

• Seventy kilometres north of Nelson and Castlegar. Follow Highway 6 to the south end of Slocan Lake.

• Two rooms. One person $40; two people $45. Ensuite and private bathrooms.

• A B&B in a small village at the south end of Slocan Lake in the Slocan Valley, at the trailhead to Valhalla Wilderness Park. Backpacking, hiking, and cycling from the B&B. Five minutes' walk from boating, fishing, and swimming on Slocan Lake. Fifteen minutes' drive from a nine-hole golf course. An hour's drive from Nelson's restaurants, art galleries, and historical sites. The garden has a swing, a pond, and a gazebo. Light or full breakfast, including homemade jams and breads and fresh fruit in season, is served at a table set with crystal and period collectibles. Not suitable for children. No pets. No smoking indoors. **In the hosts' own words:** "Spend a relaxing night in the quiet village of Slocan and enjoy a delicious breakfast."

Mistaya Country Inn and Horseback Adventures

Sue and George Iverson
Mail: Box 28
Silverton, BC V0G 2B0
(250) 358-7787 Fax: (250) 358-7787
(area code 604 before October 1996)

• On Highway 6. Ten kilometres south of Silverton. Ninety kilometres north of Nelson.

• Five rooms. One person $45–50; two people $60–65. Double bed; queen-sized bed; twin beds. Shared guest bathrooms. Additional person $15. Riding lessons, trail rides, and three- to five-day pack trips.

• A lodge with walking trails on ninety acres in the Slocan Valley, between Valhalla and Kokanee Glacier parks. Guest sitting room with fireplace. A base from which to explore nearby ghost towns and old mining trails of the Selkirk Mountains. A few minutes' drive from Slocan Lake, hiking, golfing, and cross-country skiing. Fire pit. Full breakfast. Visa, MasterCard. No pets. Smoking on the porch.

Mountainberry B&B

Don and Debbie Law
Highway 6
Mail: Box 37
New Denver, BC V0G 1S0
(250) 358-2584
(area code 604 before October 1996)

● One hundred kilometres north of Nelson, 220 kilometres east of Vernon, and 60 kilometres southeast of Nakusp.

● One room. One person $65; two people $75. Minimum stay two nights. Guided adventure travel packages. Barbecue and dinner packages. Complimentary passes to a hot spring with packages booked before June.

● A B&B in the Slocan Valley, surrounded by mountain trails, peaks, streams, and wildflowers. Slocan Lake, which is bordered by Valhalla Wilderness Park, is a one-minute walk away. Two blocks from New Denver's historical main street, museums, small art and craft shops, and cafés. The Slocan Valley area has a rich history of silver mining. The nearby ghost town of Sandon had streetcars and hydroelectric power in the 1890s. The B&B has cedar décor. Sitting room on the upper level has a fireplace. Guided adventure travel tours and other activity packages include kayaking and canoeing on Slocan Lake; fishing, touring, and sunbathing on a twenty-five-horsepower Yamaha touring boat on Slocan Lake; guided hiking, cat skiing, and backcountry skiing; a historical tour of Sandon and Sandon Museum; a barbecue on the beach; and dinner for two. In the area are a lookout on Idaho Peak, golfing at Slocan Lake Golf Club, and mountain biking along the old narrow-gauge Kaslo and Slocan railway bed. Breakfast includes bagels and cheese, fresh fruit, crêpes or bacon and eggs, juice, coffee, and butter tarts. **In the hosts' own words:** "We invite you to Kootenay country, and we look forward to helping you plan your vacation activities."

Margo's Sunny Hill B&B

Margot and Wolfgang Haerter
357 Shakespeare Road
Mail: Box 64
Nakusp, BC V0G 1R0
(250) 265-4502 Fax: (250) 265-4502
(area code 604 before October 1996)

- One kilometre from downtown Nakusp.
- Suite (sleeps up to six). Two people $50. Bathroom in suite. Family and weekly rates.
- A quiet B&B three minutes from beaches, fishing, and boating on Arrow Lake and fifteen kilometres from Nakusp Hotsprings. New suite with kitchen, TV, and VCR. Garden area with barbecue facilities. Near fishing lakes and a nine-hole golf course. Hot springs passes. Within driving distance of cross-country ski trails and downhill ski slopes. Choice of breakfasts. German spoken. No pets inside. No smoking. **In the hosts' own words:** "Join us in the sunny and quiet Glennbank area."

Country B&B

John and Elena Walker
1012 Highway 6 East
Mail: Box 24
Nakusp, BC V0G 1R0
(250) 265-4448
(area code 604 before October 1996)

- Five kilometres from downtown Nakusp.
- Three rooms. One person $35; two people $45, double bed; two people $50, twin beds. Shared guest bathroom. Young child $10. Closed Friday nights. Accommodation for horses available.
- A quiet B&B on forty-five acres, with a mountain view, five kilometres from downtown Nakusp, one kilometre from a golf course, two kilometres from a cross-country ski area, twelve kilometres from downhill skiing, and seventeen kilometres from a hot springs. Guest sitting room with phone, TV, VCR, radio, books, and piano. Dry room for hikers and skiers to hang gear in. Bathrobes provided. Separate ground-floor entrance. Indoor parking. Guest fridge; ice available for coolers. Shady outdoor picnic area. Outdoor railed paddocks available for guests travelling with horses. Biking, hiking, cross-country skiing, and riding trails from the front yard. Full breakfast, including homemade bread and jams, fresh eggs, beef bacon, and fruit and berries in season, is served in the formal dining room or in the kitchen. Vegetarian and other diets are accommodated. Traveller's cheques, personal cheques, cash. Children welcome. No pets. Non-smoking house; smoking outside in designated area.

Paradise Lodging

Edmund Eckert
4820 Highway 6
Mail: Box 154
Burton, BC V0G 1E0
(250) 265-4379 Fax: (250) 265-4379
(area code 604 before October 1996)

• Thirty kilometres south of Nakusp, on Highway 6.

• Room. One person $35; two people $40. Double bed, ensuite bathroom.

Two-bedroom suite. Three people $70. Queen-sized bed, one twin bed, and double sofa bed. Bathroom in suite.

Self-contained two-bedroom log house. Four people $100. Queen-sized bed and twin beds. Additional person $10. Minimum stay two days. Weekly rate $600.

• A house and a guest house on twenty-five acres on Arrow Lake, between Nakusp and Burton, with views of forest, lake, and mountains. Two-bedroom suite has a living room with a double sofa bed. Guest dining/sitting room. Use of kitchen and coffee bar. German spoken. No pets. No smoking. **In the hosts' own words:** "The beautiful views from both our romantic guest house and our inviting main house contribute to a peaceful holiday experience."

Tara Shanti Retreat B&B

John and Marie Wells
134 Riondel Road
Mail: Box 77
Kootenay Bay, BC V0B 1X0
(250) 227-9616 Fax: (250) 227-9617
(area code 604 before October 1996)
Toll-free: 1-800-811-3888

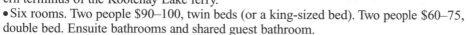

• Seventy-five minutes' drive north of Creston, along Highway 3A. Five minutes from the eastern terminus of the Kootenay Lake ferry.

• Six rooms. Two people $90–100, twin beds (or a king-sized bed). Two people $60–75, double bed. Ensuite bathrooms and shared guest bathroom. Off-season rates.

• A lodgelike wood and brick house built on five wooded acres at the foot of the Purcell Mountains, with a view of Kootenay Lake and Kokanee Glacier. Near hiking, bicycling, boating, swimming, fishing, and golfing. Ten minutes from Kokanee Springs golf course. Car ferry across Kootenay Lake from Nelson, Kaslo, and Ainsworth Hot Springs is free. Sun deck, den, living room, upstairs reading lounge, wood-fired sauna, and jetted hot tub. One of the guest rooms is suitable for families. Breakfast includes a choice of egg dishes, homemade bread, waffles, fresh fruit, juice, fresh-ground coffee, and tea. Visa, MasterCard. Families welcome. Dog in residence. Smoking outdoors. **In the hosts' own words:** "Our guests are invited to lounge on the sun deck and relax in the inviting fireside den, spacious living room, and comfortable upstairs reading lounge."

Wedgwood Manor Country Inn

Joan Huiberts and John Edwards
16002 Crawford Creek Road
Mail: Box 135
Crawford Bay, BC V0B 1E0
(250) 227-9233
(area code 604 before October 1996)

• Crawford Bay is 80 kilometres north of Creston, on Highway 3A. Crawford Creek Road leaves Highway 3A at the southern edge of Crawford Bay, 7 kilometres from the Kootenay Lake ferry.

• Six rooms. One person $79; two people $79–105. Queen-sized bed; double bed. Ensuite bathrooms. Additional adult or child $20. Open April 15 to October 15. Golf packages and Ainsworth Hot Springs packages.

• A country inn built at the turn of the century by the Wedgwood China family, on fifty acres at the foot of the Purcell Mountains. Across the road from Kokanee Springs golf course. A few minutes from beaches, fishing, and boating on Kootenay Lake. Wilderness hiking, walking, and biking from the B&B. Landscaped grounds and gardens. Library and sitting room. Guest rooms have Victorian furnishings. One is a honeymoon suite. Some have Jacuzzis. Some have fireplaces. One is wheelchair accessible. Tea and snacks served any time. Visa, MasterCard. **In the hosts' own words:** "Snuggle up in the library, sip tea by the parlour fireplace, stroll the garden paths. Our goal is to make you welcome in the most restful and beautiful surroundings."

Heighes' House B&B

Gaytha and Jim Heighes
306 Tenth Avenue North
Mail: Box 3245
Creston, BC V0B 1G0
(250) 428-9905 Fax: (250) 428-9905
(area code 604 before October 1996)
Toll-free from within B.C. and the U.S.: 1-800-249-4343

• From Highway 3 (also called Canyon Street), turn north onto Tenth Avenue. Continue for one long block. The B&B is just past the town hall.

• Three rooms. One person $55, two people $65, queen-sized bed, shared guest bathroom; one person $55, two people $80, queen-sized bed, single day bed, shared guest bathroom (private bathroom can be arranged); one person $70, two people $100, two double beds, ensuite bathroom. Reduced rates on stays of more than three nights.

• A house built in 1939 for the town judge, with a view of the town of Creston, the Creston Valley, and the Selkirk Mountains. Five minutes' walk from restaurants and shopping. Fifteen minutes' drive from hiking, canoeing, birdwatching in the Creston Valley Wildlife Management Area, golfing, and river cruises. Golf and cruises can be arranged by the hosts. An hour and a half's drive from the world's longest free ferry ride. The house is furnished with antiques and collectibles and has a fireplace, a flower garden, fruit trees, a nature walk, a patio, a veranda, a bistro deck, and a water garden. Each guest room has a TV and VCR. Books and videos available. Robes and slippers provided. Tea or lemonade is served when guests arrive. Bedtime snacks. Before breakfast, coffee or tea is served on trays in guests' rooms or on the veranda. Full breakfast includes homemade baked goods and preserves, fruit, meat, cheese, and farm eggs. Vegetarian breakfast available. Visa, MasterCard. Children welcome by arrangement. Pets can be boarded nearby. Smoking outside. **In the hosts' own words:** "Welcome to our home, our hospitality, and extra special touches."

Kootenay Kountry B&B

Brian and Dianne Grant
220 Eleventh Avenue North
Mail: Box 1368
Creston, BC V0B 1G0
(250) 428-7494
(area code 604 before October 1996)

• From Highway 3 (Canyon Street), turn north onto Eleventh Avenue. Watch for the B&B's signs on the right.

• Three rooms. One person $40-55; two people $55-65. Queen-sized bed; double bed; twin beds. Private bathroom and shared guest bathroom. Additional person $12.

• A quiet B&B in the centre of Creston, with flower gardens, a gazebo, and heritage-style guest rooms. Eight kilometres from hiking, canoeing, and birdwatching in the Creston Valley Wildlife Management Area, a wetland preserve. Ten minutes from the eighteen-hole Creston Golf Course, the Kokanee Brewery, which gives free tours, and the Wayside Gardens Arboretum. Twenty minutes south of Kootenay Lake. Twenty minutes north of the Idaho border. Ninety minutes from Nelson. Two and a half hours from Spokane, Washington. Two of the guest rooms have TVs. Full breakfast, including fresh fruit in season and home-made preserves, is served in the dining room. Not suitable for small children or pets. No smoking. **In the hosts' own words:** "Weary travellers will find an oasis in the heart of the Creston Valley."

Sweetapple B&B

Gilbert and Elspeth Doull
3939 Highway 3 East
Mail: Box 93
Erickson, BC V0B 1K0
(250) 428-7205 Fax: (250) 428-7205
(area code 604 before October 1996)

• Between Creston and Cranbrook, 5 kilometres east of Creston.

• Two rooms. One person $40; two people $50. Queen-sized bed; double bed and one twin bed. Shared guest bathroom and half bathroom. Additional person $10. Seniors' rates. Golf packages.

• A modern house with a view of the Skimmerhorn mountains and the Goat River Valley. Guest entrance, guest balcony, and guest sitting room with TV, wood stove, books, and puzzles. Line-dried linen. Snacks and beverages. Picnic area and fire pit. Guest hot tub available October to April. The hosts are golfers and offer golf packages. Full breakfast includes fruit in season, farm-fresh eggs, homemade baked goods, and jams.

Singing Pines B&B

Sandra and Robert Dirom
5180 Kennedy Road
Mail: SS 3 Site 15 Box A-9
Cranbrook, BC V1C 6H3
(250) 426-5959 Fax: (250) 426-5959
(area code 604 before October 1996)
Toll-free: 1-800-863-4969

• At Cranbrook, take the airport/Kimberley exit
to Highway 95A. Four kilometres north, turn
right onto Kennedy Road. Continue for 700
metres. The B&B is the second driveway on the right.
• Three rooms. One person $55–65; two people $60–75. Queen-sized bed; two queen-sized
beds. Ensuite and private bathrooms. Additional person $20. Off-season and weekly rates.
• A modern rancher on ten acres, with views of the Rocky Mountains to the east and the
Purcell Mountains to the west. Eclectic furnishings. Guest rooms are on the main floor. Two
of the guest rooms have patio doors that open onto a deck. Three to twenty-five kilometres
from five golf courses, two of which are executive par three. Fifteen minutes from Fort Steele
Heritage Town. Twenty-five minutes from downhill and cross-country skiing at Kimberley.
Seventy minutes from Fernie Snow Valley. Guest outdoor hot tub. Breakfast, with a varied
menu and choices offered, is served (in summer) on a covered deck with a view of the Rocky
Mountains, at guests' convenience. Dinner available on request. Deposit of one night's rate
required to hold reservation. Cancellation notice seven days. Cash, traveller's cheques, Visa,
MasterCard. Adult oriented. No pets; dog in residence and wildlfe in area. Smoking on deck.
In the hosts' own words: "Our B&B has a warm, friendly atmosphere. We take pleasure in
sharing our home and the beauty of our natural setting."

Cranberry House B&B

Gloria Murray
321 Cranbrook Street North
Cranbrook, BC V1C 3R4
(250) 489-6216 Fax: (250) 489-6216
(area code 604 before October 1996)

• Four rooms. One person $55–60; two people
$60–70. Queen-sized bed, ensuite bathroom;
twin beds, shared guest bathroom.
• A B&B with a hot tub, three blocks from downtown Cranbrook. Guest rooms have duvets, per-
cale linen, and TVs. Fax and secretarial service available. Central air conditioning. Paved
parking. Breakfast includes fresh-ground coffee, purified water, and homemade jams, bread,
and homemade baked goods. Deposit of one night's rate required to hold reservation.
Cancellation notice seven days. Visa, MasterCard, American Express. Smoking on the patio.
In the hosts' own words: "Old-fashioned comfort in a heritage house. A warm welcome
awaits you."

Kootenay Hills B&B

Roxsane Tanner
69 Cross Road South
Mail: RR 2 Site 13-14
Cranbrook, BC V1C 4H3
(250) 489-3611 Fax: (250) 489-3611
(area code 604 before October 1996)

• Five minutes from downtown Cranbrook. Take the Jim Smith Lake Road exit and cross the railroad tracks. Watch for the B&B's sign. Follow the sign's arrows and continue straight for fifty metres. Behind the Canadian Helicopter pad, turn right onto Cross Road South. Go 1 kilometre. The B&B is on the left.

• Three rooms. One person $45–55; two people $50–60. Queen-sized bed; double bed; twin beds. Shared guest bathroom.

• A country house on a hillside overlooking Cranbrook, with a panoramic view of the Rocky Mountains. Fifteen minutes from Fort Steele Heritage Village. Twenty minutes from Kimberley. Living room with fireplace. Guests watch the city lights at night from a covered veranda. Guest entrance. Close to swimming, canoeing, and fishing in nearby lakes; hiking; biking; golfing; and skiing. Breakfast includes farm-fresh eggs, fresh fruit, and homemade baked goods and preserves and is served in the country kitchen or on the veranda, both of which have mountain views. Visa, MasterCard. Some German spoken. Adult oriented. No pets. Smoke-free environment. **In the hosts' own words:** "Peace and tranquillity with a view. Relax in our décor of pine and soft comforters."

Mountain Magic Ventures

Gordon Burns and Sue Boyd
Wardner Road
Mail: Box 94
Wardner, BC V0B 2J0
(250) 429-3958 Fax: (250) 429-3958
(area code 604 before October 1996)

• In the East Kootenays. From Cranbrook, go east on Highway 3 for 35 kilometres. Turn right onto Wardner Road and continue south for 1 kilometre.

• Two cabins. One person $59; two people $69. Private bathrooms. Additional person $15. Guided adventure travel packages.

• Two log cabins separate from the hosts' ranch house, with views of the Rockies, on six hundred acres on the shore of the Kootenay River. Cabins have wood stoves and sun decks. Walking and hiking trails on the property. The hosts offer guided trail riding, sleigh rides, and extended backcountry packhorse trips, and they offer both guided and unguided canoeing, fishing, mountain biking, hiking, and cross-country skiing. The ranch has a volleyball court, a basketball hoop, a games room, and a horseshoe pit. Forty minutes' drive from Fernie Snow Valley and Kimberley Ski and Summer Resort. Cat-skiing packages can be arranged. Choice of Continental breakfast served in the cabins or full breakfast, including farm-fresh eggs and homemade baked goods, served in the ranch house dining room or on the sun deck. **In the hosts' own words:** "We offer western hospitality."

Wild Horse Farm

Bob and Orma Termuende
Mail: Box 7
Fort Steele, BC V0B 1N0
(250) 426-6000 Fax: (250) 426-6083
(area code 604 before October 1996)

• Twelve minutes north of Cranbrook. On Highway 93/95, across from Fort Steele Heritage Town.

• Two rooms and one self-contained suite. One person $58–75; two people $75–97. King-sized bed; queen-sized bed; extra-long twin beds. Ensuite bathroom and shared guest bathroom and half bathroom. Additional person $25.

• A two-storey log-faced house built by the New York Astors in the early 1900s, on eighty acres of meadows, woodlands, and gardens. Five fieldstone fireplaces, high ceilings, antique furnishings, and screened verandas. Living room with player piano, games tables, books, TV, VCR, and CD player. Self-contained two-storey suite has a bedroom with queen-sized bed, an ensuite bathroom with bathtub and hand-held shower, kitchen facilities, a sitting/dining room with TV, and a private entrance. In the area are hiking, fishing, and boating. Near golf courses and tennis courts. Coffee or tea is brought to guest rooms and suite before breakfast. Full breakfast, including fresh fruit, farm produce, and homemade muffins, is served in the dining room. Cancellation notice ten days. Visa. **In the hosts' own words:** "Step back to a time of leisure and luxury at our secluded, parklike estate in the Rocky Mountains."

Emery's Mountain View B&B

John and Joanna Emery
Wardner–Fort Steele Road
Mail: Box 60
Fort Steele, BC V0B 1N0
(250) 426-4756
(area code 604 before October 1996)

• Two kilometres from Fort Steele. Twenty minutes from Cranbrook. At the Fort Steele gas station, turn onto the Wardner–Fort Steele Road. Go downhill to a small bridge over Wild Horse Creek. The B&B is 1 kilometre from the bridge, on the right.

• Three rooms. One person $40–65; two people $55–80. Twin beds, shared guest bathroom; king-sized bed, shared guest bathroom; queen-sized bed, private bathroom. Additional person $15. Cot available.

• A new house on thirty-six acres, with views of mountains and cliffs. Guests watch sunrises, sunsets, and stars from porches and patios. At Wild Horse Creek, guests fish, look for gold dust, and watch Kokanee spawn. Birds and animals, including occasional bears, can be seen foraging for food in a marsh twenty-five metres below the property. Coal trains pass by quietly. Near historical attractions, mountain hiking trails, lakes, hot springs, golf courses, and ski hills. One of the guest rooms has a sitting room, cooking facilities, and a private entrance. Full breakfast. Most diets are accommodated. Visa. No pets; dog in residence. Non-smoking house. **In the hosts' own words:** "Come and enjoy tranquillity, relaxed atmosphere, panoramic scenery, friendly hospitality, and a tasty breakfast."

Wasa Lakeside B&B

James and Mary Swansburg
Spruce Road
Mail: Box 122
Wasa, BC V0B 2K0
(250) 422-3688 or (250) 422-3551
Fax: (250) 422-3551
(area code 604 before October 1996)
E-mail: swanys@cyberlink.bc.ca
Web site: http://www.cyberlink.bc.ca/~swanys/

• Thirty-two kilometres north of Cranbrook on the northwest side of Wasa Lake. From Highway 93/95, turn east at the north exit onto Wasa Lake Park Drive and continue for one block. Turn south onto Poplar Road, and continue for three blocks. Turn east onto Spruce Road and continue for 100 metres. The B&B is the peach and white house on the lake side of the road.

• Three rooms. One person $40; two people $80. Queen-sized bed. Shared guest bathroom and half bathroom.

Water skiing and Hobie Cat sailing rentals.

Rides and retrievals for hang glider and paraglider pilots.

Golf, skiing, and adventure travel packages.

• A newly renovated B&B on the shore of Wasa Lake with a private sandy beach, a dock, a water-ski boat, a sailboat, a pedal boat, canoes, and beginner windsurfers. Six-person outdoor hot tub on the beach and two warm-water beach showers. One-thousand-square-foot glassed-in veranda with books and ping-pong table. Media room with TV, two VCRs, CD stereo, and slide projector. Bicycles, canoe, beach toys, swing set, volleyball, and trampoline. The hosts arrange adventure travel packages. Near golf, hot springs, birdwatching, gold panning, fishing and ice fishing, skating, snowmobiling, and cross-country and downhill skiing. Full breakfast is served on a beachside patio or in a formal dining room. Guests use beachside kitchen, barbecue, and fire pit to prepare additional meals. Deposit of 50 percent required to hold reservation. Check-in between 4:00 and 8:00 p.m.; check-out by 11:00 a.m. Visa, MasterCard, American Express, traveller's cheques, personal cheques, cash. Children welcome. No smoking in buildings. **In the hosts' own words:** "Wasa Lake is an undiscovered jewel in the massive Rocky Mountains. Small, shallow, and clean, it is the warmest lake in the region and is surrounded by a recreation paradise. Stay on our sandy beach with its awesome view and enjoy all the comforts of home."

Boundary Street House B&B

Dorothy Robinson and Gerry Wheatcroft
89 Boundary Street
Kimberley, BC V1A 2H4
(250) 427-3510
(area code 604 before October 1996)

• One block from downtown Kimberley. From
the post office, go three blocks north on
Wallinger Avenue and turn left onto Boundary
Street.

• Two rooms. One person $40–50; two people
$45–55. Queen-sized bed. Shared guest bathroom. Additional person $15.
Golf and ski packages.

• A restored English cottage–style house, built circa 1920, decorated and furnished with
family heirlooms and antiques. Guest rooms and guest sitting room are on the main floor.
One block from the city centre, a Bavarian pedestrian mall, shops, galleries, and restaurants.
Five minutes' drive from two eighteen-hole golf courses and downhill and cross-country
skiing. Full breakfast. Visa. Adult oriented. No pets. Smoking outside. **In the hosts' own
words:** "Our goal is to provide guests with a relaxed setting, steeped in the traditions of a
bygone era, from which they can enjoy the activities and sights Kimberley has to offer."

McMillan Chalet B&B

Ken and Bonnie McMillan
5021 Fairmont Close
Mail: Box 504
Fairmont Hot Springs, BC V0B 1L0
(250) 345-9553
(area code 604 before October 1996)
In winter: (403) 934-5291

• Off Highway 93, at Fairmont Hot Springs. Turn
left behind Fairmont Grocery and then take two
immediate right turns. The B&B is at the southeast corner of Fairmont Close.

• Three rooms. One person $42–67; two people $52–77. Private bathroom
and shared guest bathroom. Additional person $20. Child 3 to 10 $10.

• A B&B near Windermere and Columbia lakes, at the foot of the hill leading to Fairmont
Hot Springs, near five golf courses—Mountainside, Riverside, Radium's two courses, and
Windermere Valley. Skiing at Fairmont's ski hill and at Panorama, half an hour away, and
Kimberley, an hour away. Two hours from Fernie and Lake Louise. Fine dining at Fairmont
Hot Springs Resort. Some guest rooms have TVs and sofa beds. One of the guest rooms is
a loft with a sitting area and a private bathroom. Breakfast is served in the dining area.
Deposit of one night's rate required to hold reservation. Cancellation notice seven days.
Cash, Visa, MasterCard. No pets. Smoking on deck and porch. **In the hosts' own words:** "A
warm welcome—come, relax, and enjoy the scenic Windermere Valley."

Emerald Grove Estate

Lorraine Klassen and Glenda Lindsay
1265 Sunridge Road
Mail: Box 627
Windermere, BC V0B 2L0
(250) 342-4431 Fax: (250) 342-4456
(area code 604 before October 1996)

- Off Highway 93/95, south of Radium Hot Springs. Between Radium and Fairmont hot springs.
- Rooms. Two people $80–100. Queen-sized bed. Ensuite bathrooms.
Suite. Four people $140.
Additional person $20. Child 6 to 12 $15. Children under 6 free.
Honeymoon packages.
- A new house on three wooded acres in the Columbia Valley, with views of the Purcell Mountains, Lake Windermere, Mount Swansen, and the Rocky Mountains. A few minutes from golf courses, swimming, fishing, sailing, boating, miniature golf, and horseback riding. Five minutes from shops, a museum, theatre, and restaurants in Invermere on the Lake. A few minutes from glass blowing, wood working, and other artists' studios in Windermere. Downhill skiing, cross-country skiing, heli-skiing, and curling bonspiel. Close to Panorama Resort and Fairmont Resort. Suite with loft and private entrance is suitable for families. One ground-floor guest room accommodates wheelchairs. Two bathrooms have double Jacuzzi tubs. Upper balcony and lower deck. Hosts help guests arrange small functions and wedding ceremonies. Full or Continental breakfast. Deposit of one night's rate required to hold reservation. Cancellation notice seven days. Check-in 2:00 to 4:00 p.m.; check-out 11:00 a.m. Cash, traveller's cheques, Visa, MasterCard, Diners Club/enRoute. A non-smoking house. **In the host's own words:** "You will be enveloped in hospitality from the moment you are greeted at the front entrance and are welcomed into the elegant foyer with its curved staircase and comfortable surroundings. Our house was designed for your enjoyment, to offer you the ultimate in comfort and privacy."

Windermere Creek B&B

Scott and Astrid MacDonald
1658 Windermere Loop Road
Mail: Box 409
Windermere, BC V0B 2L0
(250) 342-0356 Fax: (250) 342-0356
(area code 604 before October 1996)

• From Windermere, go south on Highway 95/93 for 1 kilometre to the south end of Windermere Loop Road. Turn left and follow the loop road past Windermere Valley Golf Course. The B&B is the third house on the right, 1.5 kilometres past the golf course entrance.

• Three rooms. $60–75. Queen-sized bed. Private and shared guest bathrooms. Three cabins. $90. Queen-sized bed. Private bathroom.

• A B&B on 107 forested acres with lawns, gardens, five hours of walking trails, a heated pool, creekside hammocks, beaver ponds, and picnic and lookout spots. Guided nature walks daily. Guest rooms are on the main floor. Living room with fireplace, dining room, sunroom with deck, and breakfast nook with wood stove in the main house. Guest cabin built in 1887 has been refurbished. Two new cabins. Bathrooms in cabins have Jacuzzi tubs. Near Radium Hot Springs and Fairmont Hot Springs, which have pools and golfing. Five minutes' drive from Invermere on the Lake and Windermere's public beach and art shops. Picnic lunches available. Full buffet breakfast. Not suitable for children. Smoking restricted. **In the hosts' own words:** "Abundant wildlife and hospitality will make this the highlight of your trip."

Delphine Lodge

Anne and David Joy
Mail: Box 2797
Invermere, BC V0A 1K0
(250) 342-6851
(area code 604 before October 1996)

• Five kilometres north of Invermere, in Wilmer, B.C., on the corner of Main and Wells streets.

• Six rooms in a lodge separate from the hosts' house. One person $45; two people $60–75. Queen-sized bed; double bed; twin bed; one double bed and one twin bed. Ensuite and shared guest bathrooms. Additional person $20. Child under 11 $10.

• A restored lodge, separate from the hosts' house, on an acre of gardens, in a small rural village in the Windermere Valley. The lodge has quilts, lace curtains, early Canadian antiques, and a double-sided stone fireplace. Hiking, mountain biking, and cross-country skiing from the B&B. Five kilometres from Lake Windermere. Twelve kilometres from Panorama Ski Resort. Birdwatching in the area. Breakfast includes homemade baked goods, eggs, and fruit. Visa. Cat in residence. No smoking. **In the hosts' own words:** "Our lodge has an outstanding garden. Guests relax, surrounded by majestic mountains."

Columbia Valley Lodge

Erwin Perzinger
2304 Highway 95 South
Mail: Box 2669 E
Golden, BC V0A 1H0
(250) 348-2508 Fax: (250) 348-2508
(area code 604 before October 1996)

• From Golden, go south on Highway 95 for 23
kilometres (twenty minutes). The lodge is on the
right.
• Twelve rooms. One person $40–45; two people
$55–60. Private bathrooms. Additional person $10. Fresh fruit, a muffin or toast, and
juices are served; full breakfast is available for an additional charge. Seniors' discount 10
percent. Off-season rates. Weekly rates. Closed November and April.
• A European-style lodge on eighty acres, surrounded by the Rocky and Purcell mountains
and the Columbia Valley Wetlands. Birdwatching, canoeing, mountain biking, cross-country
skiing, and exploring the wetlands. Within two hours' drive of four national parks—Banff,
Yoho, Kootenay, and Glacier. Some guest rooms are on the ground floor, and some are
upstairs. Some have TVs, and some have private balconies. Sitting room has books, magazines, information on local hiking trails, a TV, and a VCR. A licensed dining room has
European and Canadian specials; the host, an Austrian chef, accommodates guests' requests.
Fresh fruit, a muffin or toast, and juices are served; full breakfast is available for an additional charge. Cancellation notice three days. Visa, MasterCard. Some non-smoking guest
rooms. No pets. **In the hosts' own words:** "We offer a relaxed and friendly atmosphere—
just the place to get away from it all."

McLaren Lodge

George and Lou McLaren
Mail: Box 2586
Golden, BC V0A 1H0
(250) 344-6133 Fax: (250) 344-7650
(area code 604 before October 1996)

• Off Highway 1, on the eastern limits of
Golden. Forty-five minutes from Lake Louise,
Alberta.
• Ten rooms. One person $50–55; two people
$60–68. Queen-sized bed; twin beds. Ensuite
bathrooms.
Flatwater beginner kayaking trips. Whitewater rafting trips.
Four-wheel-drive all-terrain vehicle mountain trail tours.
• A log house between the Purcell and Rocky Mountain ranges, with views of the Columbia
Valley and the Kicking Horse River Valley. Forty-five minutes' drive from Lake Louise.
Lounge with books, wood stove, and TV. Sun decks and garden gazebo. Near hiking,
horseback riding, golfing, scenic water tours, hang gliding, and parasailing. Whitewater
rafting trips leave daily from the lodge. Adult oriented. No pets. Smoking outdoors. **In the
hosts' own words:** "We invite you to stay a while and enjoy the mountain beauty."

Kelly Lake Ranch B&B

Mrs. Karin H. Lange
Kelly Lake Road
Mail: Box 547
Clinton, BC V0K 1K0
(250) 459-2313 Fax: (250) 459-2313
(area code 604 before October 1996)

• Seventeen kilometres west of Clinton on paved road. The B.C. Rail train stops at Kelly Lake.

• Ranch house rooms. One person $40–45. Queen-sized bed; twin beds. Shared guest bathroom. Additional person $10.

Three log cabins. Two people $60–70. Shared guest showers in separate cabin. Additional person $10. Minimum stay two days.

Winter and extended stay rates for cabins.

Horseback riding rentals.

• A B&B with a ranch house and three log cabins, surrounded by lakes, mountains, and wildlife, on a two-hundred-forty-acre ranch on the Cariboo Gold Rush Trail. During the gold rush, the trail passed between the barn and the present-day ranch house. B.C. Rail runs through the ranch; trains stop to pick up and let off guests. Horseback trail riding, hiking, biking, swimming, canoeing, trout fishing, cross-country skiing, and trampoline. Each cabin has kitchen facilities, an electric stove, a wood stove, a horse paddock, a flower garden, a fire pit, and lawn chairs. Breakfast is served in the ranch house in a glassed-in sunroom overlooking gardens and corrals. Additional meals are served on request. Ranch house guests also prepare additional meals in the ranch house kitchen. Visa, MasterCard, traveller's cheques. German spoken. **In the hosts' own words:** "Guests ride the train to Kelly Lake station and spend a few days at the ranch riding, hiking, and exploring, before continuing on their journeys. Two rustic creekside cabins and one historical log cabin house hikers, nature lovers, artists, authors, fishermen, birdwatchers, and horse enthusiasts. Families can spend a white Christmas here."

Anchor Ranch

Rob and Anne Willis
Mail: Box 127
Clinton, BC V0K 1K0
(250) 459-2282
(area code 604 before October 1996)

• From Clinton, go 16 kilometres north on Highway 97 and then 3.2 kilometres east on Chasm Road.

• One person from $40; two people from $55.

Three rooms in main house. Double bed; twin bed. Shared guest bathrooms.

Log cabin. One single bed and bunk beds. Outhouse.

Bunkhouse. Four twin beds. Shared guest bathroom in main house.

Group rates.

Family packages.

Guided trail rides.

• A B&B on a working cattle ranch with a variety of farm animals and pets, near Chasm Provincial Park, in the south Cariboo. Walking trails beside a creek and two lakes. Cross-country skiing and skating. Guided trail rides for additional fees. Log cabin has a wood heater. Bunkhouse has a sitting area. Full or light breakfast, including farm-fresh eggs, hosts' ranch-raised beef, and local produce, is served on a deck overlooking the creek or by a fireplace in the dining room. Lunch, dinner, and picnic lunches available.

Ruth Lake Lodge

Klaus and Susanna Kaiser
Ruth Lake Road
Mail: Box 315
Forest Grove, BC V0K 1M0
(250) 397-2727 Fax: (250) 397-2284
(area code 604 before October 1996)
E-mail: ruthlake@netshop.net

● Thirty-two kilometres northeast of 100 Mile House, off Highway 97. Turn right onto Canim Lake Road. At Forest Grove, proceed straight ahead onto Eagle Creek Road and continue for 6.5 kilometres. Turn left onto Ruth Lake Road and continue for another 3.5 kilometres to the lodge.

● Five rooms. One person $59; two people $89. Queen-sized bed; queen-sized bed and sofa bed; bunk beds.
Three self-contained cabins (each sleeps up to six). $130. Queen-sized bed and four mattresses in loft. Breakfast not included.
Early booking discounts.
Boats, mountain bikes, and skidoo rentals.

● A full-facility lodge and three new cabins separate from the hosts' house, on the shores of Ruth Lake. Fishing, swimming, and hiking from the lodge. The hosts arrange golfing, horseback riding, dog sled rides, and fly-ins by float plane. Guest sauna by the lake. The lodge has a guest TV and video room and a guest living room with fireplace. Each cabin has a bedroom with queen-sized bed, a loft with four beds, a bathroom with shower, kitchen facilities, a dining and living area, a wood stove, and electric heaters. A restaurant in the lodge serves European cuisine. A full breakfast is served in the restaurant for lodge guests. For guests staying in the cabins, breakfast is available in the restaurant for an additional charge. Reservations required. Visa, MasterCard, American Express. **In the hosts' own words:** "The sumptuous breakfast served in the restaurant will make your day."

The Log House B&B

Dale and Joan Bummer
U81 Kitwanga Drive
Mail: C–347
108 Mile Ranch, BC V0K 2Z0
(250) 791-5353
(area code 604 before October 1996)
Toll-free: 1-800-610-1002

• Thirteen kilometres north of 100 Mile House. Thirteen kilometres south of Lac La Hache. Turn off Highway 97 at the heritage site rest stop. Turn right onto Kitwanga Drive and follow it around the lake for 2 kilometres. The house is on the lake side.

• Two rooms. One person $50–60. Queen-sized bed; queen-sized bed and twin beds. Ensuite bathrooms. Additional person $12.50. Children under 8 free. Cots and small crib available.

• A log house on 108 Mile Lake in the Cariboo. Swimming, sailing, hiking, and cross-country skiing from the B&B. Three kilometres from a golf course, tennis courts, a fitness gym, gourmet restaurants, and the 108 Mile airstrip. Half a block from riding stables. Sixteen kilometres from downhill skiing at Mount Timothy and Lac La Hache. The hosts arrange covered wagon rides, hay rides, sleigh rides, helicopter rides, and dog sled rides. Large landscaped yard. One of the guest rooms, the living room, and a sun deck are wheelchair accessible. Tea, coffee, and cold drinks provided. Full breakfast is served in the dining room or on a sun deck. Reservations recommended. Deposit of one night's rate required to hold reservation. Cancellation notice seven days. Visa, MasterCard. Children welcome. No pets. No smoking. **In the hosts' own words:** "Experience our hearty Cariboo breakfasts."

Soda Creek Acres

Robert and Bernice Johansen
RR 4 Site 15 C–7
Williams Lake, BC V2G 4M8
(250) 297-6418
(area code 604 before October 1996)

• Thirty minutes' drive north of Williams Lake and 4 kilometres west of Highway 97. Take Soda Creek Townsite Road, 2.5 kilometres north of the Soda Creek Emporium.

• Two rooms. One person $45; two people $50. Double bed; twin beds. Shared guest bathroom with shower.

Family (two adults, two children) rate for both rooms: $75.

Accommodation for horses.

• A B&B on seventy-five acres in a country setting at Soda Creek. Guest rooms are separate from the hosts' living space. Guest deck with view of the Fraser River, guest sitting room with TV, and guest entrance. Breakfast, including Yukon sourdough pancakes, is served on the deck, weather permitting. Children and pets welcome. Smoking permitted on decks. **In the hosts' own words:** "Join us at Soda Creek, once a booming town and busy junction where stern-wheelers plied the Fraser River."

Eagle Bluff B&B

Mary Allen and Bryan Cox
201 Cow Bay Road
Prince Rupert, BC V8J 1A2
(250) 627-4955 Fax: (250) 627-7945
(area code 604 before October 1996)

• From Highway 16, take the Cow Bay turnoff (Third Avenue East) onto Cow Bay Road. Turn left one block past Smile's Seafood Cafe. The B&B is next to Cow Bay Wharf.

• Four rooms. One person $45–50; two people $50–60. Queen-sized bed; queen-sized bed and double hide-a-bed; queen-sized bed and single futon. Ensuite and shared guest bathrooms. Cot available.
One suite. Two people $65. Queen-sized bed, twin beds, and one double hide-a-bed.
Additional person $10. Child 7 to 12 $5. Children under 7 free. Weekly and winter rates.

• A B&B overlooking a yacht club, on a harbour where cruise ships, sailboats, freighters, and commercial fishing boats come and go. Five minutes' walk from downtown Prince Rupert, the Northern Museum, and Mariner's Park. Ten minutes' walk from a library, tennis courts, an indoor swimming pool, and a performing arts centre. Near a public boat launch and mooring, boat rentals and charters, the Sea Walk hiking trail, an eighteen-hole golf course, a racquet centre, and a gondola to the top of Mount Hays. Two of the guest rooms are downstairs; two of the guest rooms and one guest suite are upstairs. The suite has a bedroom with twin beds and a sitting room with a queen-sized bed and a hide-a-bed. Laundry facilities available. Within a block of two seaside cafés and a neighbourhood pub. Full breakfast includes muffins and fruit salad. Deposit of one night's rate required to hold reservation. Cancellation notice seven days. Visa, MasterCard. No pets. No smoking. **In the hosts' own words:** "Experience Prince Rupert's waterfront and enjoy the sunset over the harbour."

Raindrop B&B

Bob and Judy Warren
2121 Graham Avenue
Prince Rupert, BC V8J 1C9
(250) 624-5564
(area code 604 before October 1996)

- One person or two people $70. Double bed.
Private bathroom.
- A B&B with a harbour view from bay windows,
ten minutes' drive from city centre, a golf course,
a swimming pool, hiking trails, and parks. Guest
sitting room. Gardens and decks. Pickup from transportation services. The hosts arrange
tours of the city and North Pacific Cannery museum. A choice of breakfasts is served with
linen, china, and silver, overlooking the harbour. Visa. No pets. No smoking. **In the hosts'
own words:** "Enjoy peace and tranquillity. Feed the wild deer who are almost daily in the
yard, and watch the ships go by."

Merkodei Meadows

Inke Kase
4507 North Sparks Street
Terrace, BC V8G 2W4
(250) 635-7808 Fax: (250) 635-9727
(area code 604 before October 1996)
E-mail: merkodei@kermode.net

- Five minutes' drive from downtown Terrace.
- Self-contained one-bedroom suite. One person
$45; two people $50. Queen-sized bed and day
bed. Ensuite bathroom. Additional person $10.
Winter rates.
Ski packages.
- A B&B on two and a half acres of gardens and woods, five minutes' walk from a heritage
park, tennis courts, Terrace Mountain trail, playground, and transit route. Suite has a kitchen,
a private telephone line, and a TV and VCR. Pickup from plane, train, and bus for a fee. Ski
packages at Shames Mountain can be arranged. In the area are Skeena River fishing, Lakelse
Lake, and Mount Layton hotsprings. One hour's drive south of Tseax lava beds. Computer
equipment rental and Internet access can be arranged. Continental breakfast is served at
guests' convenience. Visa. Children welcome. No dogs; cats in residence. **In the hosts' own
words:** "We would like to welcome you to the hub of B.C.'s northwest."

Berg's Valley Tours B&B

Beverley and David Berg
3924 Thirteenth Avenue
Mail: Box 3235
Smithers, BC V0J 2N0
(250) 847-5925 Fax: (250) 847-5945
(area code 604 before October 1996)

• Five minutes' walk from downtown Smithers.
• Two rooms. One person $40-45. Queen-sized bed; double bed. Ensuite and private bathrooms. Additional person $10.
Valley and alpine tours.
Ski packages.
• A B&B in a quiet residential area, next to Riverside Park, with a view of Hudson Bay Mountain. Five minutes' walk from downtown's shopping malls, restaurants, swimming pool, and spa. Smithers's perimeter walking trail is at the back door. Pickup from plane, bus, and train. One of the guest rooms is wheelchair accessible and has a private entrance. The other guest room has a private bathroom with Jacuzzi tub. Full breakfast includes fresh fruit, farm-fresh eggs, homemade bread, homemade baked goods, and homemade preserves. No smoking in the guest rooms. **In the hosts' own words:** "Since you have chosen Smithers as your stopping point, we invite you to spend an extra day or three in our home and join us on some of our valley and alpine tours."

Tyhee Lake Lodge

Gene Cole
Tyhee Lake Road
Mail: RR 1 Site 19 C–6
Telkwa, BC V0J 2X0
(250) 846-9636 Fax: (250) 846-9636
(area code 604 before October 1996)

- Nine kilometres from Smithers by paved road. Call for directions.
- Suite. Two people $75–95. Ensuite bathroom.
Cabin. Two people $75–95. Private bathroom. Breakfast ingredients supplied.
Child $15.
- A B&B on Tyhee Lake in the Bulkley Valley. Guests swim on a private beach and use a canoe. Power boat available. Evening camp fires. Near hiking, trail riding, fishing, and golfing. Close to downhill ski runs, set cross-country skiing trails, and snowmobiling areas. Accommodation for horses is available. Top floor suite has a private entrance, a kitchen, and a deck. Cabin has a kitchen. Adults only in suite. No pets. Smoking outside. **In the hosts' own words:** "Relax and enjoy thirty acres of lakeside tranquillity with a panoramic view of glacier-clad mountains."

La Mia Casa, E'Sempre Aperta B&B

Luciano and Georgina Dotto
2555 Dominion Avenue
Mail: Box 43
Houston, BC V0J 1Z0
(250) 845-7775
(area code 604 before October 1996)

• From Highway 16, turn at the forestry building onto Butler Avenue. Turn left onto Eleventh Street. Turn left onto Avalon Avenue. Turn right onto Star Street, which leads to Dominion Avenue. The B&B is on the left and has a tree-lined driveway.

• Three rooms. One person $40; two people $50. Double bed; twin beds. Shared guest bathrooms. Children under 6 free. Child 7 to 12 half rate. Queen-sized hide-a-bed available in family room. Highchair and playpen available. Monthly rates.

• A quiet house at the end of a tree-lined driveway, with a yard, a garden, a greenhouse, a patio, a woodworking shop, and a family room with fireplace. Close to shopping. Within ten minutes of a nature walk along a creek, two nine-hole golf courses, tennis courts, basketball, bowling, fishing, and cross-country skiing. Forty-five minutes from downhill skiing at Hudson Bay Mountain. In the area are sawmill and forestry tours. Coffee, tea, and other beverages provided when guests arrive. Choice of full breakfast, which includes waffles, fresh strawberries and raspberries with whipped cream, pork sausages, and bacon, or Continental breakfast, which includes toast made with fresh-baked bread, homemade preserves, cereal, and fresh fruit. Other meals by arrangement. Ground floor is wheelchair accessible. Cash, traveller's cheques. Italian spoken. Children welcome. No pets; small dog in residence. Smoking outdoors. **In the hosts' own words:** "Your comfort is our main concern, so come and enjoy your stay in our quiet, peaceful, and friendly house."

Little Madness on Francois Lake B&B

Meg and Ron Opas
Colleymount Road West
Mail: Box 606
Francois Lake, BC V0J 1R0
(250) 695-6673
(area code 604 before October 1996)

• Thirty kilometres (20 minutes) south of Burns Lake. Take Highway 35 from Burns Lake south to the Francois Lake ferry landing and follow the lakeshore road west for 4 kilometres.

• Three rooms. One person $50; two people $60. Shared guest bathroom.

• A traditional European-style B&B in a log house on five acres, with views of Francois Lake, rolling ranch lands, forests, and distant snow-capped mountains. Within twelve hours' drive of Prince Rupert, Jasper, Banff, Vancouver, Yukon, and Alaska. In the area are boating, sailing, horseback riding, birdwatching, cycling, hiking, and cross-country skiing. Garden. Living areas with art, books, music, and TV. Full breakfast. Outdoor shelter for pets and smokers. **In the hosts' own words:** "Our peaceful and picturesque place is far away from the big madnesses of other parts of the world. An ideal spot to take a break from road touring."

Cozy Corner B&B

Linda Malcolm
7131 Harvard Crescent
Prince George, BC V2N 2V6
(250) 964-7550 Fax: (250) 562-8252
(area code 604 before October 1996)

• From Highway 16, turn west onto Domano Boulevard and then left onto Gladstone. Pass Gladstone Elementary school and turn onto Harvard Crescent.

• Two rooms. One person $50; two people $60. Queen-sized bed; double hide-a-bed and extra-long twin beds. Ensuite bathroom and private bathroom with shower. Additional person $10. Child under 6 $5.

• A quiet B&B with a hot tub, on a green belt with a walking trail, ten minutes from downtown Prince George and five minutes from the University of Northern British Columbia and golf courses. One of the guest rooms has a telephone and a sitting area with a TV, a VCR, and a selection of movies; popcorn on request. A second guest room has a TV. Laundry facilities. Full breakfast, including homemade muffins, is served in the dining room. Cash, Visa. Smoking in designated area. **In the hosts' own words:** "Relax your travel-weary muscles in our hot tub."

Fessenden's B&B on the River

George and Wendy Fessenden
3311 Riverview Road
Prince George, BC V2K 4Y8
(250) 562-1807 Fax: (250) 562-1847
Cellular: (250) 613-6551
(area code 604 before October 1996)

• From Highway 97, turn west onto North Nechako Road. Turn left onto Rosia, continue to the end, and turn right onto Riverview Road.

• Two rooms. One person $50; two people $60. Twin beds; queen-sized bed. Shared guest bathroom.

• A B&B on the Nechako River, with a riverside deck and a patio that overlooks the water. Family room with TV and formal living room. Fire pit, sauna, and indoor and outdoor hot tubs. Guest room with brass four-post queen-sized bed has a TV. Laundry facilities. Pre-breakfast coffee is available in guest rooms. Full or Continental breakfast includes homemade muffins. Visa, MasterCard. No pets. Smoking outdoors. **In the hosts' own words:** "Make our home your home while you're away from home."

Mead Manor B&B

Laura and Robert Mead
4127 Baker Road
Prince George, BC V1H 1A4
(250) 964-8436
(area code 604 before October 1996)

• From the centre of downtown Prince George,
go west on Highway 16 for five minutes to
Tyner Road. Turn right onto Tyner and continue
to the first right, which is Baker Road. Turn onto
Baker and continue past the stop sign at Davis
Road.

• Two rooms. One person $40; two people $50. Queen-sized bed. Private bathrooms with showers. Seniors' rates.

• A B&B in a quiet neighbourhood, five minutes from downtown Prince George. Close to the University of Northern British Columbia and shopping. One of the guest rooms has a TV and a VCR. A second guest room has a private entrance, a Jacuzzi, access to a guest lounge with TV and VCR, and a selection of movies. Guest hot tub. Laundry facilities. Choice of breakfast is served in a sunroom overlooking a garden. Cash, Visa. Smoking in designated area.

Adrienne's B&B

Glenn and Adrienne Bowden
1467 Fraser Crescent
Prince George, BC V2M 3Y4
(250) 561-2086 Fax: (250) 562-6699
(area code 604 before October 1996)

• Three blocks west of the intersection of Highway 97 and Fifteenth Avenue.

• Two rooms. One person $40; two people
$45–50. Private and shared bathrooms.

• A quiet B&B within five minutes' walk of an art
gallery and within fifteen to twenty minutes' walk of restaurants, shopping, a railway museum, parks, and nature paths. Ten minutes' drive from a park with walking trails. Living room with TV and stereo. Large, shaded backyard. The hosts play bridge and help guests plan sightseeing and other activities. Off-street parking. Full or light breakfast is served with Royal Doulton china and crystal stemware. Check-in from 4:00 to 8:00 p.m. or by arrangement; check-out by 11:00 a.m. Adult oriented. No pets in residence. No smoking. **In the hosts' own words:** "Once you have stayed with us, you will want to come back."

A-Place-to-Rest on Foothills B&B

Cathy McFadyen
1282 Elkhorn Crescent
Prince George, BC V2M 6J3
(250) 561-2445 Fax: (250) 564-1180
(area code 604 before October 1996)

• Go west on Fifteenth Avenue. Turn right onto
Foothills Boulevard and go one block. Turn left
onto Azure, go one block, and turn right onto
Elkhorn Crescent.

• Two rooms. One person $40; two people $50.
Private and shared bathrooms. Additional person $10. Child $5. Seniors' and extended stay
rates.

• A quiet B&B set against Cranbrook Hill, five minutes from downtown Prince George, the
University of Northern British Columbia, exhibition grounds, and a multiplex arena. Nature
trails from the B&B. Guest rooms have TVs and telephones. One of the guest rooms has a
queen-sized bed, a double bed, and a private bathroom. Computer available. Outdoor hot tub
in a wooded garden. Breakfast includes homemade bread. Kitchen available for guests to
prepare additional meals. Credit cards. Smoking in designated area on furnished patio. **In
the hosts' own words:** "Our B&B is central yet nestled peacefully on the green belt. Enjoy
our warm hospitality."

Marylin's B&B

Marylin Law
2731 Merritt Road
Prince George, BC V2N 1M5
(250) 562-9833
(area code 604 before October 1996)

• From Highway 16, turn right onto Range Road
(Mohawk gas station and Costco store on cor-
ner), left onto Wiebe, and right onto Merritt
Road.
From the Pine Centre Mall in Prince George, go
south on Westwood Drive for 1 kilometre. Turn left onto Merritt Road.

• Two suites. One person $45; two people $55. Bathroom in suite and shared bathroom.
Seniors' and weekly rates.

• A centrally located B&B in a residential area, near a shopping mall, walking trails, golfing, and a warehouse store. Each two-room suite has kitchen facilities, a TV, a telephone, and
a private entrance. Laundry facilities. Breakfast includes homemade bread made daily with
homeground flour. **In the hosts' own words:** "We're waiting for you."

Bedford Place B&B

Walt and Ruth Thielmann
135 Patricia Boulevard
Prince George, BC V2L 3T6
(250) 562-3269 or (250) 562-4557
(area code 604 before October 1996)

• From First Avenue, take Queensway Street.
Turn left onto Patricia Boulevard and continue
for eight blocks to Taylor Drive.
• Two rooms. One person $65; two people $75.
Queen-sized bed. Ensuite and private bathrooms.
• A B&B overlooking the Fraser River and the Yellowhead Bridge. One of the guest rooms
has a queen-sized Murphy bed, maple wainscoting, and an ensuite bathroom. The other guest
room has a queen-sized sleigh bed and a private bathroom with a claw-foot tub. Ten minutes'
walk from three parks, regional and railway museums, and the Heritage River Trail. Full
breakfast is served in a formal dining room or on a patio. **In the hosts' own words:** "Relax
and enjoy the beautiful garden and the backyard patio."

The Tea House B&B

Elena and David
1457 Taylor Drive
Prince George, BC V2L 1A1
(250) 563-9131
(area code 604 before October 1996)

• Room. One person $50. Two people $60.
Queen-sized futon bed. Private bathroom.
• A centrally located B&B within walking distance of downtown restaurants, a swimming pool,
a convention centre, and Fort George park and
museum. If they like, guests join hosts for an
early morning walk along the Heritage River Trail. Choice of Asian, American, or not strict-
ly vegetarian breakfast. **In the hosts' own words:** "Experience Oriental hospitality and luxurious simplicity."

Seaport B&B

Bonnie
Mail: Box 206
Sandspit, BC V0T 1T0
(250) 637-5698 Fax: (250) 637-5697
(area code 604 before October 1996)

• Four rooms in a house separate from the hosts'
house. One person $30; two people $40. Double
bed; twin beds. Shared guest bathroom.
Two studio suites in a self-contained house. One
person $30; two people $40. Queen-sized bed
and one twin bed. Shared guest bathroom.
Whale watching sightseeing tours. Fishing charters.
• A waterfront B&B with an ocean view, within walking distance of airport and shops. Four
guest rooms are in a house separate from the hosts' house. Two studio suites are in a separate house with a kitchen, a sliding glass door, a patio, and a TV. Host arranges whale
watching, fishing charters, and sightseeing boat tours including tours of Haida village sites.
Eagles and other birds can be seen from the B&B. Self-serve breakfast includes homemade
baked goods, free-range eggs, granola, coffee, tea, and fruit juices. **In the hosts' own words:**
"If you would like to stop in and view our facilities, I would be more than pleased to show
you around. Enjoy the friendly atmosphere and beautiful sunsets."

Misty Island Guest House

Andrea Hunter
414 Third Avenue
Mail: Box 503
Queen Charlotte, BC V0T 1S0
(250) 559-8224
(area code 604 before October 1996)

• On the main street, across from the firehall,
three blocks west of the city centre shopping
area. Six kilometres from the ferry terminal.
• Suite. One person $60; two people $75–85.
Queen-sized bed and queen-sized sofa bed. Bathroom in suite. Breakfast ingredients supplied. Additional person $10. Minimum stay two nights. Off-season rates October to April.
Extended stay rates.
• A suite in a modern house on an acre of waterfront, high above Skidegate Inlet. Terraced
lawns lead down to a beach, where guests hike, birdwatch, and beachcomb. The suite has a
view of the water, a ground-level private entrance, a kitchen with microwave, a TV, a VCR,
a radio, and a telephone. Use of washer and dryer. The host has lived on the Queen
Charlottes for sixteen years and shares her knowledge with guests. Breakfast, including
homemade muffins, cinnamon buns, jams, and farm-fresh eggs, is self-serve in the suite. On
weekends, full breakfast is served in the dining room solarium, which has a view of the
water, docks, and mountains; eagles, herons, and deer may be seen. Reservations required.
Check-in and check-out times flexible. No pets. No smoking. **In the hosts' own words:**
"Come visit the beautiful Queen Charlotte Islands and enjoy a home-away-from-home stay,
on the waterfront."

Polly Ranch B&B and Campground

Walter and Liliane Herzog
B. J. Smith Road 2
East Pine, BC
Mail: Box 213
Groundbirch, BC V0C 1T0
(250) 788-9667 Fax: (250) 788-9667
(area code 604 before October 1996)

• From Chetwynd, take Highway 97 east for 35 kilometres. Turn right before the East Pine River bridge and continue for 1.5 kilometres on a gravel road.

• Three rooms. One person $29; two people $38. Double bed; twin beds. Private and shared guest bathrooms. Open May to October; open in winter by arrangement.

• A house surrounded by trees, with a view of the East Pine River. Deer and birds can be seen on the property. The top of a nearby hill provides a view of the East Pine Valley. Guests walk and jog on the waterfront. Two mountain bikes for guest use. Near canoeing, horseback riding, fishing, and golfing. Cross-country and downhill skiing at Powder King ski area. Half an hour from pool in Chetwynd. In the area are Kinusoe Falls, Monkman Park, the W.A.C. Bennett Dam, and the Peace Canyon Dam. Sawmill tours can be arranged. Dawson Creek has a pioneer museum, restaurants, and shopping malls. Two of the guest rooms and a living room with VCR are on ground level. A third guest room, with private bathroom, is upstairs. Refreshments provided. Full or Continental breakfast includes homemade bread and jams. Other meals on request. Visa, MasterCard.

Eleanor's House

Eleanor House and Rick Kunelius
125 Kootenay Avenue
Mail: Box 1553
Banff, AB   T0L 0C0
(403) 760-2457   Fax: (403) 762-3852

• On the south side of the river, one block above the road to the Banff Springs Hotel.

• Rooms. In spring (February to April), two people $75. In summer (May to October), two people $105. Queen-sized bed; extra-long twin beds. Ensuite bathrooms. Open February to Thanksgiving.

• A B&B in a quiet residential area, ten minutes' walk from the Banff Springs Hotel, which can be seen from the guest rooms, and ten minutes' walk from the town centre. In the area are golfing, hiking, mountain climbing, rafting, fishing, downhill skiing, cross-country skiing, heli-hiking, wildlife viewing, the Banff Centre for the Performing Arts, museums, art galleries, and restaurants. The hosts help guests plan activities. One host spent twenty years with the national park service and knows local trails and wildlife. Guest rooms are 350 square feet and have corner sitting areas with mountain views and ensuite bathrooms with soaker tubs. Guest sitting room has a fireplace, a wet bar, and books. Secure bicycle storage. Heated ski storage. Continental breakfast. From the table, elk and deer can often be seen grazing on the front lawn. Visa, MasterCard. Adults only. **In the hosts' own words:** "Our guest house reflects mid-century elegance for the discerning traveller."

Jac 'n' Sarah's B&B

Jac and Sarah Segstro
10 Riverview Place
Mail: Box 1067
Canmore, AB T0L 0M0
(403) 678-2770
Toll-free from within North America: 1-800-600-3816

• One hour west of Calgary. Take the first Canmore exit and follow signs to the business district. On Main Street (Eighth Street), pass through three four-way stops to Riverview Place, which is a cul-de-sac at the end of Main Street.

• Three rooms. One person $45; two people $65, twin beds, private half bathroom; two people $65, queen-sized bed, shared guest bathroom; two people $75, two queen-sized beds, shared guest bathroom. Additional person $15. Child 3 to 12 $10. Minimum stay two days during high season. Extended stay rates.

• A B&B with skylights, in a wooded, mountain setting, bordering the Bow River. Guests walk and jog along the dike by the river behind the house. Mountain walks and hikes from the B&B. Two blocks from restaurants, galleries, and gift shops. Two of the guest rooms have private entrances. One of the guest rooms has a kitchen and a TV. Another has a skylight. The third guest room is on the main floor and is suitable for people who have difficulty with stairs. One host is a marriage commissioner and performs civil ceremonies in the mountains, at the river behind the B&B, and in other locations; reservations recommended. Full or Continental breakfast includes homemade baked goods and fruit juice. Dutch and some French and German spoken. Dog in residence. Smoke-free environment. **In the hosts' own words:** "Canmore is an ideal place to use as a base from which to experience the Kananaskis, Bow Valley, Banff, and Lake Louise areas of the Rocky Mountains. With us you will feel at home away from home."

Cedar Springs B&B

Deborah J. Robillard
434 First Street
Canmore, AB T1W 2K9
(403) 678-3865 Fax: (403) 678-1938

• Canmore is fifteen minutes from Banff and an hour west of Calgary.
• Three rooms. One person from $65, two people from $75. King-sized bed;
queen-sized bed; twin beds. Ensuite and private bathrooms.
Honeymoon suite: call for rates.
• A quiet cedar chalet surrounded by forest, with mountain views and country décor. Guest
lounge with two fireplaces and guest loft sitting area with books. One of the guest rooms
accommodates up to three adults. Wildlife can be seen from a deck. A few minutes from the
Bow River and Banff National Park. River walkways lead to the town centre's shops, galleries, and restaurants. Host helps guests plan recreation activities. Marriage commissioner
available to perform wedding ceremonies. Full breakfast. Visa, MasterCard. French spoken.
Adults only. No pets. Outdoor facilities for smokers. **In the hosts' own words:** "Come for
the mountains, and stay for the hospitality, relaxed atmosphere, and spectacular views, in this
ideal mountain location."

Amble-In B&B

Ed and Joanne Rogers
438 Second Street
Box 744
Canmore, AB T0L 0M0
(403) 678-6497 Fax: (403) 678-3794

• From Highway 1, follow signs to the business district (Eighth Street). Turn south, toward Three Sisters Mountain, onto Second Street. The B&B is on the corner of Second Street and Fourth Avenue. Parking on Fourth Avenue side.
• Rooms. In summer (June to September), one person $60, two people $85. In winter, one person $50, two people $75. Queen-sized bed; twin beds. Ensuite bathrooms. Additional person $15. Extended stay rates. Group rates.
• A quiet two-storey house with balconies and a 360-degree view. Six blocks from shops, galleries, and restaurants. Walking along Policeman's Creek and the Bow River. Within an hour of Banff, Lake Louise, Kananaskis Country, the Canmore Nordic Centre, and five downhill skiing slopes. Canmore is at the east gate of Banff National Park. The hosts provide information on guided activities including birdwatching, para-gliding, and helicopter sight-seeing. Accessible for seniors and people with disabilities; a guest room with twin beds has a roll-in shower. Reservations recommended, especially in summer. **In the hosts' own words:** "Please do amble in."

The Georgetown Inn

Doreen and Barry Jones
1101 Bow Valley Trail
Mail: Box 3327
Canmore, AB T0L 0M0
(403) 678-3439 Fax: (403) 678-3630
Toll-free from within B.C. and Alberta: 1-800-657-5955

• From Highway 1, take the Canmore exit onto the Bow Valley Trail. The B&B is close to the hospital.

• Fourteen rooms. In summer, one person $95, two people $109. In winter, one person $65, two people $75. Queen-sized bed; twin beds. Ensuite bathrooms. Additional person $10-20.

• A Tudor-style inn at the entrance to Banff National Park, twenty minutes' drive from the town of Banff. A few minutes from the site where Nordic ski events were held during the 1988 Olympics. Within an hour's drive from skiing at Lake Louise, Norquay, Sunshine Village, Nakiska, and Fortress Mountain. Fifteen minutes from hiking, golfing, horseback riding, fishing, canoeing, kayaking, whitewater rafting, mountaineering, parapenting, skating, and ice climbing. The inn is named after an old Bow Valley coal mining community. It has a licensed guest lounge decorated in traditional British pub style, with mining memorabilia. The guest lounge and dining room have fireplaces and patios. Guest rooms have mountain views, antique furniture, down duvets, TVs, and telephones. One of the guest rooms is designed for people with disabilities and is wheelchair accessible. Meals are served in the dining room. Deposit of one night's rate required with reservation. Cancellation notice two days. Visa, MasterCard, American Express. Smoking in the lounge and on patios. **In the hosts' own words:** "We offer all the comforts of a B&B and the privacy of an old-fashioned inn."

By the Brook B&B

Lynn and Don Brown
4 Birchwood Place
Mail: Box 2927
Canmore, AB T0L 0M0
(403) 678-4566 Fax: (403) 678-4199

• In Canmore, ten minutes east of Banff, one hour west of Calgary.

• Rooms. Queen-sized bed. Ensuite bathrooms.

• A modern house on a cul-de-sac by a mountain stream and the Canmore walkway system of walking paths. Guest rooms have TVs and sitting areas with bay windows and mountain views. Sauna and fireplace. Five minutes' walk from shopping in downtown Canmore. Ten minutes' drive from the Canmore Nordic Centre. Twenty to fifty-five minutes' drive from five downhill ski areas. Forty minutes' drive from four golf courses. Gift certificates available. Reservations recommended. Visa, MasterCard. Adult house. No pets. Smoke-free house.

Wedgewood Mountain Inn B&B

Kathy Claxton and Frankie Michaluk
1004 Larch Place
Mail: Box 3035
Canmore, AB T0L 0M0
(403) 678-4494 Fax: (403) 678-5017

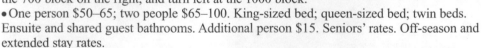

• From Highway 1, take the Canmore exit onto Highway 1A. Turn onto Seventeenth Street, towards the railway tracks. Cross the tracks and continue on Seventeenth, which becomes Larch Drive. Watch for the 1000 block on the left and the 700 block on the right, and turn left at the 1000 block.

• One person $50–65; two people $65–100. King-sized bed; queen-sized bed; twin beds. Ensuite and shared guest bathrooms. Additional person $15. Seniors' rates. Off-season and extended stay rates.

• An alpine cedar house on a quiet cul-de-sac in Canmore's west end. Outside the back gate are a forest reserve, a walking trail network, and the Bow River. Five minutes' drive from downtown Canmore. Ten minutes' drive from the Nordic Centre, where Nordic ski events were held during the 1988 Olympics. Fifteen minutes east of Banff. Forty minutes from Kananaskis Country and Lake Louise. Sixty minutes west of Calgary. Guest rooms have views of the Rockies and are decorated in a country theme. One room has a private deck, a sitting area, and an ensuite with Jacuzzi. Guest loft with TV, VCR, videos, and books. Living room with fireplace and cathedral windows. Full breakfast is served in the dining room or kitchen. Reservations recommended. Deposit of one night's rate required to hold reservation. Cancellation notice seven days. Pets in residence. Smoking outside. **In the hosts' own words:** "Your comfort is our specialty."

Reservations Jasper Ltd.

Karen Kovich and Debi Derksen
Mail: Box 1840
Jasper, Alberta T0E 1E0
(403) 852-5488 Fax: (403) 852-5489
E-mail: resjas@ycs.ab.ca
Web site: http://www.ycs.ab.ca/market/resjas/index.htm.

• A reservation service covering house accommodation, bed and breakfasts, hotels, motels, cabins, and bungalows in the Jasper area; bed and breakfasts, hotels, motels, cabins, and bungalows in Banff; and hotels, motels, cabins, and bungalows in the Lake Louise area. $15 booking fee for one reservation in one place. $20 booking fee for multiple reservations. Additional $5 booking fee for overseas clients. Visa. Non-commissionable. In the agents' own words: "We offer a fast, reliable, and informative service for our clients. You need only make one call for your Canadian Rockies vacation accommodations."

Crystal Butterfly B&B

Ralph and Maurine Heninger
321 East Second Avenue North
Mail: Box 531
Raymond, Alberta T0K 2S0
(403) 752-3100

• One person $35–50; two people $40–65.
Twin beds; queen-sized bed. Shared guest bathroom.
Honeymoon suite. Ensuite bathroom. Couch and roll-away cot available.
Additional person $10. Child under ten $5. Children under 5 free. Crib and highchair available.

• A B&B with two guest rooms, a honeymoon suite, and a banquet room. Thirty minutes' drive from shopping and attractions in Lethbridge. An hour's drive from Waterton National Park and attractions at Fort Macleod. Within ninety minutes' drive of Head Smashed-In Buffalo Jump and Pincher Creek. Banquet room has a private entrance, an ensuite bathroom, a kitchen, and a hide-a-bed couch, and is suitable for seminars, reunions, parties, and dancing. Honeymoon suite has a Jacuzzi and a TV. Full breakfast. Children welcome. No pets. No smoking. **In the hosts' own words:** "We love to pamper our guests and enjoy meeting people from all over the world."

Sweetgrass Triple "B"

Colleen and Boyd Bianchi
RR 1
Coutts, AB T0K 0N0
(403) 344-4473

• Thirty-five kilometres from Milk River.
Twenty-four kilometres east of Coutts.
• Three rooms in a mobile home. One person
$30; two people $50. Two double beds; double
bed; twin beds. Shared guest bathroom. Child
$10.
Entire mobile home. Call for rates.
• A self-contained mobile home on a working grain and cattle operation on the Alberta-
Montana border at the base of Sweetgrass Hills. Fifteen minutes from Writing-on-Stone
Provincial Park. Close to a park, river rafting and tubing, and guided horseback riding tours.
Grassland and coulees for horseback riding. Horse corrals, shelter, and bales available. Wild
birds and wildlife in the area. Kitchen with microwave. Living area with books, board
games, TV, VCR, and collection of videos. Sun deck, horseshoe pit, bonfire area, and trout-
stocked pond. Hosts share their knowledge about the area. Full breakfast, including farm-
fresh eggs, is served at guests' convenience. Diets are accommodated. Dinners by arrangement. Cancellation notice forty-eight hours. Cash, traveller's cheques. Children welcome.
Pets welcome by arrangement; cats and two dogs in residence. **In the hosts' own words:**
"Our sun deck has a beautiful prairie view of the hills. Become our guests in Southern
Alberta, to enjoy our rural life at the base of Sweetgrass Hills."

Ollie and Mike's Place

Ollie and Mike Kozicky
5424 Dalrymple Crescent NW
Calgary, AB T3A 1R3
(403) 286-9119

• Two rooms. One person $35; two people $50.
Double bed. Shared guest bathroom. Family rate
for both rooms: $75.
• An updated split-level house with air conditioning and a treed backyard. Family room with TV
and fireplace. Laundry facilities. Five minutes from bus stop; bus connects to rapid transit.
Thirty minutes' drive from downtown. On direct route to stampede grounds and shopping.
Off-street parking. Pickup from plane for a fee. Guest fridge. Guests use the kitchen to prepare meals other than breakfast. Full breakfast includes toast, muffins, juice, tea, coffee, and
a choice of hot or cold cereal, sausages, or bacon and eggs. Deposit. Ukrainian spoken.
Children welcome. Cat in residence. Smoking permitted.

Riverpark B&B

Margaret and Philip West-Daradich
86 Mountain Park Drive SE
Calgary, AB T2Z 1S1
(403) 257-0757

• Room. One person $40; two people $50.
Queen-sized bed. Private bathroom.
• A modern two-storey house bordering on a park,
with views of mountains and occasionally a flock
of Canada geese. Several kilometres of walking
and cycling tails from the B&B. Ten minutes'
drive from shopping malls, restaurants, theatres, swimming pools, and Spruce Meadows,
where international show jumping events are held in June, July, and September. Twenty minutes from downtown and the Calgary Stampede in July. Within driving distance of
Kananaskis Country and Banff National Park. On bus route. Guest living room and dining
room. Full or light breakfast with tea or fresh-ground coffee. No children. No pets. No
smoking. **In the hosts' own words:** "A place for all seasons. Enjoy a friendly atmosphere,
spotless rooms, and a quiet, convenient location."

Mountain View B&B

Anna Pockar
Mail: Box 6 Site 24 RR 12
Calgary, AB T3E 6W3
(403) 246-4838

• Twenty minutes west of Calgary. Five kilometres south of Highway 1.
• Three rooms. One person $55–60; two people
$65–75. Queen-sized bed. Private and shared
bathrooms. Additional person $15.
• A B&B on two acres, with valley and Rocky
Mountain views, one hour from Banff and forty-five minutes from Kananaskis. Indoor
swimming pool, indoor hot tub, two sun decks, billiard table, guest lounge, and tennis court.
One of the guest rooms has a fireplace. Coffee and tea provided. Full breakfast is served in
the kitchen. Other meals available. Diets are accommodated. Deposit of one night's rate
required to hold reservation. Cancellation notice seven days. A non-smoking establishment.
In the hosts' own words: "Relax in our spacious guest rooms or in the guest lounge.
Delicious home cooking awaits you in this serene setting."

A Deer Place B&B

Shari and Alan Murray
76 Midlawn Place SE
Calgary, AB T2X 1A6
(403) 254-8933 Fax: (403) 254-8933

• Room. One person from $40; two people from
$60. Twin beds. Private bathroom. Additional
person $15. Double bed available.

• A house on a quiet residential cul-de-sac, close
to Fish Creek Provincial Park. Eight minutes'
drive from Spruce Meadows equestrian centre.
Easy access to Highway 2 (McLeod Trail). Half a block from public transportation. Near a
shopping centre. Guest room with TV. Pickup from plane. Breakfast includes homemade
jams and jellies and homemade muffins and quick breads. Deposit required to hold reservation. Cancellation notice seven days. Adults only. No pets. No smoking. **In the hosts' own
words:** "I would be more than happy to help you plan a daily itinerary and point out high-
lights of the city and some favourite spots of the locals."

The Crescent B&B

Bruce and Debbie Trevitt
635 Crescent Boulevard SW
Calgary, AB T2S 1L1
(403) 287-0654 Fax: (403) 287-8009

• Two suites. Two people $70–120. Two queen-
sized beds; queen-sized bed and optional double
bed. Ensuite bathrooms.

• A B&B in a quiet neighbourhood with parks and
walkways. Close to downtown, restaurants, shopping, and the Calgary Stampede grounds. Within
walking distance of bus and rapid transit to downtown. Guest suites have fresh flowers, private entrances, garden patios, fridges, and TVs. One of the suites has French doors to a garden, a Jacuzzi, and a glass block shower. Guest grand piano in the family room and guest
gas barbecue in the garden. Children's tree house and deck. In the area are one hundred and
fifty kilometres of river valley paths. Mountain bikes and children's bikes. Near an outdoor
swimming pool and a children's wading pool, four tennis courts, playing fields, pedestrian
and bicycle paths, children's playgrounds, pedestrian suspension bridges, picnic and barbecue facilities, and birdwatching and wildlife viewing. Off-street parking. Coffee, tea, beverages, and snacks provided in the suite. Three-course breakfast includes eggs Benedict,
homemade cinnamon buns or croissants, and fresh fruit salad. Diets are accommodated. **In
the hosts' own words:** "We are located in the heart of Calgary's beautiful Elbow River
Valley. Our breakfast is a treat."

Betty's B&B

Betty and John Kennett
12427 Lake Fraser Way
Calgary, AB T2J 3T3
(403) 278-7960

• From Highway 1, turn south onto Highway 2.
Take the Anderson Road exit, turn south onto
Bonaventure Drive, and take the fifth turn to the
right.
• Three rooms. $65, twin beds, ensuite bath-
room; $55, double bed, shared guest bathroom;
$40, one twin bed, shared guest bathroom.
• A B&B with a patio and a landscaped garden, on a quiet road. Pickup from plane, train,
and bus. Bus stop at gate; one stop from light rapid transit to Calgary Stampede and downtown. Ten minutes' drive from Spruce Meadows equestrian centre. Four minutes' drive from
a shopping mall. Ten minutes' walk from restaurants. Full breakfast includes homemade
baked goods. Cash, traveller's cheques. No pets. No smoking. **In the hosts' own words:**
"Retire in comfort, and wake to the aroma of baking bread."

Klondike's Homestead B&B

Jill Bennett and Jeff Wilson
Mail: Box 1432
Cochrane, AB T0L 0W0
(403) 932-7750 Fax: (403) 932-7750

• Seven kilometres west of Cochrane on
Highway 1A. Turn north onto the Grand Valley
Road. Continue for 24 kilometres. Call for exact
directions.
• Two rooms. One person $50–60; two people
$70–80. Queen-sized bed; twin beds. Shared
guest bathroom. Hide-a-bed and crib available. Family rates.
• A log and timber frame house, designed and built by the owners, on an acreage in the
wooded foothills of the Rockies. Twenty minutes' drive northwest of Cochrane. Forty-five
minutes' drive northwest of Calgary. One of the guest rooms has a separate entrance and a
deck with stairs that lead to a hot tub. The hosts are outdoor adventure instructors who offer
rock climbing, cycling (Burley trailer available), hiking, canoeing, rafting, cross-country
skiing, and dog sledding. Walking trails through twenty acres of woods. Pond for winter
skating. Children's playground with climbing wall. In the area are a petting farm, a glass and
pottery studio, and a horseback riding stable. Reflexology is available with advance notice.
Twenty mintues' drive from golf, craft shops, and restaurants. An hour's drive from skiing at
Bragg Creek, Kananaskis Country, and Banff. Full breakfast, including farm-fresh eggs,
homemade baked goods, jams, fresh fruit, and juices is served in the sunroom or on the deck.
Vegetarian breakfast available. Children welcome; the hosts have two children. Pets welcome by arrangement; sled dogs and cat on the property. Smoking outside on decks. **In the
hosts' own words:** "Enjoy an exhilarating adventure or relax in the hammock, by the fire in
our log house, or in the hot tub. We are dedicated to helping you create an unforgettable
experience in Alberta's foothills."

Rosedale Suspension Bridge Park B&B

Elfriede Goode
46 Second Street East
Mail: Box 815
Rosedale, AB T0J 2V0
(403) 823-4599 Fax: (403) 823-4599

• Five minutes from Drumheller. Take Highway 10 east. Turn left at the suspension bridge sign. Take the next left onto Second Street East.

• Two rooms. Two people $48, twin beds; two people $55, queen-sized bed. Shared guest bathroom. Additional person $15. Child $10.

• A B&B in the Drumheller Valley, twelve minutes' walk from Rosedale Suspension Bridge Park. Near the Royal Tyrell Museum of Palaeontology. Guest entrance. Guest sitting room with fireplace, TV, VCR, and movies. Guest patio. Air conditioning. Off-street parking. European-style breakfast served with silver service. Visa. German spoken. Adult oriented. Non-smoking. **In the hosts' own words:** "Visit the Drumheller Valley. We look forward to having you as our special guest. A friendly welcome awaits you."

The Inn at Heartwood Manor

Norah Bird and Bob Hamilton
320 North Railway Avenue E
Drumheller, AB T0J 0Y4
(403) 823-6495 Fax: (604) 823-6495

• An hour and a half from Calgary.

• Nine rooms and a cottage. $50–120. Queen-sized bed and/or double bed. Ensuite and shared guest bathrooms.

Spa packages in off-season.

• An inn in downtown Drumheller, near the Royal Tyrell Museum of Palaeontology, soft (educational) adventure, and golfing. Woodwork and carvings throughout. Guest living room for reading and visiting and guest sitting room with fireplace and games. Some of the guest rooms have sitting areas, whirlpool tubs, fireplaces, air conditioning, TV, VCR, and/or private entrances. One has wheelchair access. Breakfast includes pancakes and homemade syrups. Cash, traveller's cheques, Visa, MasterCard. Children over six welcome. No smoking. **In the hosts' own words:** "Our inn offers the warmth and comfort of a heritage B&B with the elegance of a luxury inn. The fresh and fashionable rooms are an eclectic mix of new and old, with antiques and art throughout."

The Victorian House

Jack and Florence Barnes
541 Riverside Drive West
Drumheller, AB T0J 0Y3
(403) 823-3535

- Three and a half blocks west of Highway 9 north.
- Three rooms. One person $40; two people $50. Queen-sized bed; twin beds.
Shared guest bathrooms. Additional person $10. Child under 11 $5.
Ski packages.
- A two-storey house on a quiet street, with a view of river and Badlands. Three and a half blocks west of a public swimming pool. Four and a half blocks from downtown. Within walking distance of shopping, restaurants, and a seniors' centre. Guest rooms are decorated in Victorian style. Hand-made porcelain dolls and other crafts throughout the house. Living room with TV and books. Off-street parking. Beverage is served when guests arrive. Full breakfast, including homemade breads, muffins, fresh fruit, hot and cold cereals, and an entrée such as French toast, omelettes, and bacon and eggs, is served 6:00 to 10:00 a.m. MasterCard. No pets. Smoke-free environment. **In the hosts' own words:** "Come let us spoil you with warm, friendly hospitality and a delicious breakfast."

Cream Coulee B&B

Jim and Monica Bishop
Box 1118
Three Hills, AB T0M 2A0
(403) 443-7808

• On Highway 27 east. Ten kilometres east of the junction of Highway 21 and Highway 27. Twenty-four kilometres west of the junction of Highway 56, Highway 27, and Highway 9.
• Two rooms. $35–$55. Queen-sized bed; double bed. Shared guest bathroom.
• A farm house within fifty kilometres of golf courses, tea houses, the Royal Tyrell Museum of Palaeontology, and a game farm. Guests hike in a coulee. Hot tub, outdoor fire pit, lawn swing, and deck with barbecue. Breakfast includes homemade breads, muffins, and preserves. Children welcome. Dogs in residence. Smoking outdoors. **In the hosts' own words:** "Come to our quiet retreat and enjoy a great view and our warm hospitality."

Crossroads B&B

Brian and Yvonne Krause
RR 5
Stony Plain, AB T7Z 1X5
(403) 963-6095

• Thirty minutes west of Edmonton, via paved roads. On Highway 16, continue past Road 43 to Road 770, the first road south. Turn left onto Road 770 and continue for 13 kilometres to Road 627. The B&B is on the southeast corner.
• Three rooms. One person $40; two people $50. Queen-sized bed; twin beds. Two shared guest bathrooms. Child $5.
• A quiet, modern ranch-style house on a ranch, thirty minutes from West Edmonton Mall. Near swimming, fishing, golf courses, lakes, beaches, Fort Edmonton Park, the Provincial Museum, a zoo, and a space sciences centre. Facilities for guests' horses. Guest entrance. Guest rooms have TVs; VCR available. Full breakfast, including homemade baked goods is served in the dining room. Visa, MasterCard. Wheelchair accessible. Children welcome. Pets welcome. **In the hosts' own words:** "If you would like peace and quiet or an active family holiday, let our family cater to you. Horse enthusiasts, bring your horses and enjoy our ranch."

The Straw Bed B&B and Livery Stable

Helen Schiebel
c/o 15622—111th Avenue
Edmonton, AB T5M 2R7
(403) 963-1646

- From Edmonton, go west on Highway 16X for 20 kilometres. Turn north onto Highway 779 and go 10 kilometres. Turn west onto secondary Highway 633
and go 1 kilometre. The B&B's gate and sign are on the north side of the road.
- Three rooms. One person $45–55; two people $50–60. Queen-sized bed,
shared guest bathroom; double bed, shared guest bathroom; queen-sized bed
and queen-sized sofa bed, private bathroom. Additional person $15. Boarding
for horses $10 per horse, including feed.
- A new house on seventy-five acres of aspen parkland, with over eight kilometres of trails
through rolling terrain for walking, cross-country skiing, and mountain biking. Guests who
have horses ride on the trails. Guest veranda, sun deck, fire pit, living room with fireplace,
and sunroom with hot tub. Robes provided. Evening wine and liqueur. One of the guest
rooms has an iron queen-sized bed. One guest room has an oak double bed. The third guest
room has a queen-sized sleigh bed and a queen-sized sofa bed. Down duvets. Within thirty
minutes of West Edmonton Mall and ten golf courses. Five minutes from more trails for hiking, horseback riding, and biking, and from groomed ski trails. Full breakfast. Children welcome. Smoking outdoors. Two cats in residence and two large dogs in the yard. **In the hosts'
own words:** "We welcome you to share our secluded woods, explore the trails, watch the
birds and wildlife, and enjoy the comforts of our home."

Sentimental Journey B&B

Monica Iliffe
6 Diamond Drive
Hubbles Lake, Stony Plain
Mail: Box 17 Site 5 RR 2
Stony Plain, Alberta T7Z 1X2
(403) 963-3215 Fax: (403) 963-6022

• Twenty-five minutes west of Edmonton. Eight and a half kilometres west of Stony Plain. From Highway 16, turn north onto Range Road 14 (Hubbles Lake Road). Turn right onto Diamond Road and take the first left onto Diamond Drive.

• Two rooms. One person $40; two people $50. Double bed. Two shared guest bathrooms. Double sofa bed available.

• A lakeside cedar house built into a hillside, close to the town of Stony Plain, a multicultural heritage centre, wine cellars, a Victorian tea house, golf courses, and shopping. Twenty-five minutes' drive from West Edmonton Mall. Guests picnic at tables on the beach and canoe on the lake to watch the loons. Cross-country skiing. Five minutes' drive from downhill and cross-country skiing at Eden Lake Ski Hill. Spa, solarium, and sun decks. Guest lounge area with TV. The host is an artist and loon enthusiast. Full breakfast is served in the dining room, which overlooks Hubbles Lake. Children over twelve welcome. Dog in residence. Smoking outside. **In the hosts' own words:** "Ideal for special occasions, anniversaries, birthdays, and get-away weekends. Every spring, loons migrate to many lakes in the North. We welcome their sentimental journey back to Hubbles Lake."

Wetlands B&B

Raymond and Margaret Rondeau
4801 Sixty-sixth Street
Mail: Box 5523
Bonnyville, AB T9N 2G6
(403) 826-2471 Fax: (403) 826-4430

• One person $50; two people $60. Private and shared guest bathrooms. Additional person $10.
Anniversary packages.

• A house built in 1936 that was originally a hospital. Near a golf course, lakes, camping, fishing, birdwatching, and bicycling. Bicycles built for two. Guest sitting room. Hot tub, games room, licensed tea room, forty-seat meeting room, and lounge with TV, VCR, and fireplace. Parking with plug-ins. Wheelchair accessible. Visa, MasterCard. A non-smoking facility. **In the hosts' own words:** "This beautiful building built in 1936 was once the Duclos Hospital, and we have turned it into a bed and breakfast. We will be pleased to give you the history of the site on our place mat when you visit us at breakfast. Try rest and relaxation here and you won't regret it."

Field Stone Inn B&B

Roger and Angèle Field
Mail: Box 295
Grande Prairie, AB T8V 3A4
(403) 532-7529 Fax: (403) 532-1066

• Turn south onto 116th Street and continue for 2.7 kilometres. Turn right at six graineries and follow the lane to the end.

• Four rooms. Two people $75–100. King-sized bed; queen-sized bed; twin beds; extra-long twin beds. Ensuite bathrooms. Closed December.

• A B&B on a country lakeside farm, six minutes' drive from downtown and the airport. The lake has trumpeter swans and is on a migration route for ducks and geese. Guest rooms have prairie furniture, fireplaces, duvets, and robes. One of the guest rooms has a private veranda and a steam room and is wheelchair accessible. Two ensuite bathrooms have Jacuzzis. The B&B was designed by one of the hosts, who is an architect. Six minutes' drive from restaurants, Dunvegan Tea House, golf courses, shopping, tourist sites, balloon rides, and cross-country skiing. Four hours from Jasper. Recreational vehicle parking. Breakfast, including produce from the hosts' two-acre garden, is cooked on an Aga cooker and served in a variety of locations on the property. Reservations required. Cash, cheques, Visa, American Express. French spoken. Children welcome by arrangement. The hosts have a Belgian sheep dog to herd deer from gardens. Smoking on veranda. **In the hosts' own words:** "We serve Peace Country residents as well as people making Grande Prairie their destination for business, shopping, visiting, or a relaxing escape. We specialize in romantic get-aways for married couples, from wedding nights to senior anniversaries. Come experience true Peace Country hospitality."

Kozy Quarters B&B

Irene Kelly
11015—99th Street
Peace River, AB T8S 1L7
Mail: Box 7493
Peace River, AB T8S 1T1
(403) 624-2807 Fax: (403) 624-4912

• Four rooms. One person $45; two people $55. Double bed; twin beds. Shared bathroom.
Honeymoon room on request.

• A renovated two-and-a-half storey house with a garden. Built by the RCMP in 1916. A few minutes' walk from downtown. Near a museum, an indoor pool, shopping, riverboat tours, golf courses, a ski hill, art and crafts, a trout farm, jet boating, water skiing, a water park, a market garden, a farmer's market, and nature trails. Guest living room. Fireplace. Large backyard with garden furniture. Parking. Snack served when guests arrive. Full breakfast, including homemade baked goods and menu choices, is served on a closed-in veranda facing the river or outside on the lawn. Smoking restricted. **In the hosts' own words:** "Book our B&B accommodation for your sales representatives, consultants, colleagues, friends, or family, and make their stay in Peace River a delight."

A Selection of Other Books by
Gordon Soules Book Publishers